WHERE ARE YOU GOING?

WHERE ARE YOU GOING?

...It's About Choice

LARRY B. BACHMAN

CITI OF
BOOKS

CITIOFBOOKS, INC.
3736 Eubank NE Suite A1
Albuquerque, NM 87111-3579
www.citiofbooks.com
Hotline: 1 (877) 389-2759
Fax: 1 (505) 930-7244

Ordering Information:
Quantity sales. Special discounts are available on quantity purchases by corporations, associations, and others. For details, contact the publisher at the address above.

Printed in the United States of America.

ISBN-13:	Softcover	978-1-963209-28-0
	eBook	978-1-963209-29-7

Library of Congress Control Number: 2024900553

Table of Contents

FOREWORD

This is a book about dreams, about promises made and broken and a life lesson for all. The author uses his wit and humor to bring to life the experiences that makes him who he is: an entrepreneur, a husband, a father, a friend, and a man of God.

His unique writing style grabs your attention and as you share in the experiences, one cannot help but reflect on his/her past. By the end of reading this book, you will have a special appreciation for your childhood experiences and the impact the experiences made on your life today. You will also have a greater awareness of who you are and your role in the society and the world at large.

The sixties were definitely a time of upheaval, growth, exploration, innovation. Seen through the eyes of a group of kids makes for an interesting journey. The innocence of childhood, the comfort and protection of family, the challenges of adolescent, woven with the contemporary issues of the day, create a masterpiece that elicits varying emotional responses from the reader.

When I first placed my hands on this book, I was delighted to see that this was just not another story book. I encourage you to dig in, to contemplate and to reflect on the various themes that resulted in the ultimate decision.

Vennor Hackshaw
Aeronautical Engineer
Church Elder

PREFACE

It is hard sometimes not to laugh about my young daughters many concerns. What we grownups consider minutia are very real and pressing issues to our children. It has been suggested time after time; "Children don't come with instruction manuals", or do they?

Amazingly as we watch our children grow the insights and concerns that my parents had for my brother and I become 20/20. Many times I have found myself reciting the lessons I was taught to my children. Nothing changes, same lessons, just a new medium perhaps, a new format and a new presentation of old ways tried and tested being made anew.

It has been written, "There is nothing new under the sun". So let's refer to the greatest instruction manual ever made, "The Bible". Christ, the Rock, the Anchor; how do we impress upon our children just how important it is to have the foundation of a Bible based spirituality?

Consistency in the Bible's reading and prayer; children have eyes with which to see . . . they see everything. Children come equipped with ears . . . they listen to every whisper. Children come with feelings too . . . they respond to love just as they respond to all the opposites; hate, indifference, deception, prejudice, lies, anger, injustice, war . . . you get the picture. We shall reap what we sow and our sins will find us out.

That's scary to think about isn't it; we shall reap what we sow and our sins will find us out? Looking at my own past I tremble. My works, even the best ones, are like filthy rags in the Lords presence. But, I thank my heavenly Father for sending His greatest gift of all into this world's miasma; His Son the Lord Jesus Christ is our intercessor. Without His blood, His sacrifice we are lost. Thanks be to Him . . . let the world say; Amen

Childhood experiences compelled me to write this book. Those times, my friends and neighbors I review fondly and lovingly. Where each of us stands today is a compilation of our past and the choices we made. No one person or event in this story can be held as fact or fiction but only to the artistic license I used to create this story.

CHAPTER 1

The Really Great Idea

SSSSSkklaammm! The old squeaky screen door met the door frame dead on closing with as much authority that one little boy could muster. And that was that . . . I had all the abuse I could take for one day. Since I just celebrated my twelfth birthday I shouldn't have to pick up after me and my little brother too! He made more mess than I could ever think about making. And he did it in less time. He was a mean mess making machine. The swing set under the old apple tree was my point of refuge. Here I could sit all by myself and work things out to my heart's content.

It was July and the weather was hot and muggy. Mom said it was so hot in July when I was born that the heat could have melted the paint off the face of the old wooden Indian statue outside "Tittles Five and Dime Store". She said she didn't think she could stand much more if I didn't show up when I did.

Speaking of mom, here she comes. I can hear her footsteps and she is heading for the back door. It seems she is always looking for me. Maybe I'll just head for the barn. Yup, it will look like I'm on a mission to help dad with something important. Better hurry up before she gets outside.

Locking on with her mom radar she calls out bringing me to a halt in mid stride. "Hey, hold on mister! Where do you think you are going in such a big hurry? There are chores in the house to be done! You haven't finished with them yet! Before you go running off pretending to be busy doing something important; clean up one mess before you make another."

Rules to live by and what could I say? There's no point to argue because I always lose. So, I will do an about face and return to the house. "Okay mom . . . I'll be right there", I begrudgingly called out!

When I went back into the house mom was busy washing the breakfast dishes. Of course, right there in the middle of the floor sat my little brother playing with his toys. Without missing a swipe with the drying towel mom went through the rules recital: "*If you make a mess, you clean it up . . . drop it on the floor, you pick it up . . . dirty clothes and dirty towels go in the laundry hamper, and . . .*"

"I know, I know mom", I assured her as I finished what I knew she would say; "don't forget to make the bed."

How many more times must I hear that sing songy poem? This is just too much pressure for one little kid. Especially right now, I'm on summer vacation! Doesn't mom know that?

While still standing behind mom with my hands in my pockets and sporting a sheepish look I timidly made a request. I cleared my throat and spoke up, "Ahh . . . Mom."

"Yes Larry", she replied.

Trying out my best manly voice I started out with, "Ya know, I've been thinking."

"Oh really . . . and what might those thoughts be about", mom inquired?

Then mom stopped me. "You should wait . . . you should save your thoughts for lunch time when your father comes in from doing the morning chores? Then we could all share in your ideas. What do you think?"

Slowly I rolled my eyes and looked down at the floor. Disappointed with mom's suggestion, I drew out the words . . . "Well . . . yeah . . . I guess so."

"Good", mom said feeling good about the decision, smiling back at me. "It'll be lunch soon then we can all talk about it. I'm glad we agree."

My idea wasn't to have a big family meeting. I just wanted to bounce a few ideas off of mom to see her reaction before a formal presentation to the commander and chief. So at this point I didn't push the conversation any further and retreated upstairs.

Once in the safety of my room I started thinking about my idea as I finished my chores. I put away the toys. Picking up my dirty clothes, after grabbing the wet towel from the bed, I put it all into the laundry hamper. And lastly I made the bed. There . . . once again . . . all done . . . everything is neat and tidy.

My little brother, the pest, could be heard coming up the steps. Don't take what I say the wrong way. It's not that I don't love my brother. It's the big age difference. He's not into the more grownup things that I'm into. He can't even throw a baseball correctly. He can't even hit the ball or catch it when I throw it to him without getting bopped in the head.

But, the one thing he is good at . . . coming into my room when I'm not around and messing with my stuff. Little brother doesn't pick up the toys after he's finished playing with them. But guess who gets the rules recital when that happens? Yup, you got it . . . me. He's not old enough to fully understand the intention of the rules recital. Mom and dad tried to explain accountability to me one time but it seemed very complicated. I sorta came around to their way of thinking after the spanking. When my brother begins to understand accountability, that's where it ends. No more Mister nice guy. He's going to have to carry his own weight around here.

The familiar drone from the engine of Dad's old Ford tractor could be heard as he was plowing the field behind the barn. A breeze coming through the open window carried the smell of the overturned earth. Living on this small farm had its advantages. In the country life was different as compared to being a "Townie".

That's what my dad calls the people in the town where I go to Elementary School, "Townies". Dad wakes up at 4:00 am every day to work in town at the dairy station and he noted to me the differences between town and country life. He said it was too hot in town during the summer and it stank because of the tannery located next door to the dairy station. Both businesses were located right in the town limits.

The tannery was a place where people would bring raw animal hides and have them processed into leather goods. The processing of the hides included putting the raw hides in large vats of tannic acid. The stench from doing that was horrendous. On certain days when the wind was just right it would capture and deliver that odor right to our front door.

And the dairy station where my dad worked was where farmers brought milk to be sent off to New York City for processing. The dairy plant was a holding station where they received and chilled down the milk before they piped it into tanker trucks for delivery.

Dad's observation was that there were too many people in town and they all lived on top of one another. Living that way he said, being so close together, you could even smell the aroma from whatever your neighbor was cooking for breakfast. No privacy there, he said. And who needs that? It's of no one's concern whether I am frying bacon with my eggs, drinking ersatz or regular coffee or if I elect to have a meal at one o'clock in the morning. It is just nobody's affair.

I'm going into sixth grade this year and I knew exactly what dad was talking about. Odd words don't bother me anymore. I just go to the Webster's. When mom and dad really didn't want my little brother and I to know what they were talking about they spoke in Sweiss Deitch. Believe me, there is no dictionary on the planet for that language.

There were different sounds and smells out in the country too. Some smells I was sure I'd want to remember. Others, like when I had to help dad clean out the chicken house or the cow stable, those I wanted to forget. But I have dear memories of other experiences: the smell of the fresh mowed lawn and cut hay drying in the field, waking up to the aroma of brewing coffee, breakfast cooking on the old hand fired cast iron stove that mixed it all together with just a hint of wood smoke, the smell of autumn in the forest, the smell of the inside of the barn where the harvest was stored. The tractor shed also held distinct scents of dust from the field mixed together with the smell of gasoline, oil, grease and labored engine parts.

Then we have to address the worst smell possible to an up and coming big league baseball prospect. It always seemed that just when we gathered enough kids together to have a ball game, mom would tell us that we better come inside because she could smell rain coming. We would all get upset because we didn't understand how she could give a weather forecast by sniffing out an approaching storm. Eventually I too would come to know what she was talking about, but not back then. As kids, we were all filled to the brim with impatience. We didn't want to hear about rain. There was no telling us to come inside, not when there was the proposition of a big game to play.

Wait a minute. What is the sound that I no longer hear? The sound of the old Ford tractor has stopped. That means dad will be coming in to have lunch and I need to think more about my request. From my bed I continued to stare out the window looking at the trees beyond the field. There was a really neat area on the other side of the creek at the end of the field. It had a bare area underneath some very large hemlocks that would provide good shade. That would make an ideal camping spot.

My little brother broke into my daydream. "Will you play trucks and cars with me", he asked?

"Not right now", I replied.

"Why not . . . you're not doing anything", he asked insistently?

"Look kid, I am in the middle of making some very big decisions right now and you are bothering me", I said emphatically. "Okay?"

"Don't look like you're doing anything. You're just staring out that old window like you always do. You never have time to play with me", my brother said complaining to me.

"After lunch maybe I'll play a game with you. How would that be", I asked? "Just give me some space right now."

"Alright", he agreed finally conceding, "But you have to promise to play catch with me after lunch." He paused for a moment and then asked, "What is so important that you're just lying there with a dumb look on your face?"

"You wouldn't understand. Its big people stuff that I'm thinking about", I quipped.

"Oh yeah, big people stuff, you're acting funny alright", my brother observed . . . "Like how dad gets when he drags barn dirt in the house . . . cause he forgets to take his boots off! When mom catches him . . . he gets a goofy look? That's how you look. You must be in big trouble?"

"No, I'm not in trouble", I answered, paused and then assured him. "At least I'm not right now."

"Are you gonna be in trouble", my brother asked? "Are you thinking about getting in trouble?"

"No! And getting into trouble is not something you think about . . . it just happens! And you're startin to be a pest", I said. "So shoo fly, just go away!"

"Lunch is ready!" Moms' voice suddenly stopped our brotherly conversation.

My father also yelled out. "Come on boys it's time to eat! Come and get it while it's hot or they will throw it out!"

Down the stair steps we ran to have lunch. My dad was already at the table. Mom and grandmother were busy taking things from the stove and putting the hot food into the serving dishes.

Grandmother also lived with us and helped take care of my brother and me when mom was working.

Finally all was ready and grandmother gave the blessing. After the prayer dad started passing around the food and mom served my little brother his meal.

We were about halfway through eating and now that dad's stomach pains were repealed he decided to pop the question. He wanted to satisfy everyone's curiosity about my big idea. Mom and he must have had one of those secret talks before lunch. It's the conversation about how to proceed when they know one of the boys might be up to something. They'd want to nip it in the bud before the problem gets out of hand.

"So Larry" . . . as he got my attention dad went on to say, "Your' mother tells me you have a big idea that you would like to share with all of us?"

Grandma's attention was now averted from her plate of food as my brother had to throw in his two cents. "Yeah dad . . . he was up in his room looking out the window. He had a goofy look. Sorta like the way you look. You know when ya drag dirt in the house and mom yells at you?"

Mom got a good laugh at my little brothers statement. Dad got a grim look on his face, grandma chuckled too but then the faces of all at table turned in my direction.

"So what's your big idea", mom called out?

There's nothing like being on the hot seat. I felt like I was on the TV show "You Bet Your Life" and Groucho was asking me the big money question. Say the secret word and the duck will come down and give you a hundred dollars.

You bet your life he will if I could only speak. Speak, Larry speak! I was desperately searching for the secret word. I was looking for a magic genie in a bottle hoping she might pop up and grant me a wish to disappear. The tick-tock of the Grandfather clock kept getting louder and louder in my ears.

I finally mustered the courage to present my case and there was no stopping now . . . so I blurted out, "I want to leave! Go out on my own for awhile!"

There was dead silence from the family gallery and the tick tock, tick tock of the grandfather clock.

It was little brother who broke the deadlocked silence, "Cool . . . Wow . . . Great big idea! Can I have his room? I want all his neat junk and comics!"

Mom and dad glared at my brother and both said in unison, NO! Then their attention and eyes snapped directly back to me.

Again there was nothing but the tick-tock of the Grandfather clock.

Finally dad said in a calm voice, "I see."

"And where are you thinking of going", asked mom?

Grandmother then jumped into the conversation as she stated, "This idea is totally ridiculous and a waste of words!"

Continuing to explain I said, "Well, I've thought about it. I know mom doesn't like my toys all over and my clothes on the floor. In fact I feel like I'm in everyone's way around here. I want to pitch my tent across the creek under the hemlock trees. There's shade and I would be right there if anyone ever needs me."

"You think that we don't need you", inquired my mother?

Dad waved his hand at mom as if to tell her not to worry and said, "Well Larry you are getting old enough to make some bigger choices on your own. You want to move out? Is this what I am hearing?"

Just barely managing to squeak out a non committal answer I said, "Well yeah . . . sorta kinda . . . move out, I guess." I was treading in unfamiliar water here.

Startling everyone dad smacked the table and stated, "You all know what? I think that is a great big idea Larry. That's just what you need. Grab life by the horns and set out on your own. Take responsibility head on . . . wash your clothes down at the creek side and cook your meals over the campfire. I think I might even have an old camp stove somewhere to help out just in case it rains and you can't get the fire started."

With a strange dreamy look on his face dad continued. "My son, nothing compares to sleeping out under the stars, having your back right against mother earth. When there's just between you and the great outdoors the mere fabric wall of the tent, yes-sir-ree now that's living . . . yup, in my estimation there's nothing better! Oh, the chorus of the crickets, the croaking of the bullfrogs mixed with the voices of other unseen creatures of the forest at night . . . that is music to my ears. I am sure son that you will be as excited as I was when I heard all those noises for the first time . . . all alone . . . out there in the forest."

Aside from the Grandfather clocks tick-tock you could have heard a pin drop on the kitchen floor after dad's speech. I would later believe that he should have won an Oscar for his oratory. Mom was speechless, grandma thought the rhetoric an over loaded manure spreader and said as much. With a "humph", she immediately got up and started clearing the table forgetting about the uneaten food left on her plate.

Little brother just sat there clueless as to what was said and quietly asked, "Does this mean I get his room?"

Mom looked down at my brother, silently mouthed the word no as she shook her head negatively affirming what she was saying.

I was also at a loss for words. Dad broke the silence with . . . "Okay kid, are you ready to set up camp?"

Talk about kicking it into high gear. I hadn't said that this is what I **wanted** to do . . . or, did I? What was that old saying that grandma was always quoting that seems applicable right here and now? She had a million of them. Oh yes, it is; *Be careful what you wish for, because it just might come true.* Yup, seems appropriate right now doesn't it?

CHAPTER 2

A Camping We Will Go

Mom watched in disbelief as I followed dad down into the basement. Dad saw her concerned look and assured her that this was a great idea and that I would be just fine.

I heard dad say. "Don't worry mom it'll be a great learning experience for him . . . one of those things he'll remember for the rest of his life."

I was beginning to question my big idea. That is, if this really was such a big idea, or not? Would this be something I would remember? For right now I was caught in the slipstream and going with the flow. Dad found an old camp axe, the camp stove he was talking about and other antiquated looking outdoor equipment. He also grabbed my tent that was new last year and my sleeping bag from out of storage.

Last year a few of my baseball buddies and I had camped out in the back yard. We had access to the house, the barbeque grill, TV and late night "Horror Theatre". After "Horror Theatre" we all grabbed our sleeping bags and slept on the back porch. That was the extent of my camping out. I was now on an express elevator graduating from the back porch and heading for the big woods across the creek. At this point what was I thinking? I would be in the woods at night . . . all alone . . . lions, tigers, bears or worse . . . in the dark . . . oooh nooo!

Mom and grandmother looked on from the back porch. Their faces offered concern as they witnessed dad and their young boys pack camping gear into the pull behind trailer hitched to the old tractor. After all the gear was stowed little brother and I hopped into the wagon and dad settled into the tractors driver's seat. He called over his shoulder as he eased the throttle up to give the engine more gas. "Hang on boys! It is a camping we will go!"

My brother and I waved goodbye to mom and grandmother. We were driven through the yard and onto the dirt road that would lead us past the barn, the field and eventually to our destination. The camp site I was dreaming about while staring out my bedroom window was becoming a reality there beneath the spreading branches of the hemlock trees. Be careful what you wish for came to mind.

It was a little bumpy riding in the back of the wagon but kind of neat too. My little brother was enjoying this more than he ever would have playing catch. He was just chirping away. "This is fun! Wow! I never got to ride in the wagon before! This is great helping you to move out of the house Larry!"

"I'm not EXACTLY moving out of the house", I said trying to stifle my little brothers' unsolicited excitement.

My little brother thought for a second . . . "huh . . . I thought that's what you are doing . . . moving out? Well, ain't that what mom thinks? She looked sad. Grandma just looked like she always looks . . . grumpy. She's always grumpy!"

"The word is, isn't not ain't little bro", I said correcting him. And I AIN'T exactly sure what mom thinks. I think most times I am just a bother to her."

Dad made a left turn and pulled the throttle back to slow the engine as we were going to cross over the creek and start up the hill. He looked back and smiled approvingly when he saw we were still holding on to the side rails of the wagon. We crossed over the stream and dad pulled over into the area where I was apparently to set up camp. He pulled the brake and shut off the engine.

"Well here we are boys", dad said rubbing his hands together enthusiastically. He pointed and gestured towards the trees and sky and then commented, "Just look at all this nature and breathe deep boys. You can smell the pines and the freshness of the air and listen . . . you can hear the babbling brook. Wait until tonight Larry your senses won't be able to take it all in."

After he made that last statement he just chuckled.

"What did you mean by that . . . I won't be able to take it all in", I asked?

"Don't worry about it . . . forget about it . . . I was just being funny at your' expense", dad said and changed the subject.

"You know Larry I went to fill the tractor up with gas this morning at the station and it cost me almost a five dollar bill . . . yes, five dollars to fill up the fifteen gallon tank on this old tractor. Gas is now at thirty one cents a gallon. Back when this tractor was built in the forties gas was about ten cents cheaper than it is right now. Everything is going up in price. It's a good thing we're on the farm because at the store people think that chickens are laying golden eggs too. They're paying close to half a dollar a dozen for em. Can you believe it?"

"No", I said, as I wasn't really sure what dad was rambling on about but I believed "no" to be the appropriate answer. My little brother looked confused about the conversation too and just shrugged his shoulders.

All in the midst of discussing the plight of the American economy dad began unloading the wagon. Usually he talked about egg, milk and bread prices to mom. Since ours were the only ears available I guess he thought it would be a good time to bring us up to speed on such important matters. In between his complaints about out of control spiraling prices on goods, he fretted too about the fact of not knowing where this would all end up if people didn't stop spending money they didn't have. More good rules to live by.

Dad became the Gunny Sergeant of the outpost commanding us to put the tent over there and place the pegs here. "Don't forget to place your fire ring over there well away from underneath the hemlocks, he called out. They'll go up like gasoline if they catch on fire and will set the whole forest ablaze!"

"Not a good idea", I agreed. Within my own thoughts I was wondering if this really was going to be a permanent situation. This seemed real serious and we were going through a whole lot of trouble building this campsite.

There was a stone altar that someone had built along with several benches attached to trees about ten feet away from where we set up the tent. Dad said this had been built by the prior owners of the farm and was their personal outdoor church. I thought it to be a very appropriate spot. It was peaceful here. I placed the old camp stove on one of the benches and began gathering stones for the fire ring. Dad instructed my brother to pick up all the dry wood he could find and stack it for the campfire.

Grabbing some clothes line from the back of the wagon dad tied it between two trees and then gave instructions. "In the morning when you wake up you want to hang your sleeping bag on the line so the moisture dries out of it. You don't want it to become moldy. You can also hang your hand washed clothes on it too."

Dad gave me a wink and then added. "We'll bring the old tub and washboard along with some bars of lye soap after supper. In all the hustle to set up camp I forgot that you'll need the tub to wash yourself and your clothes. Sorry about that."

"Cool", said little brother.

I just sort of made a smirk and said, "Thanks dad."

"Glad to help son, just glad I can be of help", dad chortled.

After having toted the stones over to the place for the fire circle I grabbed the spade shovel to dig out the middle. How big in diameter should I make it, I asked?

Dad gave out my instructions. "Dig down about ten inches and make it about three and a half feet wide, set the stones around the perimeter and put the ground you take out of the middle against the outside of the stones." Dad continued to explain that I should also dig up the grass around the campfire about one foot around it just to be safe. "Cut the weeds down from around the rest of the camp area with the sickle that's in the back of the wagon."

What was I thinkin? Did I not realize that there was so much work to setting up a campsite? Whew! I was going to need a bath after this was over and wondered if I would be taking my next one in the stream next to the camp or in the old wash tub with a bar of grandma's lye soap.

We chopped up dead trees for more firewood and cleaned up brush around the whole area for about thirty yards in every direction. My brother started complaining that it was too hot and he was tired and getting hungry too. My stomach was also calling out for some attention.

It was a good thing we brought along a thermos filled with ice water because mom was dead on when she said it was hot in July. I guess I never noticed the heat until right now. When you're playing ball or doing fun things the heat is not a factor. But working like this is a different story. Dad was even looking a little drawn. Sweat was running down his face and his shirt was soaking wet with sweat. I had to give him credit. When dad helped us to do something he was in it for one hundred and fifty percent.

Finally dad conceded. "Boys", he said. "I think we need to call it a day and head for the house and get cleaned up for supper. We can come back this evening and set up the rest of the camp as the hard part is done. Now the fun begins for Larry. He gets to enjoy the fruit from all this afternoon's labor. Your new home is set up and ready for occupancy buddy. You can have one more bath at home and a change of clean clothes before the real move this evening."

Dad finished the sentence with another wink.

I was wondering what all the winking was about. It seemed like things were getting much more serious than I had ever intended this to be.

Little brother chimed in and asked. "Heeey . . . daaad? What about me? I helped too? Don't I get to have fun? I want to camp out too . . . just for one night though? Not like Larry."

"We will see what mom has to say about that", dad said. "You know she's the boss when it comes to certain things."

The wagon clunked and squeaked as the tractor pulled away from the camp site. Brother and I had fun bouncing around in the back of it all the way to the barn. Dad backed into the shed and we jumped out. I pulled the pin from the hitch so dad could pull away and park the tractor next to the wagon.

Hearing the cackle of the chickens reminded me that there were evening chores to do before washing up for supper. Little brother and I got the chicken feed and mash from the feed barrels and prepared to gather what dad referred to earlier as golden eggs. He left us in charge of the small critters.

The two steers and our one lonely riding horse were dad's job. He told us about the time a mean bull had purposely pinned him against the barn stall and tried to crush him. If grandpa hadn't been there dad said, he would not be here today. His rule for my brother and I was very simple. We were to never, ever go into the stalls with the steers. We weren't sure at the time what he was talking about, but he said. "Even though all the steam had been taken out of their boiler you still can't trust them."

Little brother loved taking care of the pet rabbits so I left him do that while I went to feed Danny and Mike which were dads prized hunting dogs. They were a pair of perfectly matched beagles. Dad said it was better than perfection to see how those two worked the brush and briars to flush out wild rabbits and ring neck pheasants. This year I would go along hunting with dad. I had already passed my hunting certification class. This was something that just about every twelve year old boy growing up in the country looked forward to doing. Hunting was something passed down from father to son.

But for now the only thing I wanted passed were serving dishes. My belly felt like it had a new best friend as it shook hands with my backbone. Waiting for me was a glass filled to the top with mom's ice cold lemon aide that would be on a collision course with my waiting kisser. The smell of fried chicken and corn on the cob cooking in the stew pot caught my attention.

The routine of the evening chores were overshadowed by thoughts of bright red fresh tomatoes sliced on a plate, diced cucumber salad, mashed potatoes and a large portion of grandma's coconut custard pie for dessert.

A little tiny voice way far away in the back of my head whispered a question that resounded like last weeks' thunderstorm; YOU WANT TO MOVE OUT AND INTO A TENT, AND YOUR REASONING BEHIND THAT IS WHAT . . . ?

Of course being a young man of principal I had to submerge any negative thoughts. At this point I had gone too far and I had reached the point of no return. I had my honor to defend. Besides, I had not yet contacted my buddies who were absolute camp out fanatics. Surely I would not be alone? Could there be a method to this madness? Dad didn't say I couldn't invite my buddies to stay.

CHAPTER 3

Something's In the Air

Grandma yelled from the kitchen window. "Food is at the table, hot, ready and waiting!"

The stable door closed behind me and I knew that dad had heard Grandma's call too. "Let's go get it while its' hot", he said.

"Yeah I know", I agreed. "Or before they throw it out, right?"

"That's right, you got the idea", dad asserted.

Looking around I didn't see my brother anywhere. That clever little guy . . . there he was. His face was pressed against the screen door. It looked like he was eating something as I could see a chewing motion going on and at the same time he had a big grin. Was he poking fun? "Hey you", I called out. "What's the big idea cutting chores and sneaking into the house before us?"

He started laughing and yelled. "Ha, ha you're a bunch of slow pokes. The last one in is a rotten egg!"

Off I went racing for the back door because I didn't want to be the rotten egg. I guess there was no race because I was the only one running. Dad was carrying the "golden eggs" we had gathered from the chicken house and was headed for the basement wash room to clean up. When I reached the screen door little brother was nowhere to be found. "You little stinker", I called out. "When I find you I'm gonna . . ."

"You're gonna do what", asked grandma?

Looming in front of me like a military soldier was Grandma standing ready with her corn broom in hand to swat any intruder brave enough to enter the house. I'll bet she had a lot of practice in her day. Mom said she grew up in a family with six other brothers and sisters. I could only imagine the amount of whoopins that would happen on any given day. Grandma without a doubt would have a swing as good as that of the "*Great Bambino*".

Dodging the broom I scooted past Grandma and headed for the wash sink. Just around the corner was all that food. My mission as I saw it was to be seated at the table in thirty seconds or less.

As I plopped down in my assigned seat next to dad in error my hand mistakenly reached for an ear of corn. It was so out of character and I knew better. To help me with my lapse of sanity grandma reeled me back in with a swat on the hand. "Not before God gets his thanks young man", she affirmed.

"Sorry", I said.

Mom and dad seated themselves along with my brother. Grandma offered grace.

The meal was much needed, and not many words were spoken as the food disappeared into the hungry mouths of all at the table. While mom got up to get dessert I started talking about making some phone calls to my buddies for the campout.

Dad thought that would be a good idea. And then he elaborated, "Now all the nonsense has been worked out of your system. Larry this campout will be for only one night. I could see it in your face as we worked ourselves to exhaustion today. You had thought better of the idea of moving out. It was fun going along for the ride while it lasted! Ha! Ha! Ha! I guess the jokes on you!"

Patting me on the back while giving me the Ha, ha, ha, dad said, "I really must admit that I wanted to see you down by the camp taking a tepid bath in the old laundry tub. Watching you lathering up with a bar of lye soap would have brought joyful tears to my eyes. But, I don't think your mother would have appreciated me taking it that far."

Along with that statement a sigh of relief was heard from mom. Grandma peered at us from over the top of her glasses and said, "I'm glad to see that we have not all lost our sanity!"

A lot of weight had just been lifted off my shoulders. Hey, didn't I state a little while back that I was on vacation. Don't need that kind of pressure, self inflicted or otherwise.

"The camp out will happen as long as some basic rules are followed", dad commented.

A huge grin appeared on my face as I chimed out, "Yes sir!"

Dad continued proposing a list of requirements. "As a matter of fact, my concerns are about the safety of the kids, the campfire and getting to bed at a decent hour. I do not mind that you are inviting friends. Oh yes, and about the one very important rule which I have written in stone before . . . *there will be no bike riding on the main road at night*! Are we in agreement mister?"

Giving dad the thumbs up sign, I thought that said it all but he didn't take it that way.

"That's cute and everything Larry . . . the thumbs up sign", dad said. And dad made the thumbs up sign back at me. "Don't take what I say about the bike riding loosely", dad warned. "I mean it. If my rules are not followed there will be punishment. You won't see daylight until next year. Your buddies will think you have moved outta town because they will see so little of you."

My face looked grim as I nodded in understanding.

Deep inside though, I was bursting. It was now stated that I would not be moving out of the house. That was a relief. Parents sometimes know best. I was even happy that dad had laid the groundwork for some rules to follow about the camp out. He had gone to a lot of trouble for me and I liked that. But the one thing that was so way cool and off the charts, was the night of freedom to camp out with the guys. Oh boy!

Mom came back with the custard pie and a surprise. Watermelon was on the menu too. Then she dropped the bomb. "You know what Larry? And I hate to be the bearer of bad news. When I went out onto the back porch to get the watermelon from the ice box I smelled rain comin. Its' coming from the west I believe."

"What", I exclaimed?

Grandma had to add her two cents. "Yes daughter I believe you are correct. My bones started aching about half an hour ago. I can feel that rain is on the way. Should be here in about ten to fifteen minutes I'd guess." She ended the conversation by rubbing her elbows.

"What are you guys anyway", I asked disgruntled, "The bad news weather-people?" "We worked all afternoon to get that campsite ready. I haven't even made one phone call yet!"

"What? . . . Do think they're saying this purposely just to get you upset", questioned dad? "They don't have any control over the weather."

"Well . . . yeah I guess . . . sorta", I blurted out. "I mean, I know they don't control the weather. But it just seems like when I have made plans, mom always says she smells rain coming. How can she do that?"

"And geez whizz", I continued my protest! "Most of the time she's right! She's got a better batting average than Roger Maris or Mickey Mantle. Certainly better than that stupid groundhog that pops out and always predicts a longer winter. Mom should be on Channel 8 TV with the evening report."

Lowering my voice to sound like a grownup I continued my lamentations, "Mrs. B says she smells rain for this evening giving way to gradual clearing and spreading light early in the morning."

"Cool mom . . . you on TV", little brother blurted out. "That would be great!"

"Ok, ok you guys that is enough", dad said as he looked at me sympathetically. "Look son, I helped on the project too. And I want you to use the campsite, but you can't go out there in a thunderstorm. That's just not going to happen."

Looking down at the table I mumbled with my chin on my chest, "I guess so. But I hope it doesn't rain."

"Me too", said grandma. Because I have a tent revival meeting tonight! I'm looking forward to that, praise the Lord. It's going on for a week and you children should go along sometime. It would do you some good. I'm just not talking to the wee young ones ya know. And by the way they are having a guest speaker who will be talking about the human rights situation that is occurring in the south. That is a nasty business. I can't believe that after all these years we are still dealing with that. We had to fight for the women's right to vote. We're still fighting over racial equality. Down there they got separate eating arrangements for the white and the black folks. It's ridiculous. No one's gonna tell me I can't sit down and eat in the same dining area with Ruthy Page. She and I been friends for years. They can kiss my white . . ."

"Okay mom, maybe I can go with you one or two nights. But speaking about church things here at home", mom said. "Larry your Bible school teacher Luara called and said that Bible study classes will be offered soon after school starts. She also wants you boys to sing at church and practice will be tomorrow at 1:00 pm sharp at the sanctuary."

"Don't know if I want to go", I said still pouting.

"What do you mean you don't know if you want to go", mom questioned?

Uh, oh . . . here comes grandma jumping into the conversation.

Grandma looked at mom and then down at me, pursed her lips and then opened fire. "As if the boy has a choice in the matter . . . you are twelve years old young man and you need to start making a decision. Where are you going with your life? And it should be now before the world bites too big a chunk outta you."

I looked at Grandma and told her, "I have no idea what you are talking about. I am just twelve years old."

"Course not", snapped grandma. "How could you be expected to know, and that's the point."

Dad all this time was leaning back in his chair with his arms folded watching whoever would speak up next. I think that he was enjoying the exchange because he was just sitting there smiling away.

"You're going Larry and that's that", mom said. "All your friends are going and you might learn something too and not even realize it. It will be fun."

Now dad looked at grandma.

"Hrrmmph! Fun, snorted grandma, that's all people think about nowadays is . . . fun. I grew up on a dirt poor farm and came up through the great depression. Now that was some fun let me tell you.

Here comes one of grandmas now and then speeches. She doesn't mean fun in like WOW THIS IS FUN! No, she means fun in like, lets clean out the cow stable because that is so much fun, NOT!

"Those were some hard times!" Grandma went on to say. "Just trying to make ends meet was tough. We were sometimes starving so bad we ate opossums and raccoons. My belly button was rubbin my backbone most times. Snakes were even on the eatable list back then. If I'd seen a snake I would have it skinned, cooked and ate all in ten minutes time.

Dad shook his head agreeing with grandma. But for me dad said, "I could never bring myself to eat an opossum, a raccoon maybe. Opossums look too much like a giant rat with brush bristles for hair and to eat a snake . . . I don't know? I guess it really does depend how hungry you might be?"

"Well Ben", grandma said, "You grew up in the better situation. You were lucky that you had better choices about what you could eat. You got to eat raccoons rather than opossums and snakes."

My dad then said, "Yes grandma, but let's not forget about the slimy eels we caught out of the creek. We did eat those and they were terribly hard to skin and very messy to clean."

With that being said and out of the way Grandma gave my dad a look and went on with her story. "Well ask your mother Larry if ya don't believe in what I say. God is my witness and you don't need any more truth than that. Son you are living the gravy train life now. Your parents provide for you a thousand times more than I ever could for your mother and kin. It grieves my heart to see the disrespect in the children today that they have for their parents. In my day there was family and that is all you could rely on. The government or anyone else you cannot trust. The government! With one hand their given and smiling and the other hand is taken away your freedom. It was family and only by the real grace of God that you survived back then."

Dad now looked over at mom. .

"Okay . . . ok mom, I think you are scaring the kids and there are nicer things we can talk about", mom suggested. And now mom looked over at dad and said, "And what are you doing just sittin there smilin away not saying much?"

"Hey ladies, I am in agreement with what you're talking about", dad said.

"Well anyway", grandma said getting right to the point. "They ought to be afraid of something!" With that final statement grandma abruptly got up and started clearing the table.

"See there", dad said. "I agree with that too."

Both mom and grandma looked at dad and then at me and gave us each a look. Don't know what that meant, but it was a look none the less.

Gee, had it been ten minutes already? Right on time and directly after grandma's speech a bright light flashed outside. A few seconds later . . . bang, you heard the thunder boomer. Yup, mom and grandma were right on. Here comes the rain.

I questioningly looked over at dad and he raised his eyebrows, shook his head as he shrugged his shoulders. "What can I say", he said. "They know the weather."

"Ok, I guess camping is cancelled", I responded giving out the schedule as I saw it. "There will be choir practice tomorrow, church the next day and Bible school coming up soon. Where do I sign up?"

"Don't sound so dejected Larry", grandma said seeming to have a change in her mood. "When we finish with the dishes come to my room and I'll help you get started on those Bible studies. After all, my tenting event will be cancelled too."

"Oh, I don't know, I grumbled . . . maybe?"

"Who better to get help from", queried mom. "Grandma knows more about the Bible than most people alive and maybe even more than our own Pastor Wright."

Grandma was an authority on the Bible and Christianity alright. She had volumes of books on every related subject to prove it. She had books on the beginning of the Protestant movement. She had books about the breakaway from the Catholic Church. She had books on Evangelism too. And books about every denomination and offshoot of the Christian movement lined the shelves in her room. If you got questions about Christianity grandma could probably find the answer.

She explained the reason concerning the variety of her books along with a warning. "There are many deceivers out there and false Profits abound. You can never be too careful and you need to study. Search for the truth. Life is a journey and you never stop learning so treat it as such."

My camping definitely would not happen this evening. It rained hard and the thunder showers kept on coming.

So off I go to my room to look at my latest super hero comic. Also mom bought me a magazine that had a story about the new X-15 aircraft. This rocket powered rocket plane moves faster than any manned aircraft ever did before. It flies at speeds up to mach-6. That's 6 times the speed of sound. It can fly as high as 63,137 miles above the earth. That is pushing past earth's atmosphere into outer space.

Little brother suddenly came in looking for something to do and starting pulling out from under my bed the set of Lincoln logs and a few trucks and cars. See, just like that he comes in. He doesn't even knock, doesn't even say hi or excuse me. I get no privacy. "Do not make a mess", I cautioned him. "And if you do . . . clean it up!"

"Okay . . . don't have to always yell at me", he said. "I know the rules. You're mean cause you're not camping."

Little brother went about his business and I went back to my magazine. I can't even imagine going faster than the speed of sound, or flying to the edge of outer space. It says here that once the pilots go past 50,000 miles high that qualifies them for a set of U. S. Air Force Astronaut Wings. Yeah, that's what I need to do, be an astronaut. How cool would that be!

The air smelled fresh and clean coming through the window. I loved listening to the rain hitting on the metal porch roof and running into the rain gutters and down the spouts. That silly song itsy bitsy spider came to mind. I thought about grandma's offer about spending some time with her. Why not? I read all my Hardy Boy books and I didn't get any new ones recently. Yeah, why not spend some time with grandma? Maybe she needed some company now that her tent meeting was cancelled.

Leaving my brother to trucks, cars and Lincoln logs I semi-reluctantly took the short walk to grandma's room. I peered in from around the door and I could see her sitting on the couch studying a book using a magnifying glass. I pushed the door slightly and she said, "Ah Larry, you've come to visit your old grandmother."

"How'd you know it was me", I asked?

"Let me see", grandma mused. "Could it be that I know your footsteps. Or how about the fact; I knew you were wondering about whether or not you wanted to come in. So you peer in-between the door and frame, hesitating before pushing on the door. I am not deaf and I am not yet entering into dementia."

Grandma explained that all without looking up from the page she was reading. She then laid down her magnifying glass and closed the book. "So where do we begin you wonder? First come over and sit beside me. You know we haven't sat down and had a good talk in a long time."

She motioned for me to come closer . . . "Really . . . come in here and sit down."

Slowly I walked over and sat down. She took my right hand in her hands and looked at it and turned it over and held it to her face. "You know Larry", she said. "You have the hands of a doctor or a musician. You have a temperament that could allow you to do great things. That is of course, if you don't become your own worst enemy."

"How do you know that grandma", I asked?

"History Larry", grandma said tapping her head with her forefinger. "I hold a lot of history inside this old worn out shell. My mind feels keen and poignant like it did a lifetime ago but the flesh is weak. And remember, I watch you growing up day after day. I see you have a little dark side to you. You have a desire to get ahead but sometimes you make short cuts. I see that too. What do you say we get you started in discovering the Bible. Let's learn about the greatest teacher of all."

"I guess so grandma", I said. "But where do we start?"

"Where does anyone start a journey Larry", she asked?

"From the beginning I guess?"

"Exactly", grandma affirmed!

She got up and brought from the shelf one of the biggest books I had ever seen. Centering her rolling reading table in front of us she adjusted so we could both look at the book. The Bible was leather bound and was also illustrated with beautiful pictures.

"And God created the heavens and the earth", grandma stated. "We will start where He started, right here in the front of the book, in the beginning."

We went over some stories that I remembered from Bible class. But grandma told them in a different way which helped me to understand their meaning better. Grandma taught me about creation and how long it took. She made a strong point that God had rested on the seventh day and deemed it His Holy Sabbath. It became very clear just how important the Sabbath really is.

She talked about Adam and Eve and their falling out because of disobedience. The first sacrifice occurred when God clothed Adam and Eve with the skins of animals to hide their nakedness. That was something I did not know. I wondered why they would disobey God when they had it all going for them. Now they had to labor and toil in order to survive.

Sharing my thoughts with grandma I said, "Boy I wish I could talk directly to those guys. I would love to kick Adam right in his shins. What were they thinking I wonder? Adam left the influence of a girl sway him to disobey God. I promise you grandma . . . I will never let that happen to me!"

She just smiled.

Grandma went on to explain. "God is an understanding, loving and forgiving God. So He provided a way for us to come back into his good grace and save us from that original sin."

"How did he do that? And why would he do that, after Adam and Eve disrespected Him", were my questions?"

"After you do something not to their liking, don't mom and dad still love you", asked Grandma?

"I guess they do. You yell at me sometimes too grandma", I said. "And sometimes if I am really bad . . . you guys give me a spanking. I guess that depends on how bad I was."

A story came to mind about one of those really bad things that I did and I related it to Grandma.

"It was the time", I told her. "I accidently left the door open to the beagle's cage after I fed them. Dad was so mad he said that he was seeing red. If he wouldn't have gotten his prize hunting dogs back . . . and he chased them half way across the county you know. He would have skinned me alive. I took a serious whoopin for that one. I felt the sting on my butt for breakfast, lunch and supper the next day and then some."

Grandma pointed out, "Your dad still loves you . . . right?

"Well yeah . . . I guess so", I answered.

Well you see even after leaving the dogs' cage door open your dad still cares about you and loves you. Grandma went on to explain. It is because of love we forgive. Sometimes it is very hard but we must strive do what is right because God made us in His likeness. God loves us so much and knew about the shortcomings of being human. He provided a way for us to come back to Him. Eve was tricked by the great deceiver who holds dominion over this world. God also made some provisions for him too but we won't get into that right now. Just know, God gave the greatest gift that He could and delivered Him to earth to save us."

Remember and think about this because from the first chapter of *John 1:1-5 (NIV)* comes the simple keystone for all of Christianity; "*In the beginning was the Word, and the Word was with God, and the word was God. He was with God in the beginning. Through Him all things were made; without Him nothing was made that has been made. In Him was life, and that life was the Light of men. The Light shines in the darkness, but the darkness has not understood.*"

"Sounds like a riddle", I surmised. "The verses are talking about Jesus . . . right? I know that God sent His Son here to save us. That is what I have understood since I went to church and that Jesus was born on Christmas."

Grandma paused for a second as if to think and then continued. "First let me make it clear to you that we don't exactly know when Jesus was born but most Christians celebrate His birth on December 25th. That's another story. Let's just stay with what we are discussing now."

"That scripture tells us about the God Head", grandma tried to explain. "Jesus has been with God since the beginning of time. And what the scriptures in the book of John imply is that they are one but also separate. And there is more to this we will discover later. I'll tell you what the God Head encompasses; God the Father, His Son Jesus Christ and the Holy Spirit."

"Three . . . how can that be", I asked? "Sounds like he is everywhere?"

"God is everywhere in all creation. That is what I want you to think about", grandma suggested.

"Wait just a minute. What is the Holy Spirit", I asked? "That sounds like a ghost or something? And I've got a lot of other questions too."

So now I blurted out in my best; *hurry up I need to know now voice* . . . "I have questions about the Bible and Jesus and what the Pastor was talking about; you know . . . about being saved. And saved from what exactly?"

Grandma held up her hand and gave a chuckle. "You need to know . . . yes, but you need to slow down as well."

"It's all about Jesus", I said. "I know that. But where does this ghost fit in all of this?"

Again grandma laughed and then quietly said almost in a whisper. "My boy you have no idea how happy you have made me", and patted me on my knee. "I believe that your mother will be very happy to hear about these questions of yours as well."

Then grandma got all excited and blurted out; "Praise the Lord Larry! You will see . . . knock and the door will be opened unto you! Knock and the door will open! Oh, the Spirit is working!"

"I didn't know I was knocking on anybody's door", I said.

Grandma got her composure and said, "First and before I answer anymore questions let's say a little prayer."

I shook my head in agreement as this meeting took on a more serious tone.

Taking my hands in hers grandma started the prayer. "Dear Lord our heavenly Father in your precious Son's name Jesus Christ we humbly come before you this evening. We ask that you surround us with the presence of your Holy Spirit and that You be with us as we search your Word for answers. May the words, thoughts and intent that come forth be Yours heavenly Father and not of our own. Please Lord we ask that You bless this child with Your knowledge. He is now searching. Provide him with wisdom so that he may hear that which is Your will to be done. You have said that where two or more are gathered in Your name you will send the Holy Spirit as a guide . . . please let Your will be done. In Jesus name we pray, Amen

"Wow", I exclaimed! "You sounded like the Pastor just before he gives a sermon. Are you going to give me a sermon?"

Pausing for a second grandma took a deep breath and then without missing a beat she went on to try and explain my question like this; "According to my understanding. The Bible says, the first time you begin to think and ask questions about Jesus is when He considers that as knocking on His door."

Grandma went on, "You want to know more. You want to gain wisdom and knowledge. So the Holy Spirit is called in to help you and lead you on that journey. Now you've taken steps to go through the door of understanding and have opened up your heart. That allows the Holy Spirit to enter, to speak to you and guide you. The Holy Spirit will help you to learn more about Jesus so you can live more like Him."

"Have you understood what I have talked about so far", grandma asked."

"So far . . . yeah, I think so", I said.

"Okay good", grandma smiled and proceeded. "For you to be more like Jesus means being kind to others. Simply stated; Treat others as you would like to be treated. You like to be treated in a kind way don't you", she asked?

"Sure", I agreed. "I don't like to be pushed around or bullied! And I don't like other kids that do."

"Right", grandma said. "So you agree. Treat others like you would like to be treated. That's fair and simple."

Understanding what she said I folded my arms on my chest and shook my head in agreement.

"Good, I am glad that you are grasping these ideas", said grandma.

Then she moved on with the study. "The Holy Spirit will help you to place your faith in God and less in mankind. All the treasures of heaven will be opened to you as you study God's Word and place your faith in Jesus Christ. The Bible will become the roadmap to live by. Your faith will become a well spring of peace and knowledge that you can rely on. Nothing on this earth can cast you aground as long as you're anchored to the rock of Jesus.

Grandma gave pause and took a sip of tea which she had on her night stand. I had a few moments to try and digest what she was telling me. I thought for a second and then said, "You know sometimes when I think about Jesus and the Bible He seems so far away. He seems distant and sometimes He doesn't seem so friendly. I don't understand why He lets bad things happen."

"That's good to say how you feel." Grandma seemed pleased and continued. Your' needing to know more is why we're sitting here tonight."

She thumbed through some pages and turned to the book of John Chapter 15:13-15. Here grandma started to read, "Jesus is talking to His Disciples"; 13: *Greater love has no man than this, that he lay down his life for his friends. 14: You are my friends if you do what I command. 15: I no longer call you servants, because a servant does not know his masters business. Instead, I have called you friends, for everything I have learned from my Father I have made known to you.*"

Looking for confirmation as to what I understood, I asked. "So Jesus is saying that He is our friend if we follow what he says, right?"

Shaking her head yes grandma went on to say, "Jesus is saying to His Disciples and to all of us; when you accept His teaching you become His friend. He claims that he has already paid the price of sin by dying in your place and given you the free gift of salvation and acceptance into the kingdom of heaven.

Grandma clapped here hands and exclaimed out loud, "Bang! Boom! Done! Free gift! Got it? All you need do is accept it and it is yours to keep. No man can take it away from you!"

Being more dramatic grandma got up close to me and looked at me over her glasses. She quietly said, "What is most important, you will give up your slavery to all the sin in this world and the entrapments that go along with it. The choices are important and should never be taken lightly."

"Sounds kinda scary grandma, when you put it in those terms", I said assuring her that I did take what she said seriously.

"Don't be frightened child", she said telling me that it was never God's intention to scare us into believing in Him. Rather he wants us to come to Him through grace and mercy and He will never force us to love Him.

Grandma then went to the book of Romans in the Bible and pointed out. "Larry right here in the Book of Romans the Apostle Paul reaffirms what Apostle John was saying." Romans 5:8 says, "*But God demonstrates His own love for us in this: While we are all sinners, Christ died for us. Christ's sacrifice wiped away our sins and His grace is our gift.*" "All we have to do is believe in Him to be saved."

"You see you are headed in the right direction", grandma observed and then stated. "Planting these seeds of salvation within your-self now is good and one day they will take root and grow. I believe the seed has already been planted in your heart. As it grows you will realize a difference. Knowledge will take hold and fill you up to the very depths of your soul."

Grandma mussed my hair and smiled saying, "This is a whole bunch to digest kiddo. She then asked me, "Do you have any questions?"

"A lot of questions grandma", I said. But I got one big one and that is . . . once I settle on this thing of being saved by Jesus . . . how much is that gonna hurt?

Surprised by my question grandma asked, "What in the world do you mean by asking, is it gonna hurt? Where did you ever get that idea?"

"Well the way I figure it grandma", I surmised. "I've been kinda bad these last few years and for all that badness to come out . . . it's probably gonna be kinda painful . . . don't ya think?"

Laughing about my concern she said, "No I don't think. And you won't feel a thing."

"Yeah, well that's what the nurse said when she gave me a shot at the Doctor's office", I retorted. "I had worries then and I seem to have them now too."

"It's not that something goes out of you . . . rather something enters because of your asking", Grandma explained. "When you ask Jesus to be your Lord and Savior the Holy Spirit comes to guide you. Everything we do to learn more about Jesus such as; coming to Him in prayer, singing praise songs in church, studying our bible lessons each week, helping those around us and telling others about Jesus help us to grow in his likeness."

"Then to answer your question of concern", grandma went on to say. "All those things are a witness to His goodness. As the good things take over inside, you can hang a sign outside that reads; *No Vacancy*! There will be no more room in your heart for bad things because you will be too full of the Holy Spirit."

"Grandma", I said. "The Pastor told us that the Bible study is to prepare us for accepting Jesus as our Savior."

I explained to her that the one thing I keep hearing about is to let the Holy Spirit speak to our hearts and allow Him to guide us. So I asked her about her opinion on the Holy Spirit guy.

"Not sure I am getting this Grandma", I said. "What or who is the Holy Spirit. And why should I trust something that sounds like a ghost? It is supposed to be part of Jesus in some way, but it is kind of hard to understand."

Grandma sat there contemplating and then looked at me, smiled and put her one forefinger up to her lips as if to tell me to be very quiet. Then she gave me a wink. "Just one minute", she said as she stood up and went over to her bed and got one of her pillows. When she came back she was hiding something behind her back and wouldn't let me see what it was.

She sat down in front of me. "Close your eyes and don't open them until I tell you" asked grnadma. Keep them shut or it will spoil the surprise. Okay . . . agreed?"

Shaking my head in agreement I then closed my eyes. I couldn't wait to open them to see what she had up her sleeve.

Then she said, "Okay open them wide!"

There were feathers flying everywhere! It looked like it was snowing!

Grandma was turning her fan on and off. As she pointed it this way and that the feathers kept going up and down and in every direction. "What do you see", grandma asked?

"Feathers . . . everywhere there are feathers", I said excitedly!

Winking at me again grandma said, "You are stating the obvious. Feathers yes . . . but what don't you see?"

"Just feathers grandma and nothing else", I said. "They are floating around, up and down or side to side whatever way you push them.

"What causes them to float", grandma asked?

"The air of course", I answered. "They're light in weight so they float. When you blow on them with the fan the force of the air . . . aha, I got it . . . but you don't see the air, right . . . it is the force but you don't see it! Like the wind outside, you don't see that either!"

"Eureka!" Commented grandma as she snapped her fingers. "You've got it! You've hit the nail on the noggin. It is there but you don't see it until it affects an object that it places its' influence upon. The Holy Spirit acts very much in the same way."

"You're telling me that the Holy Spirit was the force that touched my heart to make me want to learn more about the Bible. Is that right grandma, I asked?"

"Yes, you are absolutely correct", said grandma.

Grandma went on to tell me that the Holy Spirit acts upon us and can change us in ways that we can't even imagine. She told me that the Holy Spirit was there when the universe was created and that it was right there in the room with us. It was the inspiration that impressed upon the prophets the need to write the Holy Scriptures.

"For instance, if you see someone who is angry and mean", grandma pointed out. "And that mean and angry person suddenly stops to think and has a complete change of heart. That is the Holy Spirit working on them and guiding them in a new direction."

"Sometimes I wish the Holy Spirit had showed up in the nick of time when I was making some dumb decisions", I said to grandma. "Or maybe He could have showed up when dad was thinking about punishing me or not. Maybe the Holy Spirit could of talked to dad or mom and said", "*Gee Mr. or Mrs. B don't you think that is a little cruel for such a small thing?*"

Grandma was chuckling to herself and then said, "I believe that is what the Holy Spirit is all about but you never can tell. He shows up almost anywhere, at any time when his will needs to be done."

"Well, I guess I can trust in what you tell me", I said.

"I would hope so after all these years", grandma said as she went on to try and make it clear to me from the evidence of Scripture what Jesus said about the Holy Spirit. "We are going to look into the Book of John", she said. "There are just a few more verses to share with you before you go to sleep. I see it in your eyes that you are about ready for bed."

Stretching and yawning I confirmed what grandma had observed and said, " I am getting tired but I think I can last for a little while longer.

"Okay then we will go on. Here we are in John Chapter 16." Grandma quickly pointed to Verse 5. "This is where Jesus teaches the Disciples about the Holy Spirit", she said. "I will try to point out and clarify things from my understanding as we move along." Jesus says in Verse 5 – *Now I am going to Him who sent me, yet none of you asks me, where are you going? 6 – Because I have said these things, you are filled with grief.*

"What I believe is happening here", grandma explained. "Jesus has told His Disciples that He is going away from them. He had already told them of His death. They are so occupied at this point with their own selfish feelings. The Disciples are wondering what would become of them without Him. They did not even ask Jesus the simple question; Where are you going and why?"

Continuing on in Jesus' conversation grandma took us to Verse 7 – *But I tell you the truth: It is for your own good that I am going. Unless I go away, the Counselor* (Holy Spirit) *will not come to you.*

"Hopefully you see Larry", grandma said. "Here in Jesus own words it sets the scene for the coming of the Holy Spirit and the reasons behind it. If Christ hadn't accomplished what he came to do on earth, there would be no salvation, no spiritual hope for any of us. If Jesus did not die, there would be no course of action for the removal of sin from the world. If he did not die, he could not rise again and defeat death. Christ's presence here was limited to one place at one time. By leaving earth he would now be able to be present to the whole world all at once through the Holy Spirit."

Grandma went on about the whole purpose of the Holy Spirit but I wasn't totally clear on that. There were three reasons as I saw it; 1). The Holy Spirit was to show the world its sinful nature and call us to repent. 2). The Holy Spirit was to reveal God to anyone who would believe in Jesus in His absence. 3). The Holy Spirit was to demonstrate God's judgment over Satan.

For a kid my age this was a lot to have heaped on me and have stay put in my scatter brained mind. It was a lot to have held in my brain and locked in my heart. There are many distractions out in the world and at age twelve I was really just starting to take note of that. Grandma of course was the first to point that out. She considered the many attractions of the world her biggest pet peeve.

During one of her many speeches before this meeting I recalled grandma talking vigorously about her pet peeve. Usually speeches started at dinner. This particular time she held me captive. She prepared my favorite breakfast and I couldn't get away from that.

"This world", grandma started to say, "It is but an illusion Larry!" She said this while waiving her arms all around. Then she started to walk funny like a match stick man and continued her dialogue. "We have to walk a fine line trying to balance ourselves between the real things that we should be caring about and all the rest. By all the rest I mean the glam . . . the glitter . . . these worldly things are sssoooo cool."

With that being said grandma stuck an ice cube down my back.

"Hey, what's up with that", I yelled out loud! I took the ice cube from out of my shirt and asked, "Why'd you do that?"

"To get your attention", grandma said giving me a smirk.

"Well, you've got it", I said. Must admit it did wake me up.

"Anyway, these worldly things", she went on to tell me, "Are cold and have nothing to offer us in the form of love for one another and hold no spiritual value. But listen . . . and here is the kicker young Larry . . . that is what attracts us. Like moths to the flame. Everything that we should not want is our hearts desire. The world draws us near. Just as the moth goes to the flame we too get closer and closer and our delicate wings are burned up by desires flame and we die. The world will consume you Larry if you are not careful and it will burn you up from the inside out. That is how we die spiritually and physically too."

More words to live by I noted. I listened at that time but I don't know if I ever heard.

"Are you still listening to me or have you fallen asleep", grandma said as she gently shook me?

"No I'm good grandma. I was just thinking about something else you said a while back. That's all. Choices, I heard you mention choices. I believe that's where you are going", I said.

Grandma pulled out a large dictionary and spoke about the word choice. She said, "Choice . . . it is not a big word. It is not a small word. I suppose it to be a medium size word which provides a whole bunch of inferences. Please read what it says here Larry if you would be so kind. My eyes are telling me its bed time too."

Moving closer so I could see I started to read out loud. "Choice; An act or instance of choosing from selection: *a wise choice of friends*. The right, the power, or opportunity to choose an option. The person or thing chosen or eligible to be chosen: Green is my choice of color. An alternative to. An abundance or variety from which to choose: a wide choice of styles."

"Good, very good . . . thank you for doing that", said grandma. "Now out of this I gather what I believe is the most applicable to our Biblical situation; something that is preferred or preferable to others; the best part, something worthy of being chosen; excellent, superior, something which is carefully selected. I have always believed Larry in those who stand by their faith through thick and thin. They are the chosen ones. And I must again quote from the Bible; "*For many are invited, but few are chosen.*"

"There is another important verse I want to point out for you", grandma said. "I will write down book, chapter and verse on a piece of paper so you can look it up for yourself."

She wrote it down and handed it to me and I read it to myself. It said; Mathew 22:1-14 "*The parable of the wedding feast*".

When I looked up at her, grandma smiled and said, "What the parable means, and it simply states that Jesus calls upon us all and invites us to become part of His Kingdom. He calls us time after time up until the time that it will be too late. At that moment, only those who have been faithful, only those who are believers will be chosen. Those who have not accepted Christ will be as the man in the parable; *As if bound hand and foot and thrown into the street, into the darkness, where there will be weeping and gnashing of teeth*. I understand the wedding clothes to be the cloak of the Holy Spirit that surrounds us when we accept Christ as our Lord and Savior. You let me know if you agree when you read the whole parable in its context."

"Wow, there are so many stories", I said referring to the fact I was noticing the variety of situations we were discussing. "These people we talk about come from different places and

times. But at the same time their problems and experiences fit what happens to us today. Just like us they are trying to figure out how best to relate to God."

Grandma I see how big of a word choice is. I think I am listening and hearing it's meaning too", I said. The word affects us in many ways. Like, it is my choice. It is your choice. It is our choice. Every move we make and everything we do is a choice. The choices' of others affects what happens to us too."

"It is about you and your relationship with God, grandma explained. It's about how you choose to go about living. And the other observation you made is that what we all do affects one another. You could say that we are all our brothers and sisters keepers. Think about what we learned tonight. We're on a quest to see where we are going. You cannot know where you are going until you understand the past. To unlock the future we must find the keys to unlock the past."

"This is kinda cool. I didn't think this would be like going on a treasure hunt, but it sorta is", I said.

"It is the best kind of treasure that we are seeking", grandma assured me. "It is the kind that won't get lost or stolen and will always be a foundation to build your life upon. You go get some sleep because the time has just flown by, it's almost nine o'clock."

"Ok", I said. "See you in the morning."

"Hey, aren't you forgetting something", asked grandma?

Retracing my steps I gave grandma a hug and said, "I love you in spite of the terrible weather report."

"I am so glad you can forgive me for that and I love you too . . . and that's forever", she said with a smile.

CHAPTER 4

Lateral Thinking

Back in my room I sat at my desk and turned on the light. The rain was now falling slow and steady and would provide a great rhythmic background for falling asleep. My demeanor was high from the grandma to grandson meeting. I never thought that we would have the world of discovery in common.

Looking at my book shelf I took note. My collection of books ranged from children's mysteries, comics, stories on UFO sightings and science fiction, cowboy stories, stories about baseball, quite a few novels that my mother said would be required reading for high school. Those I hadn't gotten to yet and there was my collection of baseball cards too.

Coming out on August 15th, I had heard from one of my buddies, there's a new comic book which I can't wait to get my mitts on. There will be the introduction of a new super hero called the spider something or other.

DC Comics is at that time releasing Amazing Fantasy #15. But maybe I shouldn't get all caught up in this junk. These things will never amount to much.

Along with the card and comic collections and the other stuff I guess my bookshelf is a little shallow compared to my grandmothers. I will have to start to take a closer look to see what her small library has to offer. What she related to me really had me thinking. These Bible stories are as fascinating to me as the supposed landing of an alien spacecraft in Roswell, New Mexico in 1947.

And this is very interesting too; our new President Kennedy is saying that we are pushing to land a man on the moon by the end of the decade. Hey, maybe I could be an astronaut? I wonder if there really are moon men or other beings somewhere out there in space.

Earth calling Larry . . . oh yes, as grandma and I had talked about there is one supreme creator being. So far I have found out He is multi-faceted in purpose. If He truly is the One Creator God of all, who sent His only Son to save us from the original sin of man, and His Son is truly God in the flesh, He must also be everywhere at once.

You could say that God is like the rain falling on the roof. The rain falls from the clouds. It provides life to all it touches. Whatever is run-off flows into the creek in the field. The creek flows into the river and the river to the ocean and evaporates and becomes a gas. The gas goes up into the atmosphere and becomes clouds again and the process is repeated making it eternal. Giving life to all it touches. Of course sometimes it also takes away like when there is too much rain and there is a flood. But then doesn't God also take away? He took away grandpa on my mother's side of the family right after I was born. Some people say that grandpa went to heaven. All the votes aren't in on that one for me. I've been to funerals and they just look asleep to me. I'll make a mental note to find out more about that later.

Grabbing the dictionary I went looking for the meaning of being everywhere at once. Remembering something from English class about what the teacher was saying concerning the usage of the word form omni, meaning "all", made me go to the o's. There I found a variety of uses for the prefix omni; *omnipotent, an adjective meaning infinite power, omnipresent meaning present everywhere at the same time, omniscience a noun meaning infinite knowledge and omniscient an adjective meaning having complete or unlimited knowledge, awareness or understanding like an omniscient being.*

Water or H2O is considered *"ubiquitous".* Now there's a word. This sounds like my little brother because he is everywhere all at once making one mess after the other and you never see him but you know that he's been there. This adjective also means existing or being everywhere, especially at the same time; omnipresent. God exists ubiquitously. You have to love the dictionary. I made a note to ask mom to get me *a word tool book kinda thing* that sounds like a dinosaur, oh yeah, it's a *Thesaurus.*

Oh man, its ten o'clock, sleepy by time for this guy, so its lights out and under the covers I go for the sound of the rain will just take me away.

Pretty soon I found myself along with my buddies standing in the baseball field behind our house. The dew glistened on the grass like diamonds as the sun came up and its' light reflected off the tiny droplets. A whippoorwill was calling too. That bird was very clever at hiding. You would hear its' song but never would you find its' nest. I loved listening to the whippoorwill and the bobwhite quail singing. But wait a minute, during the morning? They sang mostly right before sundown. What's up with those birds, don't they know what time it is?

Well anyway, here we all are on the hill sitting in the grass and oddly enough we're playing cards. It's the game of hearts. For some reason the cards are huge. They're about ten times the size of a normal playing card. Everything's looking kinda like the mad hatter tea party in the story "Alice in Wonderland". Things are beginning to make less and less sense. There it is! I chose the ace of spades from the draw and I'm looking at it.

"You know what guys", I asked as I threw it down on the ground and stood up? "Do you want to see what I can do with that card?"

"What", they asked?

Quick as a wink I laid down on my stomach right on top of that playing card and away I flew. Just like one of those whippoorwills. Yup, it was hard to believe, but I went flying all around the farm and up through the small village. And back I went to the baseball field.

When I got back the guys weren't even there! No one was around to say, "Wow! That was really cool!"

No one was there to congratulate me on my new flying skills. In fact my buddies must not have found that interesting at all and simply went home. Looking down at my bare feet I notice that I am standing in the middle of the ball field wearing just my pajamas. The grass is wet and so are my feet. It is cold and I'm feeling rather silly.

Looking down at the house I decide to get back there before someone missed me. So I'll just walk down the path leading from the ball field to my home. Walking up the back porch steps I enter the house. Through the kitchen and up the steps I go to my room and fall back into bed. That's when I woke up. I'm thinking so much for being an astronaut. Maybe that dream will qualify me to fly the next X-15 project . . . or maybe not?

CHAPTER 5

Baseball, Camping and Buds

Looking out the window beside my bed I saw a beautiful day on the rise. Wow, there was that bob white calling out, but no whippoorwill. And there was the familiar sound of the click-clack clatter of baseball cards on bicycle wheel spokes. We kids used clothes pins to attach lesser known player's baseball cards to the frame of the bike. Positioning them just so the cards would hit the spokes with the turning of the wheel gave the bike what we considered an engine sound. I estimated about four bikes approaching from a northerly direction. Then the noise stopped.

A clinking noise could be heard coming from the roof and then another. Pressing my nose to the window screen I looked down in the yard to see the same guys who were in my dream. Abe had tossed a few pebbles on the metal roof to get my attention.

"Hey Larry", Abe yelled! "You gettin outta bed? Or you gonna sleep all day like Susie whats-er name . . . or what?"

"Or what", I yelled back! "Give me a minute to get dressed!"

Each boy one after the other kept firing words towards the window. "We're headin to the ball field! "We can't wait around for you . . . daylights burning!"

"Hey, saw you and your dad building a campsite down by the creek", yelled another!

"How'd they know that", I wondered?

"HEY LAR . . . and when do we get to camp out", Abe yelled at the top of his lungs?

"Anytime", I yelled back! "Just as soon as I put on my socks, pants, shirt, find a hat and tie my sneaks!"

"Cool man, we'll make plans! The Midnight Bike Marauders will ride again", yelled Abe!

"Yeah, the MBM's will ride again", said another boy confirming the deal.

My bedroom door was slowly opening and a soft motherly voice inquired. "And who might the MBM's be . . . known as the Midnight Bike Marauders? Sounds like the only place you boys are ridin is into trouble."

"Mom, you scared me", I said. The mom radar had locked on again and she snuck up behind me after eavesdropping on the not so secret conversation.

She grabbed me and started tickling me and threw me on the bed. "Hey, I'm too big for this", I called out!

Little brother was there too and he jumped into action. I was being overtaken. Mom had me pinned and little brother was tickling my ribs. "Hey, hold on here I have to go", I complained.

"Your ball team will wait, and you have to eat breakfast", mom scolded.

"No, I mean I have to go to the bathroom", I said. "So let me up before it's too late . . ."

Mom let me up and little brother ran for his room thinking that he was next on the tickle list. I went to finish getting dressed. Breakfast was waiting when I got downstairs. Grandma reminded me to say grace and asked me how I slept. I told her, "like a rock."

Not saying a word I inhaled my food and headed for the back door. Grandma didn't say a word either and just shook her head. She watched me as I bolted past her. On the way I grabbed my bat, some balls and my glove from the back porch.

"Don't let the screen door hit you in the back side", yelled mom! "Don't forget choir practice! Don't make any other big boy plans!"

"Okay mom", I yelled as the screen door slammed behind me!

The guys were A. O. K. in my book. They were the boys from the village that we lived near. There were at the most thirty families that lived there and everyone pretty much new one another.

Dad fashioned a little baseball field up on the hill behind the house so we would all have some place to play. This would keep us out of trouble. And for the most part everybody in the village knew where their kids were because we all played together.

The small ball diamond had a backstop and a few benches along the first base line and the third base side. The field was kind of on a tilt but it still worked out. Dad gave up a field that he could have planted and handed it over to us kids to play on. There were flatter areas around but the old guy who owned them was too finicky to let us use it.

Going to first base was a breeze because it was flat. Heading to second sloped upward. Once you got to second it was flat going to third and then it was all downhill from there as you headed for home.

We had to use old baseballs and mended bats from dad's baseball days when he played with the town team. Some balls were taped with black electrical tape to hold them together and others had just a few seam threads missing. Bats were glued and screwed back together. When you hit the ball wrong with one of those bats they sent out painful rippling vibrations that stung your hands. Most of the old bats were considered too big and heavy for us to use but we still managed.

Once in awhile one of the parents could be coaxed into buying a new bat or baseball. But most times we'd end up losing the balls in the brush somewhere or hit them foul into the creek and ruin them. Old feed bags stuffed with grass or straw served as bases and we cut a piece of old plywood in the shape of a home plate and painted it white. It wasn't a pretty baseball field but that's how it was back then. You made it work the best you could with what you had available.

Because the ball field was on the side of a hill our teams' name said it all. We were the Ridge Runners aka the MBM's or Midnight Bike Marauders. But you didn't tell anybody that we were the Midnight Bike Marauders under penalty of being kicked out of the secret club. That was our secret.

On our potential ball playing roster there was; Abe, Bob, Skin, Roger, Jerry, Skeeter, Lynn from up on the hill, another Lynn and another Roger from on the hill. Dennis and some of the older boys would come around when they didn't have anything better to do than to play ball. I was the only Larry. Even though we were small in number most of the time we had enough guys to play ball.

The MBM's were mostly comprised of the boys who showed up early that day to practice; Abe, Skin, Skeeter, Roger, Bob and I. We were all close to the same age and the guys who were into camping out.

Our bikes were fixed with make-shift flashlight headlights taped to the front fender or handle bars. Those lights would allow us to cruise around at night on the back country roads. We ran silent at night so we took off our clacker noise engines. It was a lot of fun biking at night and since there were very few cars we kids didn't think it was dangerous.

The really cool thing was to bike over to the big creek and go night fishing. We also would catch fish by other means when we were bored with the regular drop the line in the water routine. When you readily need some fresh fish to fry? A well place firecracker will quickly produce a few floaters from a local pond. But, I am getting ahead of myself.

The morning was clear and fresh and we put a small practice game together. As we took turns batting and fielding the subject quickly turned to the campsite. A plan was needed for a camp out. So we went back to my house and started making a check list. I grabbed a pencil and some paper from my room and we all sat together on the front porch.

"My umbrella tent will hold four people but we should have at least one more tent to be comfortable", I explained.

"Yeah", said Abe. "Hold on a minute here guys. All these big plans are great but who is really gonna be camping out? Has anybody even asked permission? Last time we were going to have a camp out at my place . . . remember? Yeah, and what happened? Nobody shows up. My folks were pissed. They bought all sorts of necessary stuff; hamburgers, hot dogs, soda, ice cream and even some watermelons. You know how my mom gets. She was a little more than peeved. She didn't blame anybody but me. I took all the heat! She said all my big ideas were just in my imagination. To make matters worse, there's my big brother giving mom . . . I told ya so!"

Roger Dodger jumped into the conversation. "That's true guys, I remember that. I think we made plans but it was the weekend of the carnival. Just about all our parents decided to go on that same night. To be fair we all need to get permission and confirm that we are coming.

Roger told us how his parents had him on a short leash but didn't get into the reason for the lock down.

He was one of our best ball players and we didn't want to take any chances. So we told him not to ask even if he wanted to. We had a game coming up against the "Townies" our arch rival team and we wanted all the good players available. Roger was our Roger Maris.

"Look Rog don't feel left out or that we don't want you there", Abe said. "You can come out first thing in the morning for breakfast and hang out all day if you want. What's wrong with that?"

Roger agreed to sit it out for the team if that's what it took.

"Ok, so we know Skeeter will be there", Abe observed. "His parents let him do anything. And Bob . . . what's your story?

"What day guys", asked Bob? "We haven't even set a day."

"How about Monday night", suggested Abe?

"That sounds ok", I said. "What about everyone else? Everyone in agreement for Monday say aye."

All said aye. It was to be a Monday to Tuesday camp out pending permission from the parents.

Our front porch meeting was interrupted by Abe's mothers call. Not a phone call but her call from the front porch of their house. She was our choir director, music co-coordinator and Bible study teacher.

Abe's mom Luella had a voice that you could hear from one end of the village to the other. Birds in trees would suddenly take flight. Leaving their nests in fear they would circle the village until they were sure that all danger had passed. The sound started with a tenor aaaaaa and would reach a high shrill soprano pitched braaahaaam to finish. This was repeated several times. If Abe was within a half mile radius from the event there was no problem in hearing his mother's call. I am sure that if the wind was blowing in the right direction the exercise in vocal acrobatics would project up to a mile away.

Abe's real name was Abraham, named after Abraham Lincoln our 16th President of the United States, who served from March 1861 until his assassination in April 1865. His dad thought it honorable to name his boy after the President. Abe was a good egg and he brought a lot of character to our gang.

By the time we sorted out our plans it was time for lunch and I had to get ready for choir practice. My little brother came running to tell me that mom had lunch ready and that anyone who wanted to could stay. Skeeter was the first to agree to stay and then Bob but Abe and Roger headed for the door.

See you in church Larry, said Abe. Roger said he wouldn't see me till Monday and probably not until ball practice in the late morning.

After lunch Bob and Skeeter headed for home. Bob lived on the east side of the village and Skeet went to the west. He had further to go as his home was up in the hills about a mile from my house. Skeet had a rough life and it was hard for him to get away from his chores on the farm. He was part American Indian and as a friend he would do anything for you. Skeeter really enjoyed fishing and he and I never missed the first day of trout season in the spring. Bob was a good friend too. He was raised with a strong faith and was more cerebral than any of us. I always felt that Bob would go into politics or be a preacher and try to make changes to better the world in some way.

At lunch Grandma told me that she was proud that I was singing in the choir. She assured me that she would be in the first pew just to hear me sing out loud for the Lord.

Before I left the table grandma reminded me, "When you get back from choir practice we have a date to continue our discussion. Don't forget."

Wow! I thought to myself. This is a lot of church information for one kid. Maybe if I was lucky she had a tent meeting to go to tonight. Some of the best TV happened tonight. I missed Rawhide last night and the Twilight Zone.

After my bath I was combing my hair and looking in the mirror when mom popped her head in and said, "You're looking pretty spiffy there kid. Is it a little dab'll do ya or are you waxing your top knot today?"

"Just wax today on the flat top", I answered. "And who is that on the radio", I asked?

"That's a boy from the area of Pittsburgh, Pennsylvania" said mom. "His name is Bobby Vinton. The song that's playing is Roses are Red."

"Why do you like it", mom asked?

Taking a break from combing my hair I stopped to listen to "*Roses are red my love, but not as sweet as you*" and then I said, "I think he has a good voice. But that's all too mushy for me. The girls will probably go . . . ooohh wow . . . getting themselves all goofy and go ga, ga over it."

"Someday soon young man you'll be looking in that goofy direction", mom cautioned.

Looking back into the mirror I checked and made sure my flat top was standing up right.

"Aaahh, come on mom that stuff's just not my style. "I got more important things to do than think about silly girls", I said. "Besides mom, aren't you my number one? That's what you tell all of us, right . . . that you are our number one."

"Say it is nice to hear you to say it, but what else right now could be more important than girls", mom asked me with a twinkle in her eye?

"Come on mom! You've got to be kidding!" I exclaimed and then retorted. "There's my buds, baseball and camping . . . and there's fishing too. Girls don't like worms, bugs and stuff. They think all that's yucky. If a girl can't even bait a hook . . . what good is she? They can't even throw a baseball right. They're worse than my little brother. And have you ever seen how a girl rides bike? Man, now that's funny!"

"Really?" . . . said my mom in awe, "I didn't even know that! You're absolutely right Larry! What good are ya if can't even bait a fish hook?"

"Come on mom", I pleaded. "I think you're making fun of me."

"Maybe just a little", she said smiling and gave me a wink. Mom tapped on the bathroom door frame . . . "Hurry up! You don't want to keep Luella waiting."

Mom was right. I did not want to keep the choir waiting. I was out the door and up the street like Flash Gordon. The little white church was only about three blocks from my house if you wanted to call it that. There was no street layout to the village and no sidewalks just a little winding road that went right through the middle. There was however, a general store, a gas station and one church. Everything was here that anyone needed. You could feed your body and your spirit, fuel up and get your car fixed, all within walking distance. You really didn't need a car unless you really, really needed to get somewhere.

I wasn't the first one but not the last to arrive at choir practice. There were about twelve boys and girls in our little choir and it seemed that everyone eventually showed up. Reverend Wright was even there to listen. We went through about four songs and Luella chose three out of the four for church.

We finished rehearsal and I was about to leave when Reverend Wright pulled me aside.

He told me that both my grandmother and my mother confirmed that I was interested in learning more about the Bible and Jesus Christ. He related to me that he had two other boys who would be interested in taking Bible study as well.

Thinking for a moment I then said, "I guess I'll take the classes with the other fellas. When do they start?"

The Reverend answered, "Classes will commence the same week that school starts. Bible classes will be on the same night as prayer meetings which are on Wednesday nights. Both will take place at the same time here at the church. Classes will go on for eight weeks."

He then added, "We made the classes on Wednesday so it will be more convenient. Those who attend prayer meetings can place their children in the class. They can be here at the same time and they won't have to make two trips. It's also a good way to get more adults to attend prayer meeting and to get their kids in Bible study."

"Geezz wizz", I gave a whistle and said. "That's a pretty big commitment, eight weeks in a row. But I'll do it. Grandma and I are discussing the Bible right now too. So I'll be getting a double dose."

The Reverend smiled and said, "You make it sound like you're taking medicine. But it is a good medicine, I assure you."

The Reverend stood up, shook my hand and said, "I look forward to investigating the scriptures with you Larry. I am sure you can add some different perspectives to our lesson study . . . and, especially multiplying that by your grandmothers' in home tutelage . . . well, let us just say, this study should prove to be very intriguing for you and all of us."

Whatever he said I just smiled and agreed with him. Then I said goodbye to everybody and went to walk home. It was a beautiful day, just a little humid from last night's rain but still great. There were but one or two clouds in the whole sky.

I picked up a few stones from the side of the road and pitched them over into Mr. Zechman's pond. If he would have seen me do that he probably would have yelled at me. He was known to have threatened kids when they were playing Halloween pranks. It was reported that he had a double barrel twelve gauge shotgun that was loaded with shells that had rock salt in them. It was said that he actually came out onto his porch with his shotgun and threatened to open fire on any and all pranksters one dark night.

Now I've seen him working in his garden a couple of times when I walked by before. He always waved and smiled at me and asked, "Hey, how ya doin Ben number two?" My dad's name is Ben. I guess he couldn't remember my name or he didn't know it. I became Ben number two to him. Yup, I guess I'm Ben number two. So how do you do too?

As I was just about to round the corner next to Moyer's General Store and head down the hill to my house I heard Abe yelling out my name from his yard. "HEY LAR! We still need to make a list of goodies for the camp out! I can get my two man tent and set it up next to your tent!"

Talk about a set of lungs! I had no idea. He's louder than his mother! Why not let the whole universe know what we're up to. Geezz! Whizz! And yet he continues!

"My older brother Snail said he wants to camp out too! I don't want him to! He smells bad! He wears those stupid colognes!"

Doesn't Abe take a breath! "Okay, okay . . . I'm coming up", I said as I tried speaking over his news broadcast!

Abe's news, "Live at Five" continues. "We need to make a list man! My parents are going to the grocery store right now! Let's cash in man! Come on! Take a detour up to my house!"

Reluctantly I went up to Abes. "Look", I said. "First, I can't believe you are shouting this at the top of your lungs. The whole village will be on alert to the fact that we are camping out. The older kids will think about sabotage. They like throwing M-80s into campfires. Like when we're asleep? And there's every body's favorite; the really cool trick of pulling out tent pegs and dragging the tent along with the people in it down into the shallow creek. I got about five minutes here kiddo because mom's expecting me back right now. So what's up and so darn important?"

"Chill man, you need to relax. I got everything under control", said Abe. "Look, my mom just called your mom and told her this is what we're doing. So you got an easy thirty minute delay before curfew."

That's about how much time it took as we argued the finer points of camp out cuisine. Abe's mother threw in her suggestions and told us we needed to choose a healthier menu. "You kids need to eat more fruits and vegetables." In fact she explained, "If you didn't know it already cheese curls, potato chips, soda and ring bologna do not exist on the healthy food chart."

She did concede on one point as she said, "Just because it's you guys. If you need something sweet, I will bake a wet bottom shoo fly pie for you to take along on Monday's camp out. On one condition I'll do it. You have to skip some of the junk you got on that list."

Geez whizz that was a tough sell. I knew how tasty the baked goods were that Luella prepared. My vote was in favor. Abe gave up the cheese curls and chips and went for the hard Dutch pretzels and shoo fly pie. We also agreed to drink orange and grape juice rather than drink sodas. Abe's dad also gave us a big ice chest to keep things cold.

It was about time for me to get back to the house, so I left Abe in charge of the list. His mother said that she would be calling my mom to bring her up to speed on the food selections and preparations.

I got home just in time for the evening chores and supper. Mom told me that Luella had called and they spoke about the camp out menu and both agreed we should not be eating a bunch of junk food. I felt as if the freedom code of the MBM'S was being compromised.

Dad pointed out. "You have a camp stove and a campfire and you can prepare just about anything with that combination."

"If you want me to", dad went on to suggest, "I'll come down and fix you and the other boys' breakfast very early in the morning. How would that be?"

"That would be great if you want to dad", I said.

"You know", dad explained, "We could even make a Dutch oven and cook a whole meal with a chicken if you want."

"What's that", I asked?

Dad went on to explain how to build a Dutch oven. "What we will do is dig about a two foot deep hole about one and a half to two feet in diameter and line it with rocks and put hot wood coals on the bottom. Then we will get grandma's big old stew pot, put in a whole chicken with all sorts of vegetables and about tree cups of water. Put a lid on it and wrap the whole thing in heavy duty aluminum foil. After that we set the stew pot into the pit and put more red hot coals around and on top and cover it with ground and more rocks. You just bury it . . . forget it, and presto, in three hours you got a fresh baked chicken with all the trimmins."

"That sounds really neat dad", I said. "So that could be our lunch."

"That's right", dad said agreeing with me. "And when I get home I'll help you guys dig it up and we can all have lunch together."

Thinking about how agreeable and helpful dad had been I said, "Thanks dad for all your help. I think this will be our best camp out ever."

He gave me a smile and said, "I'm glad to do it for you. I just hope everything turns out the way you boys want. This is what makes things special. You can look back later on in life and have fond memories about these things that you did when you were a kid."

CHAPTER 6

Where Did We Come From; Grandma's History Lesson

My little brother and I usually watched Beany and Cecil and the Roy Rodgers and Dale Evans Show but tonight grandmother had other plans for me.

When I walked into her room I noticed that both mom and grandma were seated on the couch. Both of them had a big grin on their face. They also had a pile of photograph books and shoe boxes containing photographs stack on the floor in front of them. It looked like school had opened early for me this year. The look on my face probably told them how I was feeling.

"Don't worry", said mom trying to assure me, "we're not here to weigh you down with anything heavy tonight. We thought it might be fun to show and tell you about your ancestry. This way you will see why we believe in what we do and the history behind it. This will help you to better understand who you are."

"Oh", was all I could muster verbally. Right now I was clueless as to what they might be up to. Sitting down between them I was ready to see what they had in store for me and asked, "So tell me again. What are we doing?"

"Like your mother said its family show and tell time", said grandma.

And away we went rummaging through many photos that were described as being great grandparents, uncles and aunts. There were even older photos that they called tin types. The men mostly had long hair and beards. The ladies had their hair in tight buns and were dressed in tight waist floor length dresses. Dark colored clothing predominated in all the photos. In some pictures both the man and woman were seated, and others showed the men standing and the ladies were seated.

In one of the photos a regal looking gentleman was seated holding a cane with carvings on it. The cane also appeared to have a silver handle grip. He had snow white hair, a well trimmed beard and a slight handle bar moustache.

Mom pointed at the man and said, "That is your great uncle Ben. Or you could say, your dad's uncle Ben. However you want to look at it, he was your dad's favorite uncle. Your dad's mother Mary forbad him to come around."

"Why if dad liked him so much would she do that", I asked?

Mom continued telling the story of great Uncle Ben. "He would come up from Lancaster and take your dad fishing. While they were passing the time away talking and fishing great Uncle Ben would teach your dad how to speak Sweiss Dietch. That was the cause which upset your' grandmother Bachman. Sweiss Dietch was the language from the old country. Grandma Mary Bachman had certain agendas. She believed that since they were in America all the old ways should be left behind. She also felt that Lancaster where he lived was sin city. She believed that in that city, evil lurked around every corner. So it was guilt by association for your great Uncle Ben along with the fact he was teaching you father Sweiss Dietch that your father's mother felt he was a *bad influence* him.

Sounds like a *bum rap* to me, I said. Besides I don't think I ever met dad's mom did I?

"No", said mom. "She passed before you were born." "And besides, where did you hear that term, *bum rap*", mom asked?

"On Dragnet", I said.

Grandma jumped into the conversation. "See daughter! Nowadays we don't need our strange relatives influencing our young people. We have television. It is teaching kids brass and sass just like the criminals in the programs. Bum rap, now that's bad influence if I ever heard it said.

I just rolled my eyes and hoped that we would go on looking at more photos and thought, yup, poor old great Uncle Ben got a raw deal.

There were pictures of people standing in yards in front of old whitewashed clapboard sided houses. Some of the buildings looked like they never had been painted. The people in the pictures looked stern and determined. I did not see many smiling faces. In fact the faces were almost void of smiles, as if smiling was not the thing to do at that time. When you got your picture taken back then you had better look serious or else. Today when you are photographed, what do they say . . . *smile, say cheese*!

The faces, dress and settings in grandma's photos reminded me of the actors and places I would see early Saturday mornings on Covered Wagon Theatre. It was a TV program on Channel 8 that ran western movies. All the great cowboys were on there like Gene Autry and Roy Rogers. Roy Rodgers had a dog named Bullet, a horse named Trigger and a sidekick named Pat who drove a crazy jeep he called Nellie Bell. There was also the Cisco Kid, Audie Murphy and of course, who could forget the Lone Ranger and Tonto. Great character actors like Gabby Hayes, Slim Pickens and Walter Brennen were stars in their own right. And they made varying appearances with John Wayne, Randolf Scott, Hop-along Cassidy, Roy Rodgers and Gary Cooper in full length features.

Enough has been said about Saturday morning TV. Mom explained to me the reasons the Bachmans and Saltzmans, who were on my father's side of the family, left Switzerland in the first place.

She said, "Many families in those days left Europe to escape religious oppression and persecution. Your great grandfather Saltzman Larry was an engineer who designed bridges and horse drawn carriages. On my side of the family the Walters and Schrawders came from Germany escaping that country for the same reasons."

Mom I found out was a D. A. R. which means a Daughter of the American Revolution. This honor was bestowed on her because one of her great uncle's fought in the American Revolution. Surprisingly we learned that he was buried less than a mile from our home. His final resting place was in a cemetery located behind a little white church along the main road.

Learning about my family history was fascinating. Grandma told me that they had traced the Schrawder family's ancestry all the way back to the King of Holland and at that time the family name was Von Schroeder. She said it was not the best of times for the family because King Von Schroeder was asked to leave Holland and sought asylum in Germany where he was later murdered for political reasons. Beheading was the common choice at the time for removing the unsightly crowns from the regal heads of unwanted kings and queens.

Mom also said that great grandfather Saltzman had a contract to build Model "A" cars for Henry Ford. Henry Ford had chosen him to build and design his cars because of his engineering abilities as a carriage maker. But he lost the whole business on one turn of a card in a hand of blackjack. This caused the breakup of that whole beautiful family. Great grandfather Saltzman went home and was so distraught over the situation that he ended his life. The choice for suicide during that time was a well aimed pistol I had learned.

The children consequently were scattered and sent off to boarding schools. Without the family business and its income great grandfather's widow could not possibly have made it by herself. Not to mention the stigma attached to such an unfortunate tragedy would most certainly be the cause of certain social disgrace.

In my hands I was now holding great grandfather's daughter's pictures, my great aunts; Addie, Henrietta and Florence were featured boarding a train. "Wow", I exclaimed, "You mean tell me that the Saltzman family lost their dad because of a silly card game?"

"Your grandmother Mary", mom explained, "Whom you never met because she passed before you were born, was the fourth sister. All were affected not because of the turn of a card but rather because of the choices that their father made. He liked scotch and playing cards more than he loved his family I guess. You can't choose your relation but you can certainly learn from their mistakes, so you have no reason to be ashamed."

Grandma added her own thoughts. "Believe me Larry, every family has a few old bones rattling around in the closet. I can tell you some stories about people right around here that will make your hair stand on end. There's nothing stranger than truth that can put an edge on a good story. I can tell you about a family that lived up in the hills not far from here. The father was a crack shot with a rifle. He was commissioned by Winchester or Remington. It was one of those gun companies that hired him to go on the road and do shooting demonstrations. They believed his incredible expertise with a firearm would do well to sell their guns for them."

Mom cautioned my grandmother, "I know where this story goes mom. I don't think it is a good example to use just to show Larry how every family has problems lurking in the past. Admittedly that tragedy certainly out does our little mystery. Even though the story is true it is better left untold. We will not spread trash. It is not right to bring up the past if it hurts people in the present."

"Must be a doosey, huh? And I like shooting dads twenty two rifle", I exclaimed. "Come on now you two have to finish the tale."

See what you started grandma, my mother said.

"Your mother is absolutely right Larry and I am sorry", agreed grandma. "I was wrong to bring that story up and my lips are zipped about it. Sometimes I speak before thinking and God forgive me. It is a problem I have been working on all my life. Someday you will hear about it but it won't be from me."

Later in my life I did hear about the tale of the crack shot and his family who lived back in the dollar woods. Like my dear mother said, "Admittedly the story about my great grandfather paled in comparison."

Conceding to the wishes of my elders I went back to looking at the beautiful young faces of my great aunts in the photograph that I was holding in my hands. I thought about how pretty they zwere and how happy they looked. It seemed as though their lives were full of all the things that dreams are made of.

It was a really cool picture too. From the story I knew about them this photo opportunity was very proper and almost prophetic. In it, they were getting on a train. Each was in a different stage of boarding. All the while they were holding onto the step rail. Smiling and looking at the camera their faces seemed to beam with hope and promise.

Maybe at that time each was headed to a new magical destination in life. One became a teacher, the other an army nurse during World War I. One I know married a game commissioner. And my dad's mother, who was the oldest sister, married my grandfather. My dad's father was a simple farmer. Of course if she hadn't simply married that farmer then I would not be here to simply tell about it.

"So what have you learned so far about your past", mom asked abruptly, extracting me from my daydream?

"I've learned that everybody came to America because they were escaping from being put into a situation that would stop them from worshipping and living in the way they believed was right. Is that correct", I asked?

"That is exactly right", said Grandma. "There were many people persecuted for what they believed. And to name one which would be the best known to you would be Martin Luther. Others who believed in a one to one relationship with God and were Bible based in their thinking were the Waldensians and Lombards. They took a more humble view to preaching the gospel. These Bible based groups tried to take the path of the Apostles and steer clear from all the pomp and circumstance of the Roman Catholic Church. These people saw the folly of having mediators other than Jesus Christ to represent them before the One true living God. They saw the corruption over money and power that was the Roman Catholic Church at the time."

"There are many stories about persecution Larry", my mother added. "But what it all boils down to is that we all can have a one on one personal relationship with God. All we need do is ask Him and it will be given. There is no need to place coins into a plate or light a candle or confess to another person in an effort to win God's grace. God already knows your needs, he knows your misdeeds and all you need do is simply get down on your knees at night before you go to bed and talk to him. Tell him about your day, tell him about what is bothering you and ask him for forgiveness of your sins from the day and tell him what it is that you need. You can ask him for his blessings and his forgiveness. It is that simple. Of course there is much more to the road of understanding but this is an excellent place to start."

"I'm already praying mom", I told her. "It is not every night like I did when you came to my room. You still pray with my little brother I know. But I try to talk to God. It's only like when I remember to do it or when I really, really need or want something. There are so many things that I need to remember. I guess I need to place Him at the top of the short list. Maybe I'll hang a sign above my desk or above my bed that says; Hey you! Yeah, I'm talking to you! Remember Me! Don't forget about me . . . signed God."

"It would be good to make Him a priority in your life", grandma added. "At this time it would be best to ask God to give you understanding as we search His word for truth within the message."

Like I said the other night, "This is like a treasure hunt. I didn't know that our family came from those countries and the reason they left. They must have thought it very important to get out of there."

"This is enough for tonight", said mom. "Grandma and I wanted to show you where you came from."

"However before you go", mom stated as she tapped on my head. There is one other thing I want to place in your brain for future pull out and reference. Because the people came to America to avoid persecution, that was a fulfillment of prophecy.

"What in the world is that and what does it mean", I inquired with a puzzled look on my face?

Both grandma and mom gave me one of those looks and grandma said, "Just file that away for future reference and when the time comes the light will turn on."

Along with a sorta bewildered look on my face I drawled out, "Yeah, okay then it's filed."

Like they had never said something weird mom just continued the conversation, "I guess grandma will start sharing the more religious aspects with you from here on. I think you will find it very interesting comparing the little facts that grandma will provide added to what you will learn in Reverend Wright's traditional Bible study."

"Traditional", I asked, "What does that mean?"

"It means what everyone else is doing and what is popular", grandma said as she looked at me over her glasses. "Doesn't necessarily mean it's right, but it is what most people follow along and do without question. We will look into that more when we have time. But it's late and time for bed. My old bones are tired too so both you and your mom scoot and get out of here."

After giving hugs, kisses and I love you to both mom and grandma I quickly ambled off to my room for a long summers nap.

This night I remembered to spend some time talking with God. I asked Him to help me to get to know Him better. I asked Him to put Bible teachings in a way that a young boy like me could understand. I told him that I knew He was there and that He was listening. He is everywhere and I know that I told Him. I could not only see but feel his greatness and awesome power all around me. I asked Him for many things and thanked Him for his many blessings. I asked Him to please watch over my family, especially my little brother because he was too small to understand all the bad things that could happen to him. I asked God to give grandma a long life because she had so much to teach me about Him. I asked God to help my mom to understand that I am doing my best at growing up. But this growing up thing is taking a longer time than she can stand sometimes.

"God please let mom know to be patient with me and someday soon I'll get there", I said. And I also asked, "God bless my dad who works so hard. Sometimes I know that he is too tired to play with me or to help me do things, but he does it anyway. I want him to know that I know it and I love him for it. Thank you God, I know you heard me." Amen

CHAPTER 7

Church; Before the Camp Out

Mom came into my room and gently shook me while saying, "Wake up, it feels just like a summer morning."

It was indeed a beautiful morning and my day was chocked full of things to do, people to see and plans to make. Stretching my arms and breathing in the fresh morning I could smell the hay that was drying in the field across the road. Life was good. Not just good . . . life was a blessing! And I couldn't wait to get on with it.

Mom had the interesting foresight to get almost matching church clothes for my brother and me last spring. My guess is that most moms are like that. They were little guys suits with matching hats and they make nice family cameo memory shots. But man, when we get to church and all my buds see this I will get busted. Maybe not on the spot because the other moms will be there with their comments like; "Oh my goodness! Look Alice, the Bachman boys, they look sooo cute. They look like such little gentlemen."

Well behind Alice stands her son Roger with this big grin on his face. I know what he's thinking. He is looking at me like I am the lead clown for the circus that just rolled into town. What was mom thinking? Doesn't she know about the code? Yeah, like I am almost a teenager too. I should be picking out my own identity. I am matching up with my little brother. That's just not cool. This makes me look like him and we are not twins.

Of course this whole image thing didn't dawn on me until we were walking up the street to the church. As I saw the white steeple of the church Abe and his parents drove by. Abe looks at me, and then at my little brother. When he went to wave hi he suddenly stops, turns around and gets a goofy, quirky look on his face. Like he didn't know me? What's up with that? See I knew it, I knew it! Just because it was a special occasion with me singing today mom had to get us all dressed up. This was okay for the spring photo shoot thing. Now that I am twelve, man I don't know about this! I was still eleven back then. It was fine way back then, but now, I just don't know? I started to slow down and became last in the mom, little bro, grandma and me entourage.

Grandma noticed that I was lagging behind by a good ten paces. "Come on now Larry", she said trying to hurry me up. "You don't want to be late for your big singing debut!"

My mumbling, stumbling comment was, "But I am not singing solo!"

Hoping to hold up the bus with my slowing stride was so that maybe we would not arrive at church any time soon. The socializing that goes on with the meet and great before Bible study class is so that everyone can get friendly and talk about how their individual week went etc, etc. I simply wanted to take my hat off, hand it over to mom, enter and sit down in my class. No need for show and tell here. My little brother was cool with his situation. He was proud to be looking this way because he liked to please mom. Plus he was proud to image yours truly here and he had no outside influence to explain the contrary. No peer pressure on him. Little bro went with the flow.

Just wait till he grows up! Won't he be shocked about all the new things he will learn about this dog eat dog, good buddy social order? You got to go along to get along.

Of course we made it just in time for the meet and greet. All my fears came true and crashing down on me in waves as one after the other the ladies had to make comment. The men stood there sporting their approving smiles as well. Yup, one man commented, "They look like a team of lawyers . . . wouldn't want to get cross examined by them. They look pretty tough!" Later on in life my brother and I both looked back at the family photo and had a good laugh as we felt we looked more like the "Mob Squad" than attorneys.

As soon as I sat down in my Bible study class I could hear the snickers. Sitting down next to Abe I anticipated his question. "Man, what's up with the hat", he asked? "That's the same outfit your mom made you wear in the spring, isn't it? But now she added hats?"

"Yeah, it is, and now with the hat and all", I confessed.

Abe gave another two cents worth of opinion. "Wow, just the suit . . . smooth sailing, no one would have noticed. But with the addition of the hats, you're dead man", Abe snickered.

"Ok Abe . . . I get it . . . and it's over now. Can we move on to something else? Raising my voice just a little more I spoke to the surrounding class. "Besides . . . did everybody around here suddenly become fashion experts?" I could hear a few more giggles coming from the class as I asked that last question.

Speaking quietly Abe tried to work damage control. "Look, I don't want to beat you up on the subject. I know how moms are. Believe me I have to deal with my mom and it is no picnic at times. At least yours doesn't have a voice that can be heard from one end of the village to the other."

"Yeah", I sighed, "Whew, thank God for that. Just think if there were two people that could holler like that in the same village?"

Abe just sort of gave me a side long glance and a smirk as he said, "See, you think you got it bad? And what did you mean by, *two people?*

"What if . . . just sayin's all, what if", I said.

Our teacher was Abe's mother and soon she was standing directly in front of us. She wasn't a large person. She was rather petite. But she had red hair and a personality that reflected the tone of her hair. She was outspoken and willing to give her opinion as she saw fit.

"By the way Larry, those are nice suits that you and your brother are wearing and I see you got the hats", Luella said as she approached the class. "Don't let anyone tell you different . . . right Abraham? And if they do, just tell them to come and see the person with the flame red hair. I will set them straight for you."

"Yes ma'am", was Abe's answer. He hated when his mother called him Abraham in public.

If anyone had any thoughts to say anymore about my attire and matching hat their ideas quickly dissipated for the moment.

Luella's Bible lesson was delivered with the verve she put into the baking of her cakes and pies. She always made the story her own. Our lesson never followed the exact story line from the lesson book. Her recipe for discussion was flavored with ideas that were applicable to our daily lives. Luella made it interesting and that made it fun. She always seemed to pick on her own son Abe to bring out a point in the story line.

On this particular Sunday school morning we were studying the Book of Daniel. The story told about the incredible faith of four boys from Jerusalem. The King of Babylon had taken them from their homeland of Israel. The boys Jewish names were Daniel, Hananiah, Mishael and Azariah. Now that King Nebuchadnezzar had the boys in Babylon he was expecting that they should become more like the Babylonians. He wanted them to eat, drink and change their religious practices to become more like them. You know, go along to get along. Their names were changed to Belteshazzar, Shadrach, Meshach and Abed-Nego accordingly.

When the king's steward who was in charge of the boys, tried to feed them the same things that the kings court was eating the boys refused. Daniel explained that the food was unclean and would defile their bodies. The practice of eating this type of food and drinking wine went against their religious beliefs. The steward argued that the king would be upset if they were unhealthy because of their not eating. Daniel asked the steward to feed them, as a test for ten days, the vegetables they wanted to eat. By doing so the steward would see if they would become sick or be less healthy than the rest of the court who would eat and drink the King's delicacies and wine. After ten days of eating from the menu the boys required their features appeared healthier than all the young men who ate from the King's menu. So the steward took away the King's delicacies and wine and gave them the food they requested.

Luella asked Abe if he thought that cheese curls were included on Daniel and his friend's healthy list.

Abe said, "Come on now mom you're embarrassing me. Besides, I don't eat cheese curls all the time. I like peanut butter and jelly sandwiches too!" He paused and then added, "They're healthier than cheese curls."

This statement got a few chuckles from the older kids in the group.

A meager defense was put forth as Abe came back with . . . "Well they are too!"

"Okay, ok Abraham, maybe peanut butter and jelly on whole wheat bread might be a little healthier than cheese curls", agreed Luella, "But we need to get to the point. And the point is about the strength of our beliefs. That is, what we know in our hearts to be true to God's teachings should never be compromised by peer pressure. Even though Daniel and the boys were in a strange country, torn from all they knew and loved and given new names, they stuck to their believing in the one true living God Jehovah and His teachings."

"What this story implies Abraham", Luella continued, "Is just because Roger over there decides to jump head first off of the stone quarry cliff doesn't mean that Abe and Larry should go ahead and do the same."

"Why are you always including me in the story ma", asked Abe? "I'm not dumb enough to follow Roger if he did such a stupid thing. I don't know about Larry here though."

I was about to say something but Roger beat me to it.

"Hey", said Roger jumping into the conversation, "I have seen *Abraham* over there do some pretty goofy things that I would never do. Like the time you . . .

"Now come on guys", Luella said interrupting the interruption. "What is the real point here?"

Raising my hand I sheepishly said, "Well I guess that we should think before we leap rather than do something that would not be pleasing to God?"

"Thinking before doing", said Luella, "That's a good answer and clever on the inference to jumping off a cliff." She then asked, "Roger what are your thoughts?"

Roger asked, "How about in a situation when you don't go along with the crowd? Just because they think what they are doing is the cool thing to do doesn't make it right. I know in school that I have been teased or called chicken. That was because I didn't go along with what the rest of the kids were doing at that moment."

"That is also a good answer Roger", commented Luella. "Sticking to what you believe in as being right or wrong. Not going along with the gang just because they think it is the cool thing to do."

"Hey mom", Abe asked calling on Luella's attention. "What do you do when you see a bigger guy bullying someone half his size? Like there are all these other kids standing around watching and doing nothing about it. I know it's wrong and so do all the other kids watching. But it's like nobody says anything . . . like they don't care. I want to do something because that could be me getting pounded next time and I'd want somebody to stick up for me. It's like everybody's frozen and afraid to say hey, knock it off . . . leave that kid alone."

"Learn to defend your-self man", uttered one of the other boys. "If it is you getting pounded the next time, at least you can put up a good fight."

"Don't even get involved", stated one of the girls sitting beside Roger. She had her arms folded against her chest and had a sour look on her face. "Don't even waste your time", she continued, "It's not your fight to begin with." She then sat hard back in her seat and said, "Gosh! Boys are such morons! They're always going around huffing and puffing themselves up bigger than what they are, just trying to prove something. The only thing they're proving is that they don't have any brains. I find them simple, stinky and boring!"

"Well Susie", said Luella, "That is a very interesting observation."

"Thank you Mrs. Cee", said Susie while she smugly stared down every boy sitting in the pew.

Then there was a last comment from another boy named Butch. "Well sir, now Mrs. Cee if that had been me getting my butt kicked by that bully, and it wasn't. But . . . if that had been me guys . . . what I would do afterwards . . . is go on home and get my big brothers. Along with some baseball bats . . . we'd find that guy and place a hurtin on him that he'd not soon forget. We'd teach him a lesson just to make an example out of him. Trust me, nobody else would ever pick on me again."

"I've heard all your comments and they are very interesting and thought provoking as well", stated Luella. "We have as answers; *thinking before doing, fear of persecution from peers, fear of getting beat up for standing up for the person getting persecuted, self defense, indifference and revenge.* These are all good answers and most are based on basic human emotion. Several comments do show some Bible based thinking. However as you read through the Bible you will find all these emotions taking place in the stories at one time or another."

Luella went on to say to the class, "When Daniel and his friends were torn away from all they knew as family and what they were taught to believe in. They did not give up their beliefs or blame what happened to them on God and turn away from Him. They stuck to what they believed was right. They did not go and take the law into their own hands."

"Rather than revenge, indifference or just going along to be cool", Luella explained. "They chose instead to pray to God to guide them and sought a way to change the environment they were thrown into by influencing their captors. They chose instead of hate and violence to change and influence the people around them. Passive aggression is a peaceful way to overcome. Through his passivity Jesus Christ performed the greatest most perfect show and tell to which the earth has ever bore witness. You can win over and influence the mind of your greatest aggressor by this means. Jesus believed so much in what His call to duty was that He was willing to give up his life for it. So did Daniels friends, Hananiah, Mishael and Azariah."

"And that is next week's lesson guys and dolls", Luella said and concluded our lesson. "Study up on it", she advised, "It is very fitting to what we were discussing today about our own situations. The question; How can we apply Biblical lessons and truths to things we go through in our own daily lives? Remember nothing that you can go through today is new to scripture. But if you look to the scripture for answers it will help you avoid some of the pitfalls of your own everyday life."

Our choir sang with enthusiasm and was well received by the congregation. Grandmother was sitting right up front as she said she would with mom by her side. After the service the Pastor again confirmed our commitments to Bible study in the coming weeks. He said he knew and understood about the tight schedule with school and the added responsibility of Bible study, but assured us that it would be well worth the effort.

I carried my hat in my hand as we walked home.

That night Grandma called me to her room. "I know that you are perplexed", she observed and then said, "About what I said the other night when I finished our meeting with the thought of God as three people and stating the fact that we consider him as one awesome God."

As I sat there beside her I thought for a moment and said, "Yeah grandma it is unbelievable. But I think I can accept that. I thought about and listened to the rain the other night after we talked and how it affects everything that it touches. God is kinda like that. I know he is in the rain. He is creation. He simply . . . just is." I also told grandma about the words I looked up.

"That is very observant for such a young man and very accepting", grandma said. Grandma turned the pages of her Bible and stopped. But you know the older you get the less you are to believe in such miracles and Christ knew this. So in the scripture of Matthew 18:1-5 we find this:

At that time the disciples came to Jesus and asked, "*Who is the greatest in the kingdom of heaven?*"

He called a little child and had him stand among them. And he said: "*I tell you the truth, unless you change and become little children, you will never enter the kingdom of heaven. Therefore, whoever humbles himself like this child is the greatest in the kingdom of heaven.*

And whoever welcomes a little child like this in my name welcomes me. But if anyone causes one of these little ones who believe in me to sin, it would be better for him to have a large millstone hung around his neck and to be drowned in the depths of the sea."

"Here you see Jesus is talking about the kind of acceptance that children have", said grandma, "And how through humility they believe. That is the kind of faith you have."

"I do", I asked?

"Yes, and God bless", grandma said and smiled. "For right now you do."

"What about the three in one thing", I questioned?

Grandma continued, "One of the places in the Bible aside from the miracle of creation in Genesis where the Father, son and the Holy Ghost are plainly shown as being together is when Jesus is baptized by John the Baptist in the river Jordan."

Again grandma started thumbing through the pages of her big Bible and stopped. "You see", she said, "Here in Luke 3:21 it says;

When all the people were baptized Jesus was baptized too. And as he was praying, heaven was opened and the Holy Spirit descended on him in bodily form like a dove. And a voice came from heaven: "You are my Son, whom I love; with you I am well pleased".

"Wow! That must have been incredible to witness", I said. "At that point could anyone who saw that have any doubts? How old was Jesus at that time."

Upon answering my question grandma said, "According to the Bible he was already thirty years old when he was baptized and started his ministry. But here you can plainly see, as I told you before, how the three; God the Father, Jesus the Son and the Holy Spirit all work together as one but are separate."

"Amazing" I said, "But that's pretty neat."

"Okay that is enough for another day", grandma said observing the time on her wrist watch. "I am letting you know that it is past your bedtime young man."

We said our good nights, I love you and I ambled off to bed. Before hopping into bed though I remembered to pray. How did I remember? The special sign which I posted at the head of my bed called out to me. *Hey you! Remember me*! Whatever works, right?

CHAPTER 8

The MBM's Ride Again

Monday morning came along and it was just another beautiful day. The boys along with their camping gear and provisions arrived at my house as soon as the parents would allow. Next Monday was the first day of the new school year. So this was to be our last hurrah for the summer of 1962. How quickly this summer flew by. It seemed like just yesterday we were celebrating the end of last year's school term with squirt guns in the halls of learning. That was until the teachers had enough of our shenanigans and confiscated the arsenal of water weaponry held in the possession of the student body.

My grandmother told me that the older you get the faster time moves in the scheme of things. She said, "In the days of youth you look forward and are anxiously anticipating everything. You want to be twelve when you just turned ten. You want to be sixteen when you turn fourteen, because you now want a driver's license. When you are sixteen you can't wait to graduate and after graduation you can't sit still until you are twenty one."

"At my age", grandma pointed out, "Time moves ever faster . . . but oddly, I have the patience of Job."

I wasn't really sure where she was going with that but I guess someday I will understand.

Dad got home right after lunch and said he would help transport us along with our equipment and food down to the campsite. That way he said we wouldn't have to make so many trips.

I noticed a part of a bag of cheese curls peeking out of Abe's back pack and had to ask. Whatchya packin in that rucksack Abe that you don't want anyone to know about? Inquiring minds want to know.

Abe came back with one of his quirky retorts usually taken from a sitcom or movie he had recently watched. "Snoopy people shouldn't be asking dumb questions that are below their pay grade. They might not get to share in the high life at a later time. Besides, answers will only be dealt with on a need to know basis. So it is on the QT till we hit the LZ soldier."

Skeeter and Bob broke into laughter as I saluted our new CO Abe and gave a loud, "Yes sir! Duly noted sir! Not until we hit the LZ sir!"

With all that having been said my Dad asked. "Can we now load up the trailer and get along little cheese curls? Let's move it on down to the camp ground guys. How about it? Day light's burnin and I have a lot of work to do in the field? So if you guys don't want to get busted down to buck private garden duty I suggest we get a move on right now . . . quick march? Hup, one, two, three and four . . . a rotten eggs the last one out the door.

Skeeter chimed in with, "I guess now we all know who the General is. So let's load up!"

All of us gave an, "*Ooorahh!*". . . and we began to load the wagon for the trip down to the camp site.

Little brother was standing on the porch and watching us as we began loading up the wagon with groceries and camping gear. He looked a little dejected. No one was paying any attention to him. Every time I handed another item to dad to put on the trailer he seemed to move one step closer to going back in the house.

"You want to help load this wagon and ride along down to the campsite", I asked my brother?

All the guys turned around and starting coaxing my brother, "Don't be shy", Abe said.

"Come on and join us", urged Bob.

"Hey guy, we could use another hand helping us with all this stuff", Skeet suggested.

That was all it took. Now little brother was smiling. We formed an assembly line, passing the goods from one hand to another and on to my dad as he placed the items in the wagon. My brother was beaming with joy because now he felt like part of the crew. My dad looked at us and gave me a wink and smiled. I knew what dad was thinking.

Dad lifted up my little brother and put him on top of some sleeping bags and blankets in the back of the wagon and said, "Now, you are in charge of watching this stuff and making sure nothing falls out, okay?"

My little brother was beaming as he nodded yes and offered my dad a salute.

My dad chuckled as he said, "Well I guess he knows what to do! And so do you guys! Let's go camping!"

Dad started the tractor and pulled out of the yard and we quickly jumped on our bikes and caravanned behind the wagon.

The excitement of the coming camp out was electric. It was our first time at a new and what we kids considered a real camping spot. The campsite was really cool because it was far enough away from, but still located close enough to our house for comfort. The tents would be in the big woods across the stream at the far end of dad's field. The conditions seemed like we were camping up on the mountain. Anyway, as kids that's how we saw it.

As we got to the stream we walked our bikes across and pushed them up into the woods near the camping area.

Bob and Skeet had not seen the site yet. When they did finally see it they let out exclamations of approval; "Wow!" "Cool man, this is tip top!"

Abe gave me a wink, a nod and a thumb up sign.

"My dad is the one who put this all together for us", I told them. "Brother and I helped but dad directed us. So we have to thank him for this."

All the guys gave out handshakes and thanked my dad for doing this for us.

Dad told us, "You guys are all welcome. But don't forget we have a ball game to win tomorrow so make sure you get some sleep tonight."

My brother took it upon himself to try and hand the items in the wagon to dad. Along with his and dads help we pulled off the gear from the wagon and started putting things away. Abe unrolled his tent and we all helped put it up right beside my umbrella tent. Soon everything was in order. Dad talked to us as he was walking away and explained that he would be around at first light to help us with breakfast. "And don't forget I will help get the Dutch oven ready to cook the chicken for tomorrow's lunch", he added speaking over his shoulder.

As dad was heading for the tractor he stopped. It was an after-thought I believe that he had as he slowly turned around. He was deliberately intent. While he spoke his face took on a most serious look, "A few more final parting words need to be related to you fellows", he said. "Tonight . . . and this is very important. DO NOT catch the forest on fire. DO NOT throw firecrackers into our next door neighbors, Lulu and Adda's pond to get fish for a fish fry. You have enough groceries to feed a small army.

"AND", Dad continued to speak while holding one finger in the air . . . "DO make a real effort to stay out of trouble. AND, no fighting! DO NOT ride your bikes all over God's creation at night." Dad hesitated in his speech as he eyeballed Abe's makeshift headlight. Then he continued, "And especially . . . DO NOT go riding out on the main highway. If you feel the need that you just have to do some late night riding, keep it in the village. Okay . . . fellows?"

We all agreed to adhere to the rules as given. So as we looked at each other we affirmed that we understood with "yes sirs" and I spoke up with an assurance of "Okay dad you can count on me!" Dad seemed to muster a hopeful smile and managed a goodbye wave and ended with, "Hhhmmmm, I suppose."

Not exactly sure, but I don't think dad totally believed that our intentions were genuine.

Dad looked at my little brother and said, "Don't forget to find your way home mister. And make that sooner than later otherwise your mom will come looking for you." Little brother reluctantly nodded his head that he understood. Getting into the seat of the tractor, dad started the engine and drove off down the hill and crossed the stream.

Oh boy! We were finally alone and on our own in the midst of mother nature. There was a babbling brook right behind the tents. The birds were singing and the crickets and late season cicadas were putting forth their resounding calls. But I guess we weren't out there for the wonders of nature. We're just a bunch of kids camping out by ourselves in the hope of having a little fun and adventure. Now that we were away from the folks we had nothing to do but kid stuff. We were kings for the moment!

"Hey Abe", I shouted, "Did ya bring your trading cards?"

"Yeah, I got some good ones too", Abe replied. "When we went shopping over at Erdley's store he just got in a fresh batch of 'em. I got the first ones out of the box."

"Hey guys, I'd rather play pitch and catch. I want to work on my curve ball", said Skeet. "We can trade cards anytime."

"How about . . . first let's take the clackers off the bikes so they don't make any noise when we ride around tonight", suggested Bob?

"Uh-oh", my little brother said with a kind of sheepish tone. "You guys are gonna get into trouble. Don't worry, I ain't gonna say nuthin. Like the time Larry nearly blew up the house. I seen what he was up to, but I never said a thing. He got a whooppin without me have'n to say a word."

We all stopped for a moment and listened to my little brother talk.

"Yeah okay, don't worry, we'll be careful and not get into trouble", said Abe. "And Bob . . . taking off the clackers sounds like a good plan. We should do that first."

Curiously my little brother watched as all of us went over to the bikes and off came the noise makers. We were now prepared for silent running. Skeeter spoke up and the four of us cheered in agreement when he said, "The Midnight Bike Marauders will again ride the back country roads."

"Yup, I knew it", my brother said and gave a whistle. "There's trouble, I see it. No clacker's means . . . you can sneak 'round better, right?"

We tried to ignore my little brother's comments as we proceeded with our check list; tires had air, headlights and running lights were in working order, peddles and chains were tight. Our running lights were crude. They were flashlights taped to our handle bars. All were all in good working order. Now we were ready to roll.

Bob had brought his radio and turned it on so we could catch the Phillies game. They were playing the Pirates who were my favorite team, ever since those traitors the Dodgers snuck out of Brooklyn. Abe was a Phillies fan and Bob liked the Yankees. But he was also a Phillies fan when he wasn't rooting for the Yanks. Skeeter didn't really have any favorites but loved to play the game. That was okay too. Nobody said you had to be a fan of anything. We got a game of catch going until we got hungry. Then we started a campfire to make something to eat for supper. My little brother hung out with us for mealtime. Mom said it was okay for him to eat with us until it was bath time.

Dogs and burgers were the chef's choice for supper. Tonight "Abe the *Cheese Curl Man*" was the head chef. As promised Mrs. Court's shoo fly pie was on the desert menu. No cheese curls were seen, not even as a side dish. I didn't ask about them. As was proposed, it was above my pay grade, so I didn't need to know.

After supper we brought more wood over to the campfire from our stack that we had made the previous day. It was now necessary to get water to boil for washing utensils and cleaning up. My brother and I walked downstream a little way to where there was a spring. Dad said it was a good water source. The people that owned our place before us had dug it out and lined it with stones. They had used it along with the neighbors down the road who also claimed water rights to it.

Nobody used the spring anymore. It had been forgotten. But we could use it for our wash water but not until after we boiled it. We did not want to use the water from the stream, even though we knew that the stream had originated up in the hills from several natural springs. Because it flowed past too many homes in the village it was no longer safe to use. Dad said that the water had parasitic bugs called '*Giardia*' in it and they could make you very sick. Whatever they were, they did not sound friendly and I was not taking any chances.

As we approached the spring I started beating the brush and leaves. My brother asked, "What are you doing?"

"You just keep an eye out for anything that slithers through the grass", I explained. "We can't be too cautious around the water. Copperhead snakes hang around the water. Especially now since it has been so dry they will be looking for places like this."

"I hate snakes", I said emphatically!

My brother said, "I don't think I ever saw one except on TV."

"Well maybe this will be your lucky day little brother" I suggested and then added, "But I hope not. That would be all I need today is to see even a black snake. They really give me the creeps. I should have brought my camp shovel along to at least clobber it if we saw one. I know they have a place in the world. But they just need to stay out of my line of sight and away from my path."

"What's that in the leaves? I see something moving." My brother said pointing to something rustling under the leaves. The grass was waving around too.

My pulse started to race. This was all I needed. The place he was pointing to was right in our pathway. I stopped and took my stick and poked at the place where there was movement. From under the leaves several field mice burst from their hiding place. Apparently they were building a nest. Both my brother and I jumped when the startled mice decided to scramble. We laughed at ourselves for being scared by a couple of mice.

"Wow", my brother stammered. "That got me. Thought for sure it was a snake."

"Yeah, lucky us that we'd get that chance", I mumbled to myself.

Out of the corner of my eye I spied something that glistened in the sunlight. Apparently there was another creature close by that was also interested in field mice. It was watching from a distance for its chance to close in on the tiny fur bearing mammals. I told my little brother to be quiet. "Sshhh", I whispered gently touching his arm. "You are about to get your wish little brother."

The reptile was resting in the sun on a rock about ten feet from us and had been attentively watching the mice until we came along. The snake was not a large black snake by any standard, and I considered it harmless. Oddly, it had not even moved when I pointed it out.

"Guess this is my lucky day", whispered my brother. As we took our next few steps the snake decided it had enough of us and lazily slithered off into the brush and away from the spring, thank goodness.

While still tapping the brush with my walking stick we cautiously made our way over to the spring. I beat around the rocks with the wooden stick just to make sure there were no other reptilian creatures lurking about. After dipping out two buckets full of the crystal clear cool water we headed back to camp.

Walking along together my brother excitedly chattered away. "This was a fun adventure for me! I could stay with you guys tonight? What do you think? I never get to do anything fun. I've been with you and just like that, I get to see two mice and a real live snake! You and me . . . we saved those mice. We're a couple of super heroes . . . at least in the mouse world."

"Yeah, I guess you could look at it that way", I commented. "The mice are safe . . . at least for now. But they will be back and so will the snake. It is survival of the fittest out here. It moves down the food chain little bro.

Continuing on with my speech I added, "We just happen to be the biggest, baddest and smartest in this neck of the woods. Now if we lived in Africa for instance, we would be considered a part of the immediate food chain. Think about having lions, panthers, cheetahs and other large carnivorous creatures as neighbors. Even some of the snakes in South America can eat you alive."

"Wow, sure am glad we live where we do", exclaimed my little brother Scott! "Never looked at it like that. You see those neat animals on TV. To think about living in the jungle . . . now that's scary. There you are sleepin . . . the next thing . . . you're being eaten. No thanks!"

"You know here in Pennsylvania we do have large black bears", I cautioned.

"Really", Scott exclaimed and gave a whistle.

"Remember last fall, I said, when the Walter's trash got raided by a couple of bears. Then the Game Warden and a few deputies came and caught them. Now at that time they took them back to the mountain. That wasn't but a half mile from here and they could come back. Yeah, once they smell burgers and hot dogs cookin over an open fire they could come a runnin."

Scott again gave a whistle, pondered for a moment and said, "Yeah I see what ya mean. Even around here there are some big critters."

"And don't forget about the snakes", I warned. "We didn't see one today. But one of those poisonous ones could crawl into your tent and right up into your sleepin bag. That'd sure be a surprise. You might never wake up if one bites you in your sleep."

Another whistle came from my brother and he said. "Never thought about that . . . hey, ya know, I oughta maybe wait another couple-la years before I go campin. I don't think I'd never forgive myself if I was to get eatin or bitten." Scott paused and then added, "What would mom do without me?"

"Yeah, you got a good way of lookin at things kid", I said smiling and approving his decision. "She'd get pretty sore and all . . . I mean about you not being around to pick up your toys and not helping out with the chores."

"And as a matter of fact, so would dad", continuing to praise his good decision and putting my arm around my brothers shoulders.

My brother went on with his thoughts as he said, "I always thought that big brothers were pretty stinky. Like you guys are wantin to take advantage of us little guys. From what you're sayin you seem to be lookin out for me. That's kinda cool."

After patting him on the back I said, "Well, now you see that's what big brothers are for. So I guess it's almost time for you to get back to the house . . . see what mom has for you to do?"

"I guess so", said Scott. "But I'll be coming back tomorrow. And you can count on me, okay?"

"Sure man, no problem. We'll see ya in the morning", I assured him. He handed me his bucket of water and headed for the house.

I crossed over the stream to the camp with the water buckets in hand and my walking stick under my arm.

Bob called out to me. "We thought you got lost or went back home with your brother! I thought your little brother might want to sleep out with us?"

"Nahh! Not after I gave the bears and snakes in the woods story", I explained.

"Yeah, that's sure to keep any little guy from wantin to camp out", Bob agreed.

And then I added. "Besides I was getting water for the kettle so we can at least wash the utensils and ourselves. I have to brush my teeth and wash my face. I'm gettin zits. And my mom said it's because I don't keep my face clean enough."

Then Bob started to tell us his theory about why we get pimples. "My older brother puts that acne junk all over his face every night before he goes to bed. Makes him look like he's from outer space . . . he takes some antibiotic too", explained Bob. "He even gets pimples on his back. They're pretty funky looking. Some he calls blackheads. The ones on his face . . . he tries squeezing out the yellow stuff and pops them all over the bathroom mirror. My mom gets really pissed about that. She yells at him . . . says they will spread and get worse if he keeps doing it. I think they come from dating girls though. I've got it figured out too."

"Oh yeah", I said and then asked Bob as I sat down the water buckets. "And how'd you get this zits thing all figured out all by yourself . . . you got a medical degree or something?"

"You see . . . the guys who are dating girls for any length of time", Bob went on to theorize . . . "They all seem to come down with the same problem. Yup, the girls are the carriers. Just like how in our History books . . . rats carried the Bubonic Plague. Yeah, the girls carry around whatever causes pimples."

"You're nuts Bob", exclaimed Skeeter who was helping pour water into the kettle over the fire. "It comes from eating too much chocolate and sweets. That's what my mom says anyway. And she's pretty right on about most things."

"No man! Honestly for your own safety, check it out if ya don't believe me", Bob pleaded his case. "That's why I am staying as far away from girls as I can. They carry that stuff. If ya get too close . . . you're gonna get the zits. I'm tellin ya!"

"Yeah, if Larry's getting zits he must have gotten too close to his favorite girl Susie", Abe said slyly.

"Watch your mouth Abe. Or I'll come over there and dump this whole bucket of water on your head", I said threatening the "Cheese Curl Man". "You know how much I don't like that goofy girl. Besides you're the one who is always over on her porch listening to 45's on her record player. Duh! Who me, you might ask? Yeah Abe . . . it's you kiddo!"

"Wow . . . really", Skeeter and Bob were now interested and both chimed in unison! "You're the man Abe?" They looked at each other and got great big smiles on their faces. Again in unison they asked, "You're falling for the tattletale gossip queen?"

Bob shouted, "Wow, Abe my good man . . . I wouldn't have believed it . . . if I had not heard it from Larry!" Bob calmed down and then asked quietly while giving a clownish look and a wink, "Is it true Abe . . . you on the porch with Susie . . . making, I mean playing music? Inquiring minds need to know. This sounds so too serious! If so, zits are on the way, and then you won't be able to deny it."

I jumped into the chiding of Abe and I stood up and pointed at him. "Yes my boys, believe it, it is true. The young lad has been smitten and bitten as it were, by Susie the tattletale gossip queen."

Abe's face turned two shades of red as he went from being embarrassed to getting real peeved.

As his temper rose he formed the best nonsensical come back he could muster and shouted. "You guys really, really are a bunch of donkeys! Funny! Hee-haw! Hee-haw . . . AAAND! Ya know what misters hee, hee and haw . . . you will not be sharing any of my goodies. You got Susie all wrong man! She's just misunderstood! We are just good friends."

With that all said Abe grabbed his rucksack and went storming into his tent closed and zipped the flap.

Abe was mortified and we were to say the least . . . stunned.

You could have knocked us three over with a feather. Was he defending Susie, the neighborhood tattletale gossip queen?

"Say it ain't so Abe", I whispered questioning and looking at my other two comrades? "Susie . . . misunderstood? Why this can't be", I said continuing on . . . "Yes, pretty soon he will have zits if what Bob reports is true!"

"QUARANTINE, QUARANTINE", we all yelled running around the outside of Abe's tent and we all broke into laughter.

We stopped in front of Abe's tent as we heard the zipper opening. A hand popped out holding one lonely orange cheese curl and then it disappeared back into the tent with a *zzzziiiippp*. There was heard a chomping crunching sound. Then a single hand again appeared. This time it was holding a bite size snickers bar and *zzzziiiippp*. That too disappeared behind the tent fabric. We heard the wrapper being torn open followed by, *chomp-chomp*. Again a singular hand appeared holding an ice cold soda in a glass bottle. The same procedure was repeated. We heard the top being popped and then a gulping sound followed by belch. Then out came the totally unexpected final straw. There appeared a hand holding high like the Statue of Liberty a large plastic bowl. This one slipped completely past our radar. Indeed it was not a torch but a bowl of red juicy mouth watering water melon being held up high.

That really got our attention. "HEY", we all shouted, "WE WANT SOME OF THAT!

"A - HA", Abe shouted from behind the tent flap! "Wanna keep makin fun of me now don'tchya? I told you I had goodies, but you had to keep it up didn'tchya?"

"Listen wise guy", I said. "Unless you are prepared for some real rousting, you'd better get to sharing with your buds. We all kid around and nothing is meant to harm anybody. So unless you want that tent coming down around your ears and you getting pulled into the stream, alive and inside, you'd better come out here."

"That's right Abe", demanded Skeeter. "Get your water melon hoarding fanny out here and now!"

There was silence. Not a belch, crunch or candy wrapper being torn open could be heard. Then Abe quietly spoke, "Haven't heard the magic word."

Bob asked, "And what magic word might that be?

Skeeter proposed, "Seems like he's buying melon eating time guys . . . whadya think?"

Abe calmly spoke again. "You know . . . *belch* . . . the one our moms told us about."

"Oh that one", Bob acknowledged as he spoke in his best pleading down on his knees voice. "Please Mrs. Cee, can little Abraham, oops I mean Abe, come out and play with us so we can steal . . . I mean share his water melon . . . pretty please with sugar on top."

"Is that the one you meant, Bob finally asked?

"Yes Bob. That is the right word", Abe said just too calmly. "I'll accept it 'cause I know you're too much of a clown to say it the right way."

The orange stained "*Cheese Curl*" hand again made an appearance, but this time it was to zip open the tent flap. Finally he appeared, the "*Cheese Curl*" man. He had chocolate smeared around his mouth and water melon juice dripping from his chin. It looked like he tried to pig down as much of the melon as possible from behind the safety of the closed tent flaps, before giving it up to the team. Plus he had the audacity to climb out of the tent without the melon.

Skeeter was the first to speak out about his remissness and asked. "Where's the melon, curl man?"

"Oh, you boys wanted some melon. How silly of me to have forgotten, Weeelll-bers", Abe said expressing his concern using his best Mr. Ed voice.

"Yeah", stated Bob, "How silly, but let me help you find that stash."

Bob yanked back the tent flap to retrieve the absentee melon. "Wow", Bob exclaimed! "Good old Abe has been holdin out on us! He's got a whole grocery store in here! Must've had all this hidden in his rucksack and used his back pack and cheese curls as a decoy. Pretty clever there Abe."

Suddenly Abe went from being the stiff to being our hero. His dad worked in a grocery store and Abe sometimes used that to his advantage. He had a vast array of goodies. We could be sick for weeks. If we ate the right amount of all this stuff we could declare food poisoning and probably even end up missing the first day of school. That is, if we could possibly eat and consume all that junk food. But then we'd miss our big game tomorrow and we could not do that.

Abe had a huge self approving smirk on his face as he divvyed up some of the goodies. We voraciously consumed what was left of the water melon. Soon we looked like the "*cheese curl man*" himself. Melon juice, chocolate and orange cheese powder outlined our mouths.

The sun was going down and a soft breeze was coming down from the hills. With my walking stick I stirred the remaining embers of fire to life. It was ready for more wood to be added. As the first log hit the fire it sent sparks into the night and the scent of burning oak filled the evening air. It was really neat being together with the guys right then and there. The late summer swansong of the crickets and cicadas were so loud that you could barely hear the evening song of the whip poor will. We sat and watched the flames in silence, listening to it crackle and feeling the fires warmth. It was an eternal moment full of simplicity and goodness.

Suddenly breaking into the peaceful eternal moment of simplicity and goodness a disruptive shout emitted. "Let's get on our bikes and ride!" There's always one. I knew the quiet time would not last . . . especially with ants-in-his-pants Abe being part of the crew. His war cry echoed through the forest. I'll bet even my parents heard that as they were less than a quarter mile away. They slept with the windows open until the first snow flurry of the season was sighted.

Upon questioning Abe's sanity I threw a slightly over-cooked marshmallow in his direction.

"Hey, are trying to burn me or something", squeaked Abe.

"Nice going on the unsolicited political announcement, AAAAABRAAAHAM", I hissed loudly trying to show my disdain towards what I considered to be irreverence. "What, are you trying to do wake up the whole village? This is supposed to be run silent, run deep, secret stuff. We're not supposed to be cruising all over the place man. Guess you didn't hear my dad's request!"

Abe pleaded his case. "Nobody heard that man! The bullfrogs and insects are so loud I am surprised we can even hear our own conversation. They're louder than my war yell believe you me. Besides it's our last ride of the season. It's expected. Even your dad said, "*If you feel the need . . . cruise the village*". Well? We feel the need, don't we?"

Without question we all jumped up, and headed for our two wheeled war wagons. The kick stands went up and we took our bikes gingerly across the stream. We continued pushing our bikes until we got out of sight of my parent's farmhouse. Once around the corner we got on our bikes and headed for the main road. Skeet's older brother and his friends were night fishing at Royer's on the Middle Creek. This was just a few miles away by way of the main road. Riding on the main road at night was forbidden, but it saved us at least a mile and a half of peddling to get to where we were going. Most of the trek was uphill and we would have to push our bikes. We would be on the side of the road for over half the distance. After that it was all downhill. On the way back to our camp we would take the back roads and go through the village.

Cautiously we stopped and looked both ways before starting the trudge up the long incline. Trucks and cars flew by, some even honked their horns. I didn't think they were giving a friendly hello. But rather they were probably thinking; what are these crazy kids doing going out on the main road, at this time of the night?

Right after we pushed our bikes onto the side of the main road we heard a car coming from behind us and it had one of those glass packs. It sounded like a jet plane coming at ground level. The driver saw us and laid on his horn as he flew by. Loud rock n' roll music was blaring from out of the car's open windows. It must have been going over a hundred miles an hour when it flew by.

As we reached the top of the hill we were all breathing a little easier. The climb had been exhausting, but we were also a little more at ease now that we had experienced the traffic at night. Thank goodness there really were not all that many vehicles on the road at this time. The first hill was the longest and now it was down the other side and up another lesser incline. We would pass a farm and then about another half mile after that we would arrive at the bridge.

Suddenly everything was silent. There were no cars coming in either direction. Not even the sound of an oncoming car could be heard. It was our turn now. We made our break, hopped on our bikes and started peddling for all we were worth. Down the hill we raced. Our desire was to get up enough speed to make it up the next incline without having to peddle. This was a new experience. It was a little scare-crazy riding in the dark coasting on our bikes at break neck speed. Our flashlights showed a path less than ten feet in front of us. But the thrill of moving this fast in the dark, the wind blowing on my face and threw my hair, now that was the thing. It was a sensation near to free falling. That's what I felt when I would close my eyes and let myself fall off the bridge and into the water at the swimming hole. That's another thing my parents didn't want us kids to do.

When we made it up the next grade to the top of that hill we could see lights in every direction in front of us. We stopped and stared, trying to figure out what was going on. Something had just happened and there were a lot of people, cars and lights all around the bridge area.

Entranced by the lights up ahead we failed to notice a fire engine and ambulance roaring up over the hill behind us. When they were right on top of us they sounded their sirens and alarms. The emergency vehicles barely missed us. We heaved our bikes and ourselves into the ditch. An unfriendly voice shouted from the back of the fire engine as it rushed by, "GET OFF THE ROAD YOU FOOLS, BEFORE YYYAAA GEEET KIILLLED!"

Unknown to us, the reason there were no cars on the highway was because the road had been blocked. From behind and in front of us, traffic had been rerouted in both directions. We picked ourselves up out of the ditch. Each of us suffered a few scrapes and bruises from desperately piling on top of one another trying to get out of the way.

Our makeshift headlights beamed in different directions. When we tossed our bikes and ourselves into the ditch our bikes went everywhere and so did the flashlights we had taped to the handle bars. I picked up one of the flashlights that had been separated from my bike and turned it's beam of light on Bob.

"Wow", Bob exclaimed brushing himself off! "Was that close or what . . . I didn't see that one coming! I was just staring at the lights . . . standing out there in the middle of the road. I thought it must be a carnival or something. Then wham! If it wasn't for that siren . . . I could have been knocked flatter than a pancake or worse . . . lucky I made it to the ditch."

"It's an accident", Skeeter deduced. "Looks like a bad one too. I don't hope my crazy brother Ray is involved with his hot rod. He's always drinkin with his buddies and doing crazy stuff just to show off to his giddy girlfriend. He said he was just going fishing. Maaann . . . he's so full of it!"

"Don't worry Skeeter", I said. "I don't see your brothers Chevy. Looks like a truck and some kinda big black car. There's also something down over the bank too, but I can't make it out."

Abe called out, "Hey, you guys wanna shine that light over here?" He was busy picking tiny stones out of a wound in his arm and brushing dirt from his jeans. I think he took the worst of it. We all seemed to have ended up on top of him.

"You all right Abe", Bob spoke up inquiring about his condition? Bob picked his bike and turned his flashlight that was still attached towards Abe.

Skeeter was noticeably concerned about Ray. Ray was his brothers nickname. His given name was Raymond and Skeeter was staring towards the bridge trying to make sense out of the chaos.

"Yeah I am okay", Abe mumbled. "I always end up getting the worst of things. But that's okay I can take it. I'll be alright. It's just my ankle overturned on a rock and I landed on some nasty gravel."

Disgruntled by it all but, still rarin' to go Abe expressed out loud, "Let's get going before something else happens!"

So we picked up our bikes, fixed our lights, straightened out handle bars and brushed the dirt from our clothes and made our way towards the bridge.

A bit of smoke could now be seen coming from the truck and a larger crowd was gathering. As we got closer Skeets picked out his brother. "Over there he is", he pointed out. Ray's there among the people who are watching something being pulled from the creek. As he gave a sigh of relief he said under his breath, "Good . . . good there he is. I think he's okay, thank goodness."

His brother was holding a fishing rod in one hand and it looked like a bottle of something in the other. Hopefully it was just a soda. Skeeter loved both his brother and his dad but he hated it when they drank. He said it changed them. His dad was never mean to his mom and brother, he

just got kind of distant, like he wanted to be somewhere else, just not here he told us. He believed that was why his brother drank too and believed that it was just his way of dealing with problems. Right or wrong Skeeter seemed to accept it . . . didn't like it, but he accepted it.

Approaching the accident site we could smell burning tires and burning fuel oil. Skeeter's brother turned around and saw us and walked hurriedly over to us and said emphatically, "You guys shouldn't be here man! This is a mess you boys don't need to see!"

Skeeter asked his brother, "What happened?"

And all of us rapid fired questions as to, "Who, where, anyone dead, hurt, how many?"

Ray rolled his eyes and said to us while waving his fishing rod and drink bottle, "Hey, slow down and get over here out of the way!" He then continued to explain, "Me and my buddies, Hank and Steve were fishing under the bridge. You know Skeets, over there at the deep hole where we always start out fishing at night?"

Skeeter shook his head silently agreeing that he knew where his brother was talking about. He made a motion with his hands for his brother to get on with it. We were all anticipating the rest of the story.

Ray straightened up, cleared his throat and continued with the story. "Now then . . . there was this revved up car coming from the north, and I could tell it's coming at hell breakin speed. Like if you don't slow down sucker, I thought, you ain't never gonna make the turn. I hear a big freight truck comin from the south and he's putting on his jake-brake for the turn at the bridge.

Well here comes the souped-up car movin way too fast to make the turn . . . I hear squealin brakes and tires and it's like Hiroshima. The truck and the car meet on the bridge. The car hits the bridge and the truck jack knifes tryin to avoid a head on and the big black car behind it is also caught up in the mess. VAARROOOM! The hot rod ends up flyin right over the bridge. Yeah! You guessed it! SPLASH! Right into our fishin hole! Just when I was hooked onto a big one too and thinkin about a fish fry! Like I said, PLOP! Right into the water in front of me drops this candy apple red, hot rod 57 Chevy.

I nearly dropped my frosty cold one tryin to get out of the way. A tidal wave of water hits me . . . I lose my fish . . . and that's why I am soaked to the skin. You know I think I still see their faces, the driver and his lady friend in the passenger's seat. The passenger came right out through the window when they hit. Man it's like on slow motion rewind in my brain. But when that car hit, she flew out that window like a bullet through plate glass. She ended up over there on the other side of the creek bank stuck in a tree, wedged between two branches.

D. O. A. dudes both of em D. O. A.! The driver was caught between the steering wheel and the seat. I believe he was dead before the car even hit the water. It burst into flames on the way down too and really messed up that beautiful paint. Man that's a crime. After seein' that angel in flight and watching her get wedged in that tree the way she did . . . well I put down my frosty cold one and grabbed a soda. I don't think I'll touch another beer for a month of Sundays. It might even be my cause to stop drinking.

The four bike trekkers were silent and just listened with mouths agape. In dead silence we listened as Ray brought the tale to life and brought it to an end. Ray looked at the ground and kicked around a couple of stones. "Yup", Ray mumbled, "That was really something to see and I hope I never see anything like it again . . . ever", he concluded.

After about ten seconds of silence . . . "What about the truck and the car behind it", Abe stammered out?

"Oh yeah", Ray said offering the rest of the explanation. "The truck's diesel tanks are still burnin as you can see", he pointed out. "And the family who was traveling in the car behind the truck, that's so amazing."

"You see the black late model car over there", Ray asked?

We were so in awe of the details of Ray's story we kept our mouths closed. This was so hard for us to do and shook our heads in agreement. Yeah we see the car we implied but motioned him to move on with the story.

"Well, that is the Reverend's car", Ray went on, "And when the truck jack knifed from what I can tell, that is when the Chevy caught the edge of the bridge and catapulted itself over the bridge. There was just an instant when that black car could have squeaked through and got past the truck."

Now that we got Ray going, he wouldn't stop and lived up to his nickname. He was on a roll. He stopped just long enough to put down the fishing pole and take a swig of soda. You'd a thought he was delivering news at eleven.

So he went on and on. "You know that the driver of that black car wouldn't have known about the oncoming Chevy because of the turn. And . . . ya got to ask yourself, what if the Chevy hadn't become air born? But that is exactly what happened. The black car has scratches on both sides where it just scraped past the bridge and the truck when the driver went for the opening instead of hitting the truck in the rear. God was on the side of the preacher man because that is what he is. They were coming home from a revival meeting, him and his whole family. Now I think he is asking mercy for the dead. They still haven't found the truck driver. Who knows, maybe he is fish food too because he slammed into the bridge with some pretty good force. I mean this accident shook the very pylons the bridge is standing on.

Speechless is what we were as we imagined the scene unfold right in front of us while listening to Ray's story. Right now I was wishing for the campfire and the warmth of my sleeping bag and some cheese curls. But something told me that this night wasn't over yet.

"Hello! Hey, you guy's at home . . . anybody in there? Or you guys all out there somewhere?" Ray called out waving his hands as he saw we had become mesmerized by all that was going on. He interjects a polite suggestion. "Maybe you guys had better get on home before one of your parents shows up and catches you here. I am sure this is all over the CB's and scanners. Abe I know your old man is into all that stuff. I'll guess for sure that he and Luella will be here any minute."

At first what he was saying wasn't on our radar but Abe sluggishly caught on and responded. "Yeah, I guess you're right Raymond we should be moving on. What do you say fellows . . . shouldn't we get on our bikes and ride?"

One at a time we quietly agreed to head for home as we pried our eyes from the accident. Our exit was slow and deliberate. After we rode our bikes for a quarter mile Abe exclaimed, "Wow!" It was all he said for a moment and then added, "Did you catch all those details?"

Bob followed with, "Yeah . . . Wow, is right. Can you believe what just happened?"

Then Skeeter spoke up. "Gotta hand it to my brother guys, he may be a screw up but he's always on top of things. I don't think he's a bad guy? He really does care, but he's just a little lost. I don't know what I would have done if that had been him on one of those gurneys?"

"So what's up with Larry back there", asked Abe who was the lead biker?

I was following a little distance behind the rest of the crew. "Just peddling and thinking", I called out. I then pushed forward and caught up with Abe.

Abe looked over at me and commented, "Uh, oh, guys . . . Larry's deep thinkin!"

"You know everything happens for a reason", I suggested. "Guys, you gotta think about it. About us being there . . . what are the chances of that? And Skeeter's brother being there too . . . what are the chances of all of this?'

"Don't mean to take the air out of your bike tires, but he was just there fishin", surmised Skeeter. "Besides, you think too much and we had this all planned a week ago."

"You're right", I stated and went on trying to make a point. "True we made plans a week ago, but you have to see how this all fits together. Yeah, like we plan things and all, but there seems to be something else going on. We may think that we have it all planned out but we're not really in control."

Skeeter spoke up and said, "I hope my brother gets something out of it . . . hope he slows his way of living down. I think he learned something from what happened at the bridge. I hope he stops his drinkin like he said he might. And he should stop actin like a fool over his giddy girlfriend."

"See, that's the point of life guys. Just like Skeets sayin", I offered up for debate. "It's about what we see and how we use the information."

Bob suddenly jumps into the conversation, "Watch out fellas! There it is. I see it clearly. There's a sign post up ahead! And it tells us that Larry's entering into the twilight zone!"

"What does the next sign say Bob", Abe asked?

"I can't see it yet but it is there . . . oh yes, it is becoming clearer . . . just a moment . . . there it is . . . and it says . . ."

"What does it say Bob", Abe asked again?

"Don't drink and ride", said Bob. He then added, "Larry sniffed too much diesel fumes . . . and standing beside the road sign is Rod Serling. He's offering me an ice cold beer. How is that for a coincidence?"

All my buddies had a good laugh.

"Very funny guys . . . you just don't get it man", I complained. "I'm not saying that anything was out of the ordinary. We just need to be aware is all I'm saying. Didn't what was going on there at the bridge tell you anything? I guess all of us were amazed more by Ray's story, the lights and fire, than what happened to those people? Oh what's the use in talking? I suppose we are all a bunch of clowns on this road show?"

Speeding up a little I tried to move ahead leaving the rest of the clowns behind. Sometimes, and not always, a little window opened. There I could see beyond the smoke and mirrors. It was a little quiet place, and it didn't happen often, like I said. But when it did happen, I landed in a place where I did not feel comfortable. Whatever this place was, it separated me from my friends. The only way to describe it was like you are standing on a ledge. There is a big grizzly bear in front of you and an abyss behind you. All your buddies are behind the bear shouting incoherently and they can't do anything to help. There's no denying the situation. You have to decide whether to take on the bear or believe in a strange voice in your head saying, go ahead . . . jump, it'll be all right. So that's what I do, I jump, whether it makes me unpopular or not. I take the risk and see where I land.

"Hey Larry, where you going in such a hurry", shouted Abe? "You got the best light! Wait up for us!"

"Get the lead out", I shouted back at them!

Every one caught up to me at the stop sign. If we made a left we would be heading up and into the mountain and when we make a right the road takes us back to the village. The village was just around the corner and over the hill.

As we stopped for a breather Bob said, "Boys I am getting a little hungry and tired. How about we roast a few dogs and hit the hay when we get back?"

Skeeter added, "Hopefully the fire is not completely out when we get there. We put some larger logs on so maybe it will be just a perfect bed of coals for weenie roasting time."

Abe spoke up like he always did giving the command to get on our bikes and ride. So we did and as we crested the hill we could see the faint lights of the village. Coasting silently into the middle of the small hamlet we stopped under one of the few pole lights located there. The light happened to be in front of Skin's house. We looked to see if he was still up, but the house was dark. Abe dropped his bike and ran up the yard to peek into the living room window. Turning back towards us as he ran he placed his index finger over his lips and whispered, "Ssshhh, keep quiet!" As if we were going give away our favorite peeping Tom.

Abe spied Skin's cat or was it his older sister's cat? I guess it didn't matter. It was all in the family. Abe quickly snagged it out from under the hedge and hurried back to us.

Skeeter sarcastically inquired, "Now what in the world are you gonna do with that Abe?

Abe did his ssshhh thing again and spoke in a loud hoarse whisper, "I don't know yet! Just try to keep quiet. Here Larry, hold this thing."

"What do you want me to do with the darn cat", I inquired and stated, "I'm allergic to the things."

"I don't know yet. Give me time to think will you guys", Abe said still speaking in a whisper.

"Why are you whispering Abe", Skeeter asked.

"Running silent man", was Abe's answer.

Rolling his eyes Skeeter said, "Yeah, running silent, right on man."

By this time we were standing in front of Susie's house and right under her bedroom window.

Bob was quick to point this out as he said, "You know Abe this is ridiculous. Here we are trying to be quiet and not be seen. We are standing under a street light. On one side of the street there is your house, and on the other is Susie's house. Yeah, we are being real cool and we are not out in the open. Everybody in the neighborhood can clearly see us out here and you're chasing a stupid cat around."

"Maybe Bob if you would not be talking in your normal voice we wouldn't be noticed", Abe suggested?

Suddenly a familiar voice could be heard coming from above. It wasn't angels singing praises to us either. "I see you Larry. I see you in your old blue Dodgers baseball cap and red hooded sweatshirt and you're holding Lynn's cat. What are you boys up too? No good I am sure", was the understated observation from a squeaky Susie voice.

For some reason her squeaky voice and attitude just got under my skin. So I opened my big mouth. "Just go back to bed 'Susie Q' this is none of your bees wax."

"I can see all of you guys too", continuing in her best squeaky snooty voice now. "Numero uno; of course is Larry. Two; there is Bob and three; The Skeeter and four . . . why I just can't believe that you of all people Abe would be part of this rabble."

"Well you see right there 'Susie Q' ", and I had to add, "That's where you are dead wrong about old Numero Uno. Old number four is the ring leader of this whole group of rabble rousers. See that's where you just can't be too smart because you missed that point."

Abe gave me his best smirking face. Looking at Abe and holding the cat out in front of me I came back with, "After all this cat business is your great big idea . . . right Abe?"

"I just can't believe that Abraham", she said.

"Abraham", most of us said in unison!

"That's right", Susie snipped. "Abraham is his real name, and Abraham, I know you better than this. I just bet that Larry put you up to this whole thing. Besides Larry, you are the one holding the cat. Just what are you going to do with that cat anyway?

"Dough boy", I mumbled under my breath. My mind was racing and I was getting a little perturbed by where the conversation was headed. Yeah, I was holding the cat or bag so to speak, but it was placed into my hands. I didn't want this feline. Like I said I had cat allergies. Why should I even be holding the fur ball? I did not know what to do?

There I was in that quiet place again. It was me, the bear in front of me or was that 'Susie Q'? And there were my buddies behind the bear again. 'Susie Q' was squeaking incoherently and of course the abyss was behind me. So I did the best thing I could think of at the moment. With all my might I heaved the cat up into the air and onto the porch roof. It landed right in front of 'Susie Q's' bedroom window. "There", I said to Susie, "now you can deal with the cat, it's your responsibility!"

"Cool", said Bob. "What a great idea. That's perfect!"

"Wow", said Skeeter with a big smile! "I would have never thought of doing that!"

Abe just stood there with his teeth in his mouth, not saying a word.

Susie on the other hand had plenty to say but her conversation faded away in the distance as I got on my bike and headed for the serenity of the campfire. The bear disappeared and down I fell into the abyss not knowing where I would land. The guys were coming up behind me but they didn't catch up until I had crossed the stream and was all ready and seated on the other side. While putting the kick stand up I noticed that the fire had died down but the coals were hot. There were red and blue flames licking and rising upward from the coals. I grabbed my stick to stir the embers and added a few pieces of firewood. I sat down on one of our makeshift seats made from a large piece of wood from the trunk of a tree.

Skeeter was the first to get to the fireside and spoke up, "What are you all sore about? You rode away like a bear shot in the backside."

"Nothin, just forget about it", I said. "Why don't you get some dogs out of the cooler for roasting?"

Coming around to my side he smiled and patted me on the back, "Sounds like a plan man."

Bob was next for arrival at the fire and started spilling his guts. "Whoa, what are you all pissed off about? That was really cool man, sailing that cat up on the roof like that. I knew you had a pretty good arm but that was quit a distance. What a shot, it landed right in front of old Susie's nose. What a surprise. I don't think she was expectin that one. All I gotta say is wow, my hats off to ya!"

"Yeah, cool huh", I mused?

I was deep thinkin about the abyss I just leaped into and how it would play out the next day? Susie would tell her parents, if she hadn't done it all ready? Next her parents will tell Lynn's parents and Lynn's parents will ask Lynn whether he had anything to do with this in-genius plan. And then . . .

It was Abe who broke my train of thought next. "Hey, Lar that wasn't quite what I had in mind but that was a good one . . . totally cool and unexpected."

"I really don't think you had anything in mind . . . because you weren't thinking", I blurted out!

"Man what crawled up your tail pipe? Talk about a sore", spewed Abe. "Now I am not going to tell you what Susie said after you hit the pavement in such a hurry. You should have stuck around man. It was priceless!"

"That is the truth Larry", said Skeets as he brought over a tray of hot dogs and buns. "You should have stayed for the public address. Susie was very colorful describing whom and what we are. She even told us where we came from and where we should be going, right boys?"

"Yeah . . . well yeah", they all agreed!

"Just so you know she didn't just come down on you, buddy", continued Skeeter. "Don't be feelin all alone in the great cat caper. We were all there. Even though you acted totally out of character we are behind you one hundred and fifty percent, right guys?"

"Sure thing . . . we are behind you", they all agreed convincingly while shaking my hand and patting me on the back.

I told them that I felt much better knowing that. All of a sudden I was the brave kid that jumped off Niagra Falls. Admiringly I lived to tell the tale but no other mother in the village gave birth to such a foolish child as me.

We placed the dogs on a grill that we had fashioned out of an old piece of tin and placed it just over the bed of coals. Soon they were cooking and the smell filled the air. In about fifteen minutes the hot dogs were ready to be placed into buns along with ketchup, mustard and some of mom's homemade pickle relish.

Over the late dinner of tube steak sandwiches we discussed the evening's events. The surrealism of the accident was the point of most of our conversation.

"It is amazing when you think about it", Skeeter suggested, "When you realize what my brother Ray was saying. You know, about the incredible possibility of those people in the black car even surviving."

"What do you mean", questioned Bob. "What's the point? Some people are just lucky, and . . . like the kids in the Chevy . . . not so lucky."

"Lucky . . . maybe", Skeeter continued. "The odds of that car making it between the bridge and the tractor trailer must be one in a million? That red car had to be out of the way before the black car rounded the turn . . . it's a blind turn man. That driver in the black car had no way of knowing. And here comes another car from the opposite direction. He took a huge risk. I would say it was a leap of faith. Like the hand of God came down and lifted that car out of the way guys. It is almost spooky."

"Yeah, but most of those people died", said Bob making a point. "Three out of six . . . now that's fifty-fifty. Would any of us take those odds? It doesn't seem right. Why do some have to die and others don't. Who gets to choose who lives or dies? How does that work? It's like the people in the black car were selected. Ray did say the people in the black car were a preacher and his family. Maybe God selected them to be saved for a reason."

Jumping into the conversation I needed to comment. "Ah-ha, that's what I'm talkin about. You guys had to put on your clown masks and make fun of me. Who's deep thinkin now?"

Everybody was quiet for a minute.

Finally Abe spoke up almost in a whisper. "Maybe it would be a good question to ask my mom about or Reverend Wright? Why do some people die while others are spared? Things aren't always fair. I thought about this after we clowned around with Larry. That truck driver probably has a family. Those two in the red car were probably husband and wife or girlfriend and boyfriend. They had their whole lives ahead of them. They were at the time doing something they shouldn't. Maybe drinking and driving . . . racing over the speed limit and . . . dead bang! They got two tickets hopefully to paradise. They leave good friends, moms and dads and everybody who cared about them behind to clean up their mess. I guess we will hear about it tomorrow."

"You said something back there in the conversation Abe", I pointed out. "It has been nagging at me since we were at the accident. I didn't put two and two together until now. That black car, could it be Reverend Wright's car? Wasn't there something about a tent meeting or revival? My grandmother was going to that meeting. They were holding it in a farmer's field somewhere near here. She didn't go the other night because of the rain. It is clear as a bell tonight."

"Shoot, maybe you're right, said Abe. "This is going to bother me all night."

"Me too", I added.

Bob and Skeeter didn't know Reverend Wright but the whole ordeal still concerned them. We were all bothered by what we had seen more so than what we admitted too. Those accident memories over shadowed the cat on the tin roof incident by leaps and bounds.

We looked up to the village towards Abe's parent's house to see if there were any lights on, which there weren't. If anybody would know about the accident it would be them. My parents were sleeping. If grandmother had gone to the revival surely she would be back by this time.

Giving some thought to going down and seeing if grandma was still awake was rejected. We came to a group conclusion. If we asked about the accident right now, inquiring minds would want know how we even knew there was an accident at the bridge.

We dismissed the idea of questioning anybody and thought it better to eat cheese curls and other goodies that might be hidden in Abe's tent instead. Oh yes, there was that shoofly pie too. We had to finish that off before breaking camp tomorrow. Abe's mom would be sorely offended if we didn't bring back an empty pie pan and we didn't want that. After stuffing ourselves we settled down. But not before the usual calling back and forth of familiar euphemisms between tents. Eventually we drifted off to sleep.

CHAPTER 9

Bright and Early the Bird Catches the Worms

Five am came quicker than expected. Someone was shaking our tent flaps. It was my dad's voice I heard next. "Hey troopers", he called out! "You ready to rally and have some breakfast chow?"

I peered out through the screen and my dad all ready had the fire stoked with wood and it was ablaze. There was a pot of water boiling sitting a-top our make-shift grill over the fire. As my senses came alive one by one my olfactory department sent a message to my stomach. There were egg omelets cooking and the possibility of biscuits baking somewhere close by.

One by one we stumbled out of our tents wiping and shaking off the affects of the sand man.

My dad was a morning person and chatted away. "Sure hope you guys are hungry", he rambled on! He drew our attention to what was on the menu; "Two omelets are keeping warm in a pan by the fire and I got two more cooking on the stove. Biscuits are cooking in a pan over there and along with the wash water they are hot and ready. Two wash pans are on the bench. Wash off the sleep and let's eat!"

All of us were like robots. Though still half asleep we automatically followed dad's orders, lined up, washed up and were ready in five minutes for the food delivery. As we sat around the fire feeding our faces very few words were spoken. Then my dad jumped in with what we were all waiting to hear. And that was information about the accident. Oddly I had somehow forgotten or at least suppressed the accident until my first desire was met which was food.

"Did you guys hear about", dad started asking with a grin and then abruptly stopped. He tilted his head to one side and looked into the trees as if he had seen something that caught his attention. Maybe he had forgotten something? Then my dad continued, "But I guess there's no way you could have known about the horrible accident at Royer's last night."

We all gave him a bewildered look and agreed that we hadn't heard a thing. Abe had to be theatrical. He pushed the issue when he suggested that we thought we had all heard a loud boom or some kind of explosion around nine thirty.

Looking for a nearby stick I wanted to clobber Abe for even opening his mouth. Not missing a beat dad asked, "Really, you say around nine thirty? That's when you think you heard that noise? Hhhmm . . . that is about the time it happened", he surmised.

"Your grandmother Larry", dad went on to say, "She was at that tent revival meeting the E. U. B. church was holding last night at the Renninger farm. She was headed back with Luella and Frank when about a half a mile ahead of them the accident occurred. Grandma said that if they had started up the highway a few minutes sooner they would have been part of that mess. What a crowd showed up there she said, and what a heart breaking shame. There were more people there gawking at that calamity than had showed up for their revival she told me. As matter of fact Skeets, she said . . .

your brother . . . Ray was smack dab in the middle of all of that. He told her that he was fishing there at the deep hole when a car suddenly flew over the bridge abutment wall at him.

If there were any beads of sweat showing up on our foreheads now it was not from the heat of the campfire. That familiar old bear was beginning to materialize right there in front of me and I could feel a cool breeze on my backside coming from the ever widening abyss behind me.

Dad was looking right through us, or so it seemed when he said, "Grandma said she also saw a couple of kids ride up on bicycles right after the fire truck and ambulance came on the scene. Too bad though she said she couldn't make them out as she was on the other side of the creek and with the smoke and lights and all . . . you know, her eyesight's not what it used to be. She saw Ray talking to them and asked him later who they were? He said he never saw them before. But said, he told them to get the heck outta there . . . they had no business being out that late. He said he also told them it was too dangerous, that they could get hurt by accidently getting in the way.

There was a pause in the dialogue. Dad again looked past us and into the woods. For the life of me I couldn't figure out what he might be looking at. So I turned my head and looked where he was staring. There was nothing out of the ordinary, just some rocks, brush and trees.

Then he went on to tell us, like he just remembered one more thing. "Grandma said too that one of the guest Pastor's and his family, who drove over an hour to get there, just about got caught up in that accident. Grandma said the good Lord was obviously watching out for them. What do you think boys?"

The rest of the guys including myself just shrugged our shoulders. Maybe we were being a little too quiet.

While eying us suspiciously dad got up and said, "You know I have a theory, and it's not really my own, it's been said that God protects fools and little children. Sometimes I am foolish but I don't like being made a fool of. Hope you guys catch my drift."

Again we just sat there politely and didn't say a word. Abe of course said, "Yes, Mr. B we sorta know what you're talking about."

After clearing his throat dad paused said, "Oh really, yes I am sure you do. But anyway that being said", dad continued, "Grandma told me that she and the Cees drove by the campsite to see if you were still awake but you guys must have been asleep. They saw your bikes parked here, but there was no one by the fire or they would have stopped. Good thing too, your moms and dads would all be upset thinking that you might be out riding around at night. And especially, they would be really upset if you were riding on the main road. That's where those kinds of crazy drivers are racing around. But you know that . . . don't you boys?"

"Oh yes sir", we all chimed at once,

"Yessireee . . . we know that the main road is way too dangerous", Bob agreed.

Abe added and I wanted so badly to rap him with my knuckles. If only dad wasn't there. He even continued digging us in deeper when he said, "We all heard what you said there Mister B . . . you know, about no night cruising on the main road. We wouldn't go against your wishes sir. Would we fellows?" The trench was opening ever wider behind me. We all took the leap and stepped into the abyss when we affirmed positively that we had adhered to his orders. My stomach was doing back flips and I felt the last few bites of omelet wanting to revisit the great outdoors.

Bob continued the drama as he stammered out yet another question about whether or not; "Was anyone killed in the accident?"

Looking around again it wasn't a stick I wanted. Now I was looking for a hole to crawl into for the rest of my life . . . someplace where the approaching bear would not ever find me.

"Yes Bob", my dad answered with a strange faraway look on his face, "There were two young adults killed and the truck driver is in critical condition. He was taken to the burn center in Allentown. The two who lost their lives were traveling way to fast and were killed instantly. The Pastor and his family suffered minor injuries. It was said to be a miracle that they even made it. No one knows at this point who the young adults were. At least the names haven't been released yet. Grandma said it was thought that they were heading west and were going to, or had been attending some sort of party."

The information to Bob's question that dad gave us was abrupt and saline. "Anyway guys", dad stated as a matter of fact, "I have to get to work. Let's put some of the hot coals from the fire into the pit to get the Dutch oven going. We will set the pot with the chicken and veggies on top of them and surround the pot with more hot coals."

Taking care to detail we did as dad had instructed.

Dad asked Bob to do a few more things to prepare the oven for baking, "Bob would you please put more coals on top of the cooker. Add more stone and top it off with some ground."

Grabbing a shovel Bob hurried to do as instructed.

"By noon time boys", dad declared, "We will have a perfectly baked chicken. I'll be back just in time to help you get it out of the pit. Sound like a plan men?"

Upon agreeing that this was a really cool idea we then waved goodbye to dad and told him that we looked forward to seeing him for lunch.

It was really neat that my dad took the time to come down and help us out. Because of circumstances this had been a little nerve racking for me. So far I think he was cool about everything. Even if he knew we were out and about he didn't let us know that. Parents are sometimes like that. They don't want you to know what they know just to keep you off balance and see what you will do.

We all argued back and forth trying to guess whether or not dad knew or anybody knew that we were out cruising. Of course the cat on the roof incident will surely let the cat out of the bag.

Just then Skeeters' brother Ray pulled up in his hot rod. We knew it was him coming down the road. We heard the illegal glass pack mufflers sound coming from a half mile away. After hopping out of the car Ray gingerly crossed the stream. His longish hair was slicked back. He was wearing an unbuttoned shirt with a white tank top underneath, tight blue jeans and black pointy shoes. Still stuck in the fifties I thought. Waving from the car his girlfriend said hello.

"Howdy lone riders", he greeted. "Just wanted to let you know I didn't give you up to granny. Wanted to . . . hah, just kiddin. She was really suspicious . . . if granny had been able to focus her aging eyes . . . you'd have been cooked like a goose for sure.

Ray stood in front of us and pointed towards Abe and said, "Lucky too . . . Abe's folks were busy helpin out the injured Pastor's family.

"So anyway", Ray chuckled and then continued, "Stick to your story if you got one . . . and if you don't . . . you know what your ole pal Ray would do . . . make one up . . . and make it a doosey. Gotta go . . . been up all night catchin fish" . . . and he gave us a wink nodding towards the car and added, "If you know what I mean?"

He sang out as he crossed back over the creek, "Ba-ba-ba-boom, splish-splash I was takin a bath, all alone on a Saturday night! See you guys and good luck! Ha! Ha! Gotta go!"

Ray revved the engine in his '56 Chevy and popped the clutch sending dirt, dust and stones flying everywhere. When the custom posi-traction kicked in and the oversize tires caught solid ground the tires cried out leaving two black trails leading away from the campsite. Just for good measure Ray hit his horn that played out the beginning to the song "Dixie Land; Oh, I wish I was in the land of cotton!" We could see his hand waving in the air from the driver's side window.

"Right there's proof positive for my zit theory and not treated it affects the brain too", Bob stated. "You could see right there on Ray's . . .

"Knock it off with the zits theory all-ready", Abe blurted out!

"Just sayin's all . . . girl plus guy equals zits and then irrational behavior", Bob mumbled.

"Man oh man, I don't know how", Skeeter spat out, "my brother can be so cool and such an idiot all at the same time! Geez . . . he and his friends are always doin stupid stuff. He didn't have to burn off right here at our camp site. Now your dad will see that . . . I know your mom and grandmother heard it . . . if not half the village . . ."

Skeeter was upset and kicked the ground sending stones and dirt down into the stream.

"Don't worry man", Abe said. We can cover up the tracks with dirt and stones. Larry's dad won't even know."

"Know what", a loud voice coming from behind us asked? "That you kids were hanging out by the bridge last night where you shouldn't have been? The fact you were riding around on the main road where you shouldn't have been! How about the one . . . you were up in the village paying a visit to Miss Susie's where you shouldn't have been? Now which one of the shouldn'ts, should not Larry's dad need to know about?"

Grandma had snuck up behind us coming back home from her daily walk about. She looked very menacing standing there carrying her big walking stick. Grandma at that moment looked like Moses parting the Red Sea. By the concerned look on her face it would appear she was ready to give someone a darn good whacking. I guess the bear had finally caught me.

"You tell me Mr. Bright Eyes Abraham, what don't you want Larry's dad to know about", inquired Grandma? "Seems like you are the answer man? Now Ray, I can understand him. He's a part of this crazy miss-guided youth business. He's just tearing all around helter-skelter the way he does because he believes it's the thing to do. But you young boys getting all caught up in this clever little web of deceit, I just don't even want to try and understand that."

With a deep sigh Grandma sat down on one of the wood stumps beside the camp fire. She invited us to sit down for a little powwow and continued her conversation. "You know you kids have a lot more going for you than I did in my day. Look at this. You've got this nice campsite and freedom. When I was a kid, making a living was hand to mouth and that was your freedom. No time for camping and running around.

Today you kids have too many distractions. Oh that television, and all the junk that's on it! It's stealing precious time away from being a family and will be the world's downfall. What's wrong with getting the news from a newspaper? People don't even need to read anymore. That's how you get knowledge and entertain yourself, by reading books. We never had time for minimalism. It was the great depression. It was all in or nothing when I was a child. Nobody had anything but the dirt under their feet from which to scratch out a living. Hard work never hurt anybody. In fact it brought the family together under one cause and that cause was survival."

I didn't know if we were being punished or getting a history lesson at this point. We all had respectfully sat down around my grandmother. Keeping our mouths shut we listened to her go on about what it was like in the days of her childhood.

"You know boys", grandmother went on to say, "We did not even have running water back on the farm. If you had to use the toilet late at night . . . well let me tell you what an ordeal that was. Guess what you did?"

Most of us agreed that we had no clue. Skeeter told us that he remembered his grandpa telling him that they had some kind of a chamber pot in a closet to use.

"Hah, he was one of the lucky people then", grandma snipped and then added. "Most people didn't even have a pot to pee in or own a window to throw it out of. First let me tell you . . . if it was late at night, you would fumble around in the dark looking for the box of matches. Hopefully you had put them somewhere close by before you got into bed. Once you found them, you would strike a match and light the coal oil lamp sitting on the night stand. Hopefully you wouldn't knock it over.

Now to make matters worse just imagine if it was January and there was a blizzard blowing outside? Reluctantly you'd pull the covers back. Drag yourself out of a nice warm bed and you'd put on a night robe and slippers. Then you'd run to the outhouse which was located near the garden about twenty-five yards from the house. Once there, you would slowly open the door to see if there were any critters inside. Sometimes a raccoon, possum, skunk or maybe a rat might take refuge inside to keep warm. Let me tell you, they can scare the life out of ya! Once inside you'd sit your fanny down on the cold wooden seat. When you had finished you would tear several sheets from the latest catalogue or circular and clean yourself. We were so poor that toilet paper was a luxury. I won't tell you what we did when there were no more circulars."

"Didn't the ink rub off on your fanny", Abe asked?

"What? I expected a smart question from you", exclaimed grandma all the while laughing and then suggested. "I don't know Mr. Bright eyes. Why not try using the daily newspaper for toilet paper. Check yourself to see if the ink rubs off as an experiment and get back to me with the results."

We all had a good laugh at Abe's question and Grandma's suggestion.

"No thanks. I'll just take your word for it that the times were a lot different back then", said Abe.

"Anyway, you are right . . . life was different. I want to show you guys something, so watch what I do", said grandma. She went over to where we had dug up some of the dirt to make the fire pit. "Not too many people know about this or probably they've forgotten", she added.

She grabbed a handful of what looked like just plain dirt and showed us what was in her hand. "Now see this", she said and then quizzed us. "Do you know what this is?"

Was she losing her mind I silently questioned? Giving what I thought was an intelligent answer I asked, "Dirt?"

Grandma pursed her lips and then blew most of the dust away from the tiny stones. "This is shale", she explained to us. "It is very abundant around these parts. Now what most folks don't realize is . . . watch." As she said this she sprinkled the shale into the fire and in about two seconds they started to snap and pop. Little blue flames shot out and danced all around the shale stones.

"Wow", we all exclaimed!

"That's really cool", expressed Bob and demanded. "How did you do that?"

"I didn't do anything", said grandma, "except put them into the fire and they ignited. If it was nighttime you would see the flames better."

"But why did they burn up", I asked? "I know coal burns but that's just plain dirt, isn't it?"

"The shale has petro gas trapped inside of it", explained grandma. "Many years ago companies came around here trying to buy up mineral rights. They were thinking of putting down oil wells because they believed the shale indicated that there was oil lying below the surface. A few did drill but nothing ever came of it. At least they couldn't get enough oil to make it pay. Someday they will figure out how to get the gas out of these rocks. But for now the smarts aren't there yet or maybe there's no money in it for them. So yeah, you can burn these tiny little stones but they don't last long and there is too much waste left behind. It's not like coal where it almost all burns up. In a pinch you can keep warm with it but you still have to add something to keep it burning. Hope you learned something today from this old woman."

We all smiled and said that it was a great science lesson. Of course we each had to grab a hand full of the tiny stones and try it for ourselves.

"Get a big kick from that, huh", grandma said as she laughed? "Yeah, I found it pretty fascinating myself when I was a kid. Burnin shale stones was as cool then as it is now."

"So what are you gonna tell dad grandma", I asked? When I asked that question everyone who was playing with their new found science experiment stopped. All eyes and ears came to focus on grandma.

The question was answered with a question when grandma enquired, "What do you boys think I should do about what I know?" With that question there was silence.

"While you are thinking", said grandma, "about how you are going to answer my question. I'll tell you a story about the merry old country during the 1500's. And I just thought of this because I was looking at Larry's father's tomato patch over there across the creek. Did you know that in those days tomatoes were considered poisonous?"

"That sounds ridiculous", scoffed Abe and he then asked. "But how could they be poisonous if we eat them today?"

"Well, bright eyes", grandma answered, "It wasn't the tomato that was poisonous. It was the plates and cups which the people of those days were using to cook, eat and drink from that were. The pewter plates and cups contained lead. The tomato products which contain a lot of acid affected the pewter and produced lead poisoning and that made people deathly ill. The poor tomato being from the belladonna night shade family got a *bum rap* due to its relationship and was considered poisonous. Guilt through association they call it."

When grandma said that she eyed us suspiciously or maybe I was just feeling guilty. She continued, "Did you get the cool language there boys, *bum rap*? See old granny ain't so old she can't pick up on a few things."

"Wow", Skeeter exclaimed and asked, "How is it that people didn't know anything about that?"

"It was not scientifically discovered yet", grandma responded. "Just as many things at that time were not yet realized."

Grandma stopped and thought and then announced. "Since you guys are fascinated by some old tales, let me tell you another science fact. During those times, like I said, people were drinking from pewter cups. At that time there was a lot of drinking going on of wine, spirits and beer. Fresh water was not always available in the city areas because much of the water was polluted. So people would drink more alcoholic based drinks. Again whatever was put into the pewter cups would . . ."

"The liquid would mix with the pewter that contained the lead and they would die when they drank it", Skeeter quickly blurted out, offering what he thought his best insight.

"Not this time Skeeter", grandma declared, "But what it would do is send whoever was allergic to the concoction into such a drunken stupor that they would become unconscious for days at a time. Many of these poor souls were found by the roadside and considered dead."

"Whoa! Hold on there", cried out Abe and then offered, "You mean that they would be *dead drunk*, like old Mr. Dougan looks when he passes out in his car from drinking too much?"

"Good deduction, that's right but it was worse", grandma divulged. "In those days they would reuse coffins. There wasn't enough space and wood was at a premium too. So they dug up the old graves and took the old bones to a *bone yard*. She then slowly asked, "Do you know what they discovered on the lids of one in twenty five coffins?"

No one said a word.

Grandma paused, looked at us real serious, leaned towards us and disclosed in a hoarse whisper . . . "Scratches . . . yes, scratches were found on the inside of some of those lids. They knew by this discovery that sometimes they were making grievous errors. Now, instead of just sticking a body into a coffin, first the bodies would be taken to the nearest friend or relative who would stay by the body for a time. Hence the term for this situation was called holding a wake."

We were amazed to hear this all coming from grandma and she did hold our attention as she went on. "To further avoid burying people alive they would tie a cord to the dead person's wrist and bring it through the coffin's lid and up through the ground and attach it to a bell. A grave digger or watchman was assigned to sit by the grave to listen in case the bell would ring. Here is where we got the term, *the graveyard shift.*

"What . . . graveyard shift", uttered Abe, "This is unbelievable, where do you come up with these things", he asked?

"I know, I know", stated grandma with a big grin, "But there's more to the tale. When the bell would ring, or should I say, if the bell would ring, the person thought to be deceased would be called *a dead ringer*. You could also say they were *saved by the bell.*"

We all cracked up because it sounded so absurd.

Grandma laughed too and then concluded. "You can learn a lot from history. You can find out where our language and the terms we use came from. The things known today that we consider common knowledge were unheard of yesterday."

I was getting nervous and impatient because I really wanted grandma to tell us what she was going to tell dad. So I once again asked her, "Grandma I don't mean to interrupt but what are you going to say to dad?"

Once more everyone looked at her with total attention.

Making a deep sigh grandma then asserted. "You know boys the good Lord loves a sinner but absolutely hates sin. He is a forgiving Father when you ask for forgiveness but he does not want you to go back and repeat the offense."

She looked at Bob and then asked, "What do you do when you want to go somewhere where you've never been before? Let's say you want to go to New York City from here. How would you find your way?"

"I guess I would look at a road map", answered Bob.

"The rest of you", grandma enquired. "How would you find your way?"

All agreed that a map would be the best thing to use to get directions.

Grandma went on to report that for this application the best roadmap we could have was what we were being taught in church. She went on to clarify, "All that you boys are learning about now will apply to all your situations during your whole lifetime.

You know Larry you asked me a question about what I am doing concerning your mischief. But a better question is; what are you fellows going to do knowing that I know? Rest assured boys Grandma never told a lie, and I am too old to start now.

Please allow me tell you one more story. I want to qualify what I have been talking about. This story is about someone who gave up his whole inheritance just because he was hungry. He was so hungry in fact that he couldn't even wait until the meal was cooked. You have to think about what you're giving up before you commit to doing something foolish."

"Sounds like a pretty neat story", Skeeter mused. Looking around he then expressed all our thoughts, "We all like to hear good stories." Shaking our heads yes, confirmed what Skeeter just said, offering grandma the go ahead.

"Okay then, I'll continue", grandma said including a satisfactory smile. "There were two brothers, twins as a matter of fact. One named Esau and the other Jacob. Esau was born first and Jacob was right behind him grabbing on to Esau's tiny foot as if to say, "*Oh no you don't, me first*!" You see the oldest is respected to all the entitlements of being first born. In other words the oldest gets the family's wealth."

"Whoa, cool man", Abe shouted nearly jumping out of his seat. "Larry that means you will get this cool campsite. Don't let little bro sell you short on that deal."

"Alright boys", implored grandma, "Let me finish the story before we all think about what we are getting or not getting out of life. Even though Esau and Jacob were twins they were very different both physically and in spirit. Esau was rough and hairy, a man's man who liked the outdoors and was a hunter. Jacob was a home body, a laid back kind of guy and liked to stick around the home and even liked to cook. One day Esau was returning from the wilderness tired and exhausted from hunting and Jacob was cooking a fine stew. When Esau saw what Jacob was doing and smelled the aroma of the cooking stew, he couldn't stand it. Esau demanded that Jacob prepare a bowl of stew for him immediately.

"Jacob", Esau said, "I am starving so give me a bowl of some of that stew!"

Jacob thought for a moment and then said, "Okay my brother, but trade me your rights as firstborn son for a bowl of this food?"

"I am dying of starvation", replied Esau, "My rights are of no use to me now."

"I hear you", Jacob said, "But first you must give an oath that your birthright is now mine."

Continuing the story grandma went on to tell us. "Esau did not even take time to think and did as his brother asked. He gave up his rights as the firstborn to his brother Jacob in return for some bread and lentil stew. Esau quickly ate the meal, got up and left."

"By this action", grandma spelled out to us. "Esau showed contempt for his God given rights as first born. It was also wrong for Jacob to catch Esau in a weakened state and cheat him out of his rights for a bowl of stew. But Esau was also wrong to give them up for so little. God wants us all to know what holds value. What holds value for you guys other than baseball and camping?"

Bob was the first to reply. "I think that my family is really important." He looked around at the rest of us and then said, "Friendship . . . yeah, my friends mean a lot to me too."

Abe spoke up next. "I guess I know where this is going", he said. "So I am going to say that our relationship with God and knowing what he wants us to do at any given time. We should be putting him first before acting out of selfishness."

Skeeter was just listening to our answers and then he added. "I see that in my family we're missing pieces. We are what everyone would call dysfunctional. Things that you guys take for granted, that's what I miss.

"Like what could that be Skeeter", I asked.

"Well guys, don't take me the wrong way", Skeeter went on to say, "I love my mom, dad, grandpa and Raymond . . . . it's just that your families are different from mine. My dad can't help it that he drinks too much. He is like one hundred percent Navajo Indian too. Mom says that has something to do with it. She says we can't blame him . . . that he's sick and all.

Your parents expect things from you guys and care differently about certain things. In my family there are gaps. Pieces are missing. I don't know why but that's where the family puzzle is incomplete. Why do you guys think I spend so much time down here? Why do you think I ride five miles on my bike one way? Is it because I need the exercise? Man, I am skinny as a mosquito . . . that's why they call me Skeeter.

Grandma is trying to say Larry, that because you are blessed by living the way you do . . . and you other guys too . . . you shouldn't trade what you have by doing something stupid. As long as my chores are done my parents wouldn't say anything about me being out and about. But you guy's parents have different ways of looking at responsibility."

"Wow Skeeter", I declared while looking at the ground, "I never knew how you felt about such things." Looking up at grandma I then enquired, "Trust . . . trust, is that what is at stake here grandma?"

Grandma smiled, "I suppose that is a huge part of it", she assured us and then proposed. "Skeeter has good insight when he said we should not trade away important things. It's wrong to trade away things that have been freely given for what you may think to be a trivial matter at the time. When a parent hands out freedom and trust they expect obedience in return. Especially when trust was given and certain boundaries are set to go along with those blessings."

"An apology and a confession go to dad when he gets here for lunch for me being stupid and making an unwise decision", I announced as I asked, "Should I also think up of some good punishments before he gets here? What do you think grandma? Would that help?"

"No Larry", grandma cautioned. "Let's not assume and make it any worse than it already is. I would leave that option up to your dad if I were you. You boys should also stick around as you were no angels either. Also about that cat on the roof thing . . . whose big idea was that?"

Grandma looked at each one of us individually and then thought the better of it. "No, no", she uttered throwing her hands in the air, "Second thought, I don't even want to go there today."

With that being said grandma grabbed her walking stick and pulled herself up and began to walk towards the stream to head for the house. She stopped and turned around and proposed some profound advice. "You know boys if you are faithful in the little things, you will be faithful in big ones. However, if you are dishonest in little things, how can you be trusted with greater responsibilities? That is a quote from Luke 16:10 taken from the road map of life, our dear Lord's Holy Scriptures."

Grandma pointed her cane towards the road as she made known to us, "Larry, here comes your little brother Scott, I am sure he'll be wanting some breakfast too. He looks hungry."

"Your grandma Larry", Abe admitted while shaking his head, "She is something. At times she seems so old and cranky. She sticks her nose in where it doesn't belong. At least that was how I felt when she first arrived holding that war club of hers . . . but oddly she makes sense sometimes. Certainly I will tell my folks about last night and take any heat for you concerning the Susie thing. I anticipate a week or more of solitary confinement though. How about you Bob? Are you into the same plan?"

Bob kicked at one of the wood stumps and paused before speaking. "Yeah, of course I am with you guys. Here I am right in the thick of it. So what can I say?"

"We don't even have to ask Skeeter", I said looking at him. "You're always a hundred percent right on with whatever we do."

Speaking for himself Skeeter added. "Of course, we come up with goofy things together. So I guess I share the blame together."

CHAPTER 10

The Sentencing and the Cat on the Roof

My little brother came running. He was all out of breath, huffing and puffing just bursting at the britches to tell us something. "Hey guys", he shouted. Breathing heavily his feet took him splashing across the stream. "Skin's on his way . . . he's madder than a soaked rooster . . . wants to beat up Larry . . . something about his sister's cat . . . up on a roof.

"Calm down", Skeeter said, "No need to blow a piston. Take 'er easy . . . catch your breath."

We all walked over to my little brother. He was bent over and had his hands resting on his knees.

"Whew", Scott said between taking breaths as he stated, "Skin said . . . when the cat . . . jumped off the roof . . . hurt its' paw . . . and now . . . it's ah, limping around."

Things were just getting better by the minute. I acted like I didn't hear what my brother said and asked him, "Do you want some omelet and a biscuit?

"No thanks", said Scott and then went on to say, "I had a bowl of stars, toast and OJ. Aren't you listening? Didn't you hear what I said? What are you gonna do Larry? Aren't you afraid of getting pounded? What if Lynn won't play in the ball game?

Being somewhat concerned I asked my brother whether mom knew about any of this?

"Oh no", spoke Scott in a cautious voice as he disclosed, "I picked up the phone when it rang. It was Skin. Mom already went to work. I could see grandma down here with you. She doesn't know. But Skin was yelling and said he was gunnin for ya."

"Grandma knows more than you think Scott", said Abe. "She knows about the cat. Susie or her parents must have called before Skin. But I'd guess it was Susie. She was looking for Larry I'll bet and spoke to grandma. Probably told her all about it? That must have been bright and early before your grandmother's daily walk. Susie probably stayed up all night rehearsing, just waitin for first light to make that call."

"Uh oh, oweee . . . Larry you're gonna be in big trouble when dad finds out", exclaimed my brother!

Then Scott went on to speculate my outcome, "The whole village will be looking for you. Its' gonna be like that scary movie . . . people with pitchforks and axes chase old Frankenstein. He leaves the castle and heads for the windmill. Where you gonna hide out Larry? Ain't no windmills around here! Maybe head for that old fallen down shack you guys built up in the big woods?"

"You should say there are no windmills Scott", I spoke thoughtfully correcting him. Then I kicked my voice up a notch as I pointedly stated, "But okay then. Let's not panic over this. If Skin shows up here I'll deal with it."

"No way", declared Skeeter as he threw a stick into the fire and stood up, "We will all deal with this!"

As I mentioned before, Skeeter was always ready as back up. He didn't even have to think about it and you never had to ask.

My brother blurted out, "Cool man, is there going to be a fight?" Scott stopped and then asked, "You all gonna beat up on Skin?"

"No little brother", I asserted looking at everyone present, "nobody will beat up anybody. I am going to apologize for whatever trouble I have caused and that will be that."

Just then some of the other guys from the ball team started to show up. There was Roger from the village and Roger from up on the hill. Both of them hadn't heard a word about any of the things that had been going on.

Roger from the hill shook my hand and said, "Hey, what'dya say, whatdya see, what'dya know!"

Well of course before I could spit out a word Abe and Bob jumped right in there. And thus, how it started; the tale of the midnight ride of the MBM's. Anytime my name came up I just cringed. My brother just seemed to beam about my exploits. He would smile approvingly like, yup, that's my big brother who did that. Out of the corner of my eye I caught a glimpse of Skin blazing a trail down the road on his bike. He indeed looked as my little brother called it; madder than a soaked rooster.

"Here comes Lynn", I announced. "And it's not your cousin Lynn", I said to Hilltop Roger."

Skeets came over to my side and whispered, "Really, are you just going to apologize to him? What if he starts to get all puffed up about things? You know how defensive he is about everything."

"Yup, apologize is all I'm going to do", I proclaimed. "And if I have to, I'll apologize to his whole family."

My little brother who has the best ears was eavesdropping and asked, "What about Susie?"

"Abe can apologize to her", I smirked.

"What, me apologize to Susie", Abe questioned?

Everybody must have good ears. I thought Abe was engrossed telling the MBM's story. I raised my voice a little to give Abe an answer, "Yeah . . . you", I said flatly and then included. "We all stick together. Isn't that what you said? Besides the cat was your hair brained idea anyway. You know Susie better than any of us. She'll probably just feel sorry for you. Maybe she'll even give you a big smooch on the cheek to make it all better."

"You know what cheek you can smooch and its right here Larry", shouted Abe as he pointed somewhere behind him.

The arrival of Skin was not a happy one. He just left his bike drop onto the dirt on the other side of the creek. It appeared that his feet didn't even touch the water when he crossed over to our side. That was his physical opening statement.

Trying to sum up what his intentions were I stiffened as he headed right for me and my face. There was no need for him to look at anyone else. Standing my ground I prepared for whatever was going to happen. As I stood there everyone stood beside me. That seemed to take some of the steam out of Skin's stride. He stopped within five feet of me.

"Why do you always have to be such a jerk", was his opening statement?

"Pop 'em in the nose right now", retorted Skeeter! "Smack him before he says another word Larry!"

"Look Skin I don't want to fight over this", I pleaded. "Not over a silly cat. I am sorry that it happened. I didn't think by tossing onto the roof it would get hurt. I just wanted to shut Susie up. Man, can't you see the humor in that?"

"I don't think it's so darn funny Larry", Skin blurted out appearing more frustrated by my attempt at being nice than if I had whacked him. He then went on, "That's my sister's cat and she is really upset. So what are you gonna do about it?"

He took another step toward me. The rest of the guys were now edging closer to me and taking a defensive posture. Skin noticed this and that took him over the edge. Now he had to show his metal, throw down or be labeled. He lunged hitting me in the mid section. It caught me off balance taking me over one of the stumps around the camp fire. While staggering backwards we caromed off Bob and Skeeter landing in the campfire and then we rolled onto the pile of shale dirt.

As I was being pushed backwards I couldn't help but wonder why a kid two years younger than me would take me on? I was bigger and heavier. Better question; why was I allowing this to happen? This was ridiculous and now I was beginning to lose my temper. Dust was flying and the guys were yelling that my red hoodie was on fire. We rolled over and over and finally I got Skin into a headlock and I held him there.

"Look", I said, "This is stupid to fight over a simple prank. It's stupid to fight over anything! I said I would apologize to everyone! What more do you want from me? I'm gonna leave you up . . . just stop fighting, okay?"

The guys surrounded us and were in a mob mode. They wanted total annihilation. They wanted to see fists flying. The guys wanted a little blood and maybe even a tear or two. The crowd desired that the beaten should skulk away in shame. This was not going to happen I resolved, not as long as I could control the situation. Skin was my friend and teammate.

Skin's face was turning red and he was looking at the faces of the guys staring down at us. I was as mad at them right now as I was at Skin and myself for putting us all into this situation. Yeah, it was my fault for putting the cat on the roof. But to take it to the dirt like this was uncalled for. Now Skin would lose face if he lost the fight. I would be in more trouble for beating him up. Skin would not play in the game that was coming up. What is a boy to do? So I did what I thought was best . . . I gave up.

Quickly letting go of him I jumped up and yelled, "You win Skin! I-AM-A-JERK, I'm a jerk . . . I am a jerk! There now I have said it. I have told the world, what a jerk I am!" I yelled it again just for good measure, "I am a jerk!"

Skin rolled over in the dirt and looked at me as if I were one brick shy of a full load. The onlookers seemed bewildered at what had happened.

Roger shook his head at me and said, "You had him man, why didn't you finish him off? Why didn't you give him a fist right on his kisser?"

"No, he won fair and square . . . he won", I announced. "He's right I am a jerk!"

Brushing the dirt and dust off my jeans I now noticed my sweatshirt also got burned when we rolled into the fire. Mom's going to be upset about this. She just bought this for me for school.

The guys looked at Skin. They then looked back at me and then back at him lying in the dirt. Hilltop Rog pointedly exclaimed, "I think your both nuts!" He then spat in the dirt and suggested. "How about let's say we practice some baseball and all forget about this none sense."

With a few grumbling comments most everybody turned away and headed for the ball field.

Skin was still sitting on the dirt pile. Offering him my hand I asked, "You want to get up off your butt and play some ball with a bunch of jerks?"

Looking at me he gave me a funny smirk and shook his head yes and finally mumbled, "Yeah I guess, but are you going to do what you said and apologize to my sister?"

"Yeah man, I said I would", then I asked Skin again. "Now, are you gonna play some ball with us jerks or what?"

"Or what", was Skin's reply and then he offered a smile, grabbed my hand, and I pulled him up.

We all meandered over to the ball field, chose who would bat first and who would pitch and the rest of us took the field. After that we took turns hitting fly balls and grounders to practice fielding and throwing to first. The incident at the campsite was soon forgotten by everyone. I knew later that day I would have to face the lingering ghosts. There were issues hovering around concerning last night's events. For now they were exorcised from memory.

The time flew by and soon we heard my dad's car horn calling us to the campsite. Everybody had forgotten about the chicken and vegetables cooking in the underground fire pit, including myself.

"That beeping horn means its lunchtime", I yelled! "Whoever is hungry follow me!"

No second invitations were needed. Down the hill we ran just to be stopped by patrolperson grandma who was the self appointee in charge of cleanliness.

"All of you scallywags, into the basement and wash up at the sink", she demanded! Cleanliness is next to Godliness. Soap is on the counter and the towels are on the rack, hands first and then the face please. Make sure you wash those hands proper. I don't want handprints all over the towels!"

As I passed grandma she gave me the hairy eyeball. She put her hand out to stop me but thought the better of it and waved me on by. I looked back with a questioning look. She pointed to her eye and then at me as if to tell me she was watching me. Maybe she had her binoculars out and saw Skin and me taking a dirt bath.

Grandma did not let anyone leave until we were cleaned up. When we were ready she instructed, "Now after lunch, you all can come back here and have some apple pie and ice cream for dessert." We started shouting about what a great idea that was. "Sshhh . . . sshhh, quiet down please", she asked and then said, "When I say three head for the campsite!" We lined up and grandma gave the count and off we ran.

Dad was waiting for us. He had taken the kettle out of the ground and sat it on the bench under the trees. Gathering around we waited for him to take off the lid. He suspected that we weren't sure whether or not he knew what he was doing. It did seem too easy just to shove a pot into the ground like that and have it cook an entire chicken, vegetables and all.

"Roger Dodger's still the fastest one on the team", dad observed and then asked, "Or maybe today he's just the hungriest?"

"I'm hungry alright Mr. B", agreed Roger. "But what is that you've got there? Is that big kettle supposed to hold the entire meal?"

"That is correct", dad answered. "I suspect that some of the fellows who were here when we put the kettle into the ground are also skeptical", dad said looking at the rest of us. "I will remove the tin foil from around the top and sides, now off comes the lid. And on the inside fellows . . . we'll just have a look at this. Here it is, a whole meal cooked; carrots, potatoes, celery, onions and of course one perfectly baked chicken."

Everyone looked into the pot with amazement. We commended dad on a job well done and this made believers out of us. Maybe this was just a guy thing. Of course you can do the same thing more easily in an oven, in the house, but this was a way cooler idea.

After grabbing paper plates dad served us one at a time. It was pleasant having most of the team relaxing and eating together under the hemlocks. Not a word was said as we ate the delicious camp food. Dad smiled approvingly as he saw that several of us made our way back for seconds.

Looking at dad I noticed he wasn't eating so I asked him, "Aren't you going to have any chicken and vegetables? It is really good and besides you did all the work."

"That's okay, you boys enjoy it", dad said. Then he told us that grandma had cooked something for him. He also heard that there was apple pie for desert and wondered if there would be any left by the time he got there. We all laughed when he said that.

"Before we go anywhere", dad ordered, "We have to clean up. Put everything into the trash container that needs to go there and utensils go into the wash tub. Then we will chase after that apple pie."

"And ice cream", yelled Bob! "Grandma told us about ice cream that's supposed to go with the apple pie."

"Well, I didn't know about that", dad said smiling. "Good thing I've got a car so I can beat you guys to the desserts."

We all got a good chuckle and then filed in line to the trash can and to the wash tub. While passing dad Abe stopped in front of him. "Mr. B", he said plainly, "We all just want to thank you for letting us camp down here and for the meals and everything. All of us know that you didn't have to do this and it really made us all feel welcome." Everyone concurred with Abe's expressed thoughts. "Oh yeah", Abe continued, "And there's something else too, that needs to be said."

"What's that Abe", my dad enquired?

Speaking up I asked, "Maybe I should tell him Abe? "After all, he is my dad."

"It wasn't your idea Larry, you just went along with us", Abe stated emphatically.

"Hey, that's right", said Skeeter and Bob both at the same time. "It wasn't your idea Larry", pleaded Skeeter backing up what Abe said.

The rest of the guys were looking dumbfounded and had no clue as to where this was going. They all sat down like they were watching a plot to a theatrical play about to unfold.

Dad gazed oddly at the four of us. He put his hands on his hips, spoke up and began the interrogation, "My inquiring mind needs to know . . . so what's the big mystery? And which of the mystery guests wants to be the spokesperson and do I need a blindfold?

I quickly put my hand up and offered a statement, "I do dad and you won't need a blindfold."

My dad looked at me and said, "Okay, you get to go first and then I'll listen to the rest of you in turn."

After I began to tell the story, not everybody got a turn. I spilled the beans about going out onto the main road. Also I told dad that we saw what was going on at the accident along with the details. Eventually I got to the second or third act that included Susie and the cat on the porch roof.

Abe did finally jump in and tell everyone that it was his big idea. "Out of frustration", Abe proposed, "And from not knowing what I wanted Larry to do with the cat . . . Larry simply had an allergic reaction to the beast and launched the animal into space. It just happened to end up landing right in front of Susie's nose on the porch roof.

The whole team went into hysterics. They imagined everything that was told to them. The guys really flipped when Abe told them how much Susie panicked when the cat landed in front of her nose.

My dad stood there smiling and intently scratched his chin for awhile as he absorbed all the drama. Finally he spoke up. "Hmm, just so that I understand all of this . . . during the morning's breakfast . . . that parade of questions and concerns . . . or should I say charade of questions and concerns was just to keep me off guard?"

"That's sort of the truth of the matter sir", admitted Skeeter. "We were scared about what you'd say and we didn't want to ruin your day."

"Thank you for your concern Skeeter", dad said. "So were you all were in on this", dad asked?

The other members of the ball team were emphatically denying any participation or relation to knowing anything about last evening's events.

"Hold on guys, not to worry, I am only referring to the founding four of this dilemma", dad said assuring the others.

"This is really something I don't quite understand", dad conjectured. Then he said, "I know what I should do to the four of you. I should keep the four of you out of the ball game and have you grounded. But that would forfeit the game and not be fair to the rest of the team."

"As I said that, I saw the disappointment in all of your' faces", dad affirmed. "But, that is what I should do and you guys know it. Larry I am seriously disappointed in you and you will be grounded for sure. Right now I don't know what other punishment there will be but I will discuss that with your mother.

"I know, I know dad", sheepishly I uttered and then I stated, "I have betrayed your trust. I am sorry."

Dad sternly looked at me and answered, "Your apology is accepted Larry, but there must be consequences. You will apologize to Susie and her parents. I hope that the other three of you do as well . . . and to whomever owns' the cat."

Skin put up his hand and as dad noticed that he sighed, gave pause and offered a calculated guess, "What, don't tell me . . . it's your cat?"

"Yes sir", answered Skin. "Well it's my sister's cat, sir."

"Well then, apologize to him and his sister boys", dad commanded as he pointed his finger at us four. "Apologies to everyone involved. Is that understood, okay?"

The condemned four amigos as charged agreed to the sentence.

"Above and beyond the fact that you went against the rules", dad proclaimed admonishing us, "You kids could have been seriously hurt. That highway is a mess during day light hours let alone at night . . . in the dark and without lights. You guys just were not thinking."

Abe raised his hand wanting to say something.

"WHAT", dad enquired?

Abe boldly spoke up. "I just wanted to make a point . . . that we weren't entirely stupid because we did have lights."

Suddenly there were chuckles from the rest of the team.

"What in the world could you possibly be talking about . . . LIGHTS . . . are you referring to those old flashlights you flimsily tape on to your handle bars", dad queried? "You consider those some kind of safety measure? That is almost better than nothing!"

There were more chuckles from the team and they seemed to be holding back from really cracking up in front of my dad.

"Nice try Abraham", dad said looking sternly in his direction, "But it doesn't solve the problem that you guys were wrong in doing what you did in the first place. Your honesty is always appreciated, even when it comes late."

You could now have heard a pin drop in the pine needles. Dad shook his head and reluctantly went on, "As much as you don't deserve it, let's get some apple pie anyway. That will be a nice way to end an otherwise sour situation. Team is dismissed for now. Go on get your dessert. Don't forget you four musketeers! After the game in town this afternoon . . . come back here to clean up and button up the campsite."

Silently, almost reverently, single file we made our way from the campsite and headed for the apple pie and ice cream. While pushing my bike across the stream I notice that a weight had been lifted from my shoulders. What was the adage grandma used? She had a million of them. Confession is good for the soul. That is one she used quit often. I did feel better now that the cat was out of the bag and off the roof. I thought that funny and chuckled to myself.

A sudden slap on my back brought me out of my daydream. "Hey man", Bob asked smiling at me, "Whatchya gonna do with all your down time? I got some great new comic books that I've finished and I'll loan 'em to ya . . . got the new Spiderman's, some new Superheroes and a few Superman's and a new Batman. Would that help you out my friend?"

"Guess maybe . . . yeah, that'd be cool", I said. "I'm just wondering what the "what else's" that mom and dad will cook up might be? They can be pretty creative when it comes to dealing out punishment."

"Ah, don't worry about it", assured Bob. "You'll do the time standing on your head. I got grounded one time when my brother and I were lighting firecrackers behind Sammy's Garage. We accidently set the old man's oil barrel on fire. When we tried to put it out with a garden hose it got worse and caught the old stack of car tires on fire too. We didn't know that the oil and gas would just float on top of the water and would keep on burning. Man, the black smoke could be seen for miles."

"Whoa man, that was you", I asked? "That was kept really hush, hush."

"Yeah, mom and dad wanted it kept quiet. They were pretty embarrassed", Bob went on to say.

We walked a few more steps and he continued. "Yup, that was me and my older brother. The bad part was man, it was Saturday night too. Sammy had all ready left for the races and nobody was home. Our parents were at the grocery store at the time. It was the neighbors who called the fire company. They also called the race track to get in touch with Sammy. Boy, were my parents peeee-oood when they got home. You could have fried and egg on my dad's red bald head he was so hot. Sammy was just upset because he had to come home from the races. He even joked about it later. Sammy was happy just because no one was hurt and the fact his garage didn't burn down."

"Wow, good thing the garage didn't catch on fire", I commented. "You would have been grounded for the rest of your' life."

"From that lesson learned let me tell you, it took a week for the fire in my butt to cool down. The walloping I got from dad was beyond any I had ever experienced before and will never happen again if I can help it", Bob explained. "I sat on a pillow for the first couple of days just so I could sit at the table to eat. Good thing school wasn't in session. My brother and I were confined to our rooms for a month without TV. Heck . . . I was even scared to come out of my room. What you'll get Larry will be a walk in the park compared to what I went through . . . yup-per, just a walk in the park my man."

Instead of riding our bikes up to the house we pushed them slowly up the hill taking our time. It seemed that everyone was thinking about something. It was kind of strange. Usually everyone was yelling or trying to talk over each other's conversations.

Dad went on ahead in Grandpa's old 56' Plymouth Savoy. Pappy as we called him was my dad's father and never drove the thing except to the grocery store and the feed mill. That wasn't even once a week. Dad said that he took it upon himself to run the car so it wouldn't stand idle for too long.

"It isn't good to leave a car sit", he said. "A car is meant to be driven", he told me.

The Savoy looked like a space ship. It was lime green and had an automatic shifter on the dash board. He said Pappy's car was bigger than his car. And it was more convenient to haul a ball team around with their equipment on game days.

Pappy's farm was fun to visit. It was only about four miles away from where we lived. I liked going there to stay for a couple of days at a time. Pappy would sometimes go out to the shed and sleep in the front seat of the old car or drive out to one of his fields and take a nap. I asked dad why Pappy did that and he just said that maybe Pappy got tired of sleeping in his rocking chair. I never could figure that one out.

When I was staying on the farm one time I remember Pappy was sleeping and snoring away in his rocking chair. I was watching TV on his oval shaped Philco. He suddenly woke up and said, "Hey, you want to go along? It's time to go look and see if the oats are ripe for harvest." It was as if an invisible alarm clock went off inside his head and said, "Wake up Pappy it's time to go and see if the oats are ripe."

Off we went driving in the wagon tracks along the fence rows going around the fields in that old Plymouth. Several times Pappy got out of the car, walked over to the wheat stalks and pulled off a few heads of the grain. He would rub the heads of grain in the palm of his hand and blow away the chaff. He then put the grains in his mouth and munched on them. Handing me some of the grain pappy said, "Chew on them. Can you tell that they are still too green and chewy to be considered ripe?"

I shook my head in agreement. As if I really could tell whether or not the grain was ripe?

Pappy then made other observations and predicted. "With the temperature being what it is today and the ground being so dry the oats will soon be ready."

Within a few days after Pappy said that, dad was driving the tractor pulling the combine. Pappy was sitting in the back of the combine bagging the grain. When the oats filled up the bag Pappy would tie the bag shut and drop the full bags on the ground to be picked up by another tractor and wagon following on behind. I was still not strong enough to lift those heavy bags onto the wagon but it was fun to watch the harvesting process. Don't know why I just thought of that but certain things like the old Plymouth Savoy trigger memories for me I guess.

We soon reached our back porch. Grandma being true to her word had bowls of apple pie, vanilla ice cream, milk, sugar and honey waiting for the ball players. Just then the last two players arrived. It was Roger's cousin Lynn and Dennis from up in the village. Grandma spoke up, "Your just in time fellas, you smelled the apple pie, huh? I'll get two more bowls. Good thing I made three pies otherwise Larry your mother would have no dessert tonight."

Grandma made the best from scratch pies. Her coconut custard and pumpkin custard pies were a mystery. Even if you had the recipe you could never ever figure out how to duplicate them. At least that's what mom said several times when she tried to duplicate the recipe. Grandma would just laugh and say, "Ya haven't got the touch girl. I seen it right off."

This would frustrate mom to the point of telling us that she would never try baking a pie again. Mom did have the touch for baking cakes. She made great chocolate velvet layer cakes dripping with peanut butter or pecan glaze frosting.

The ball team was soon over its limit with the tasty dessert. Several of the guys started lamenting that they didn't think they could play because they were too full. "Delay of game", Abe shouted! "Delay of game because we're too fat! Grandma must have been a hit man hired by the other team. They're scared they might lose. We are going to have to sleep this off before we can play otherwise we'll cramp up."

Coming out to the back porch Grandma heard Abe giving his summarization of the overeating problem. "Me a hit man", grandma questioned? "Why bright eyes I wouldn't want to keep you from winning a baseball game. Wouldn't want your friend Susie to think you are a loser. Ooops! . . . did I leave the cat out of the bag? Sorry Abe, I thought everyone knew?"

All the team broke into hoots and hollers.

Abe turned all shades of the rainbow and tried to stammer out a rebuttal, "Hey come on now, everyone knows we are just friends! Come on guys give me a break! Thanks a lot grandma. See what you started."

In the midst of all the joking and kidding dad came out to the porch to give us a time when we had to leave for the game. "You guys have about an hour and then we have to load up and head for town. I suggest you do some planning and get your team roster together. Abe you are the roster man, so get to it. Here's a pencil and the roster book. Oh by the way Larry, you have a phone call . . . I think it's important."

"Okay dad", I said, and then asked, "But who is it?"

Dad said, "Oh that's confidential", and then he gave me a wink.

Oooh's and aahhs now could be heard from the guys. I just waved at them and entered the house and headed for the phone. My dad was right behind me. "Hey son", dad spoke quietly, "It's Susie . . . and if she brings up the cat issue, just give her your apology and that'll be the end of it."

My palms were sweating at this point. My head was not in the mood for this right now. I wanted to pick my own time to deal with this. Why did she have to press the issue? And right now before the ball game? I picked up the receiver and with reservation spoke into the phone, "Hello."

"Hi Larry . . . its Susie", the voice said

"I know who this is", I replied, "My dad told me you were calling."

"Oh", was her reply.

"What do you want", I asked?

My dad was standing there listening and after hearing me ask what Susie wanted he rolled his eyes and motioned with his hands telling me to get on with it!

"What do I want Larry", enquired Susie. "It's what I'm looking for from you, that is a much better question?"

"Ok, okay I am sorry", I apologized.

"And you are sorry for what", she asked?

"You know", I replied.

Susie played dumb, "No I don't know. I think you have to tell me."

"Oh boy", I grumbled.

"Oh boy what", quizzed Susie? "Oh boy, can you say, cat on roof? Sorry for the cat on the roof kind of sorry?"

"Alright Susie", I agreed. Then in an effort to hurry up and end the pain I quickly said, "Will you Susie please accept my apology for waking you up in the middle of the night . . . and throwing the dang cat up on the roof in front of your nose."

"Was that good enough", I invited?

She paused on the other end of the phone and then quietly said, "Well, I just don't know . . . hhhmmmm, Susie pondered and then continued. "I didn't like the word dang in there, but I guess I can't expect anything better coming from you. You know you should also apologize to Lynn's sister, after all it was her poor little cat that got hurt . . . see ya!"

There was a click. She hung up the phone before I could say another word. Not that it mattered. So I finished the conversation myself with, "Oh yes, and to you too."

Dad was smiling with approval and said, "See how simple that was."

I managed a grin and said, "Oh yeah, that was a pretty simple conversation."

I headed out the back door and the guys were wondering who the important phone call was from. Bob asked first, "Who called Larry?"

I blurted out in the most deep and authoritative voice I could muster. "It was the President of these United States of America wishing us all good luck in our upcoming game against the townies."

"Whoa fella . . . and get a grip", Bob cautioned, "I was just asking. I thought maybe it was one of the other guys. After all we are only nine and we could use an extra in case someone gets hurt or something."

"We could call Abe's friend Susie", I said with chagrin and directed the question to Abe. "What do you think there Abe? Maybe she would like to be our cheerleader? Abe, why not give her a call? Maybe she would fly down here and help us out?"

Abe just gave me a questioning look. He then asked, "Man what's bugging you and what has made you so upset?"

"Nothing Abe . . . I'm sorry", I said, "I'm just nervous about the game is all. Bob's right, we should have at least one more guy. It's better to be safe than sorry. I'd just like to beat those guys for once!"

We debated amongst ourselves as to who we could get at this late time? There was Zane who lived out on the main road on a farm, but he was almost old enough and almost good enough. We needed someone who could really hit and field too.

Then Skeeter popped a question, "How about my brother Ray?"

Everyone just grumbled. "Can he even hit a ball," Skin asked?

"Isn't he too old", Roger questioned?

"Look guys", offered Skeeter and continued in his brothers' defense. "He used to play really good baseball before he went crazy over girls and hot rods. Ray can hit a ton. In fact he could easily send one into the trees down at the town park. Look guys he's not very tall and he looks as young as we do. Maybe I can convince him to wear regular blue jeans, sneakers and a baseball cap. Besides he's only seventeen. It's his act and the fact that he tears around in that old hot rod that makes him seem older."

Abe smirked and said, "Yeah great! But when he pulls up to the game in his rootin tootin rebel hot rod . . . with his tooty frooty girlfriend, they're gonna ask us for ID and they'll never let him play."

"He can ride with us", suggested Skeeter now sporting a convincing smile.

"You think he's gonna do that", I asked?

"Sure guys", Skeeter assured us, "He'll do it for me . . . and that's a guarantee!"

Within ten minutes after Skeeter ran in the house and called his brother we heard the roar of the glass packs heading through the village. And when Ray made the turn to head down to my house he sounded the unique car horn.

My dad heard the song of 'Dixie Land' and was out on the porch in a flash and exclaimed, "You guys must be kidding? Isn't Raymond too old to play on your team?"

"No Mr. B", Abe claimed assuring him.

"This is unofficial league play and he's still in high school. And we want to skin their butts. No pun intended Skin", Abe guaranteed his teammate.

"None taken", Skin concluded agreeing. "You are right . . . we do want to skin their butts."

"He's within the age limit", dad questioned? "I thought I saw Raymond playing high school basketball five years ago?"

"That was JV", answered Skeeter.

Ray pulled up and jumped out of the car sporting a huge smile. He was wearing an old, old Yankees cap and had on regular jeans and sneakers. It was unbelievable. He was carrying a very expensive baseball glove to boot. Only one thing though, he was still wearing his shirt unbuttoned, not tucked in, and his usual white tank top. It could be January with a blizzard blowing outside and Ray would still be in his dress of preference; shirt unbuttoned and a white tank top underneath.

Grandma came running out the back door and zipped past team as she started calling out demands. "Now just hold on a minute. Oh, no you don't Mr. Raymond", exploded grandma. "You can't play with my baseball team!"

Pleading his case I asked, "What do you mean grandma? Sure he can. He's still in high school! There's no problem here!"

"Well first of all . . . and as a matter of fact", grandma stated, "He has to be in uniform."

"What uniform might that be", dad wondered?

"Here you go Raymond", said grandma and from behind her back she gave Louie our official Ridge Runner t-shirt. It was pine green in color and grandma had hand stitched Ridge Runners on the back.

"Oh that uniform", Ray acknowledged. Surprised, he now sported a big smile as he accepted the generous gift and asserted, "Grandma, I wouldn't want to play without one. Thank you for thinking of me. And it is my size too!"

"You are welcome Mr. Raymond", grandma said. "And I will expect to see you in church."

"Well I don't know", said Ray showing trepidation in his voice. "I wouldn't want to disturb any of the regular customers."

"Do not tempt Mr. Raymond", cautioned grandma. "You need not worry all God's children are welcome in His house, no matter how long they've been tardy and no matter where they come from. If you have to wear just a tank top and a shirt please tuck in your shirt just for me. God doesn't care what you wear or how you arrive . . . just get there.

"I'll try to make it a date", Ray offered.

Grandma eyed him seriously and went on stating firmly, "See that you do get there and your girlfriend is welcome too. It'll be a good reason to spend some time together and I do mean quality time!"

CHAPTER 11

The Boys of Summer

We toted our gear to the old Plymouth Savoy and dad opened its' trunk. Ray of course couldn't help but be envious of dad's ride and said as much. "Cool car Mr. B! Man, you should soup up this car, fit it with chrome skirts, white sidewalls, glass pack mufflers and crank up the horsepower. This ride could be almost as jazz as my 56' Chevy . . . well almost."

Dad listened to Ray while he packed the gloves, bats and bags into the trunk. Just to be sure he heard correctly he asked, "Almost as jazz huh, but not quit . . . right?"

"Well for sure, you'd have to change the color to something else", observed Ray giving his personal opinion. "Right now it looks like a big lime on wheels. If I was doing it I would two-tone it out and add some chrome strips down the middle to bring that out."

"Seems like you've got a good eye for the classy car thing", dad observed, "Maybe you should think of opening a specialty body shop. There's good money in that."

"Oh, I don't know Mr. B.", Ray answered sadly. "After school I'll probably be joining up and go in the army or something like that. My grades aren't good enough for anything else. The military will be about my only option I think."

Dad suggested to Ray that there were other options than the military. He told him that going to technical school might be a good idea.

"My school counselor also suggested that, but I don't know if I can afford it", Ray told dad. "So I think it's off to the military for me. I don't really want a factory job. I would go crazy doing the same thing over and over again day in and day out."

The trunk was packed and now the car was ready to be jammed and crammed with ball players. How many stinky, sweaty young rabble rousers can you fit into a 56' Plymouth Savoy without starting a fight?

"SHOTGUN", Abe yelled!

Dad held up both hands and cautioned everyone, "STOP, and hold your horses! Let me just say that it will be me who says who sits where. That way we don't have any one feeling left out because they didn't speak out soon enough. Will that be understood?

How could we not agree?

The orders were given as dad called them out, "Skeeter, Larry and Bob . . . you three can sit up front and Scott you sit on Larry's lap. The rest of you guys pile in the back the best that you can and let's go.

There was a stampede as the seven designates for the rear seat clambered aboard. Comments and concerns flowed freely; "Hey, I don't want him sitting on me!", "Someone in here needs a bath!", "How about taking up the whole back seat, why don't you!", "Alright, who left the stinker?", "He who smelt it probably dealt it!", "It's probably your own breath blowing back in your face."

"All right, alright fellas", dad exclaimed with his patience wearing thin, "How about getting along so we can get on down the highway. It will only be tight quarters for about ten minutes. So hold on to your hats, hold your noses or whatever you must hold on to but get it done. Dad closed all doors and hopped into the driver's seat."

Grandma stood on the porch smiling and shaking her head and gave a wave at the Ridge Runner crew as we pulled out of the driveway.

"Hey Abe", I shouted and asked, "How ya doin back there? And did you remember the roster sheet?"

A muffled cry came from the back seat as Abe mumbled out. "I got the roster and it's in my back pocket! If I am still alive when we get there we may get to use it!"

"He's such a whiner", Roger observed, "Nobody's even sitting on him.

I looked back and the reason Abe's voice was muffled was because he was holding his baseball glove over his face. "So what's your problem", I asked?

"Man, it smells bad back here", lamented Abe, who had his face buried in his mitt. "Smells like this morning's omelets gone bad!"

"That's you ya pig", cried Roger!

"Oooohhhh!" . . . "Whew!" . . . Everybody cried out!

Everyone in the back seat protested. They started clobbering Abe with their caps. Abe was cracking up over the situation because they were all held captive. Soon the whole car smelled like that morning's egg and cheese omelets that had gone rancid.

My dad rolled down his window all the way as he complained, "One more of those gas bombs and I won't be able to see to drive . . . now my eyes are even watering . . . WHEW!

"Another one of those you knucklehead", Ray cautioned, "And I will personally come back there and murder you for being a bio hazardous contaminate. That stink is really bad, man!"

Finally we made it to the town ball park with all windows rolled down, still in one piece and noticed the other team wasn't there yet. "Good", proclaimed dad and then added, "Maybe we can get in some chops before they get here.

Then dad asked as he gave Abe a possible new deserved nickname, "Hey *Stinky*, where's the roster and who do you have pitching."

Abe walked up front and center and started reading off the line up. "Okay guys listen up! Pitching is our own fast ball hurler *Lefty* Skeets. Catching is *Never Fumbles* Bob. First base is Roger the *Dodger*. Second base is me.

"Hold on there, little stinker. You get to play second base, questioned *Hilltop* Rog?

"Where do you think I should be playing", asked Abe? And then he admitted, "I don't have the arm for outfield."

Roger answered back, "Well you're not tall enough for second either. Who do you have playing short stop?"

"I put Larry at short stop", Abe said.

Go ahead and let him be there I said. I'll try to back him up. And Roger Dodger can help out too.

"So Abe, where did you place me in the lineup", asked *Hilltop* Rog?

"Ease up", pleaded Abe, "I am getting to that. On third I have Dennis the *Slingshot* because of his arm. In right field is none other than you *Hilltop*, your cousin *Top of the Hill* Lynn is in left field and in center field is Mr. Raymond. All you guys in the outfield have the arms and you can certainly clobber the ball too. In my opinion this town team does not stand a chance."

"Aren't you forgetting about someone", dad politely asked?

Everyone looked around at each other. It was Skin who was looking a little dejected about being the odd man out.

"I know . . . I have Skin on the bench, admitted Abe. "But we need someone for rotation and to be the designated hitter . . . don't we", Abe asked looking around as if he were running for political office?

But there came no votes in favor from anyone. Everyone was silent, even my dad.

Abe stood there wondering to himself. Skin was looking at the ground in front of him. He kicked around a few pebbles. The look on his face was as if he were waiting for his name to be called for root canal.

Finally Abe appeared to have it all figured out. He spoke up, "Okay, okay guys, I have a new idea."

Skin perked up as the whole team waited for the new and hopefully better idea.

"How about . . . Skin plays second", suggested Abe, "And I'll be the D. H. I know that I am the shortest on the team and can't throw as well as you guys. So after we get about five runs ahead, can I put myself back in the regular line up?"

"Not even that long", dad affirmed. "We admire your generosity and bringing it on for the team, right fellas?"

Everybody agreed and Skin personally thanked Abe for stepping up and doing that before he clobbered him.

"Think about this Abe", suggested Ray. "We'll get the bases loaded and I'll send one past the tree line over there. Then you can take my place and I'll be the D. H."

Abe smiled and shook Ray's hand and agreed. "You got a deal! I'm lookin forward to that home run and I'm gonna hold ya to the bargain."

Ray smiled and gave Abe a wink and a pat on the back and told him, "You can count on it, kiddo!"

Skeeter called out. "Hey Abe, you wanna catch for me while I warm up?"

"Sure thing Skeeter", said Abe, "No problem!" And Abe ran off to get the catcher's mitt.

Dad started hitting practice balls to the rest of us as we took our designated positions.

As a team we had played together the whole summer. Before that we played together off and on as soon as we were old enough to throw a baseball. We rode the bus to school together, went to grade school together and most of us went to the same small country church. Today we were the rag tag "Ridge Runner" country kids playing against the townies.

The townies had a larger player pool to choose from. We never knew what we were up against when we played them. It was always a couple of phone calls back and forth between us like; Hey, you guys wanna put a team together so we can play at such and such a time on such and such a day? We'd agree on a time and day and here we were. But the town team wasn't here yet. It was only thirty minutes until first pitch.

These games were always a hoot because we alternated umpiring. Each team got to call balls and strikes on each other and the hitting team had to umpire the field. More than one time tensions mounted when one or the other considered a call to be possibly erroneous.

Several cars began showing up with some of the other team's players. Also a few fellows showed up on bikes and I recognized them from school. They must have brought some fans too. A couple of girls and what I would consider parents arrived and sat in the protected bleachers behind home plate. Two of the girls walked past our dugout and went over towards third base and stood watching our fielding practice.

One of the girls spoke up, "Hope you little boys can hit . . . because you sure can't throw the ball! Then the other girl chimed in with, "You're gonna need as many runs as you can get the first inning. After that . . . forget it, you'll never get another chance."

The first girl again harassed us, "Yeah . . . You can go on home after that little boy, cuz . . ." She paused and snapped her fingers as she added . . . "Game over!" They both giggled and made their way back to the bleachers.

There always had to be one or in this case two hecklers. I wondered who planned that little verbal chapping.

The rest of the Townies team finally showed up. My dad called us in and we got ready to meet the opposing force. It was their turn to do warm ups and as they did that their representative met with dad to check and compare rosters. We didn't have a lot of formalities but we tried to keep it as civil and professional as possible.

My dad came over to our dugout with a puzzled look on his face. He told us to gather around him and look at the other team's roster sheet and compare it to the boys who were on the field. His concerned questions were; "Do you know all those guys? Are they all from your school? Do they all live here in town?"

We all looked out to the playing field and studied the players. I had to admit that I did recognize most of them. However there were a few that I had never seen before.

Ray said, "Just wait one second! That guy playing short also plays on the real town team and the guy playing center is a senior in my class this next year. The tall guy playing first base I think he also is on the town team. They're not regular town team players but they are good enough to have made the team. They apparently have stacked the deck with at least two of those guys."

Shrugging his shoulders he finished with, "But what can we say about it?"

"Yeah, I've never seen those townie clowns before", snorted Abe eyeing suspiciously the players on the diamond. "All the rest of those guys are regulars. If that's the case that those other three aren't regular players, how is that fair?"

"If we say something about them, then what about Raymond", dad wondered giving us all something to consider?

Then he smiled trying to give us a boost as he observed. "Look over there they have about five bench warmers to our one and only Abe. We are going to have to make do with what we got. We have good players too. Let's not be intimidated by what we don't know. Just go out there, play your best, and have some fun kicking their butts. We've got first bats so let's use that to our advantage. Dave is pitching and we've hit against him before. We can do it again. They haven't seen our ace player before, so let's get some guys on, bring them home and give them a surprise before they know what hit 'em."

"Come on", cautioned Ray. "Mr. B, please don't build me up like that. I don't want to let anybody down. Yeah, I can clobber the ball if I get a hold of one, but it's been awhile. My timing could be way off."

Ten pairs of eyes were now blinking and staring at Ray poised for a positive address.

"Hey guys", Ray pleaded, "You are expecting great things but close the steam valve a little. Let some of the pressure off old Ray."

Skeets took up the teams agenda and brought it to light, "It's not that we are counting on you big brother, but . . . yeah we are! And I know you can park one over there by the church. I've seen ya do it when you weren't so distracted. You see, I remember your try out two years ago but then you hooked up with hot rods and babes instead of baseball."

A car pulled up behind our dug out. It was Abe's mom and dad, with grandma, my mom and there was also the love of Raymond's life his girlfriend Rachel.

"Speaking of distractions . . . here she comes, now you have to hit a homer Ray", said his brother Skeeter.

"And all day long too", added Abe!

Rachel came over and gave Raymond a kiss on the cheek, smiled, quickly she headed for the bleachers but suddenly stopped, turned around and said, "knock'em dead Ray and hit me a home run."

"See guys", Ray retorted, "It doesn't stop! Now I got to please the whole crowd!"

Grandma peeked around the corner to say, "Got ya booked in church Mr. Raymond. She made a fist and said, "Now beat these rascals today. I said a prayer while on the way over here so I got a good feelin about this."

"Maybe you should umpire grandma", suggested Ray?

"With the good Lord's help, I could do it by golly", threatened grandma making a fist! "At least I'd keep em honest! I'll keep em honest from the bleachers too! They'd better keep it right, or Luella and I will run down there and box their ears!"

We all cracked up laughing because grandma was really serious.

The other team's manager walked over to our dugout and asked if we were ready to play ball and we yelled at him, "We were born ready!" With that being agreed upon dad gave us the thumbs up and he went to umpire balls and strikes and our opposing team's manager went to call the bases.

My dad called out, "Plaaayyy baaallll!

It was time to put up or shut up. The uncertainty of a new school year loomed less than a week away. This would be a good game to win. It would make us feel a little bit like we justifiably earned and preserved this for us boys in the summer of 62'.

Roger the *Dodger* was our first hitter and he gave us the thumbs up sign as he stepped into the batter's box. The first pitch was low and wild as it hit dirt in front of the catcher. The next one was inside pushing Roger back. Roger had a good eye and he had power. A strike was called on the third pitch. As the next pitch came in it was a rising fast ball and Roger connected and pulled it right along the third base line just over the head of the third baseman. He got a double out of that. Our fans, what we had of them, and our team members were ecstatic. We had our lead runner on.

Batting second was Skin and you were never sure about what he might do. It was a tossup question and this time he drew a walk of all things.

Now we had two men on and it was my turn at bat. I was nerved because I didn't want to strike out. I didn't want to hit to the infield as that could produce an easy double play. I just needed to hit one right over the heads of the infielders. Sounds easy don't it . . . just over the infield . . . not a homerun, just place one right over the heads of the infield players. They weren't playing back so they didn't consider me a big threat that's for sure. The heckling of the infielders told me that; "He can't hit", they yelled, "he bats left . . . send him back to the bench, blow it past him, he can't see . . . he's wearin glasses, throw him a heater."

The first pitch to me was a strike and I looked questioningly back at dad and he just smiled.

The catcher said, "Got one on ya."

I took a couple of practice swings and then I had a big idea. The next pitch came in and I took it for a ball. The next ball came in and it looked so good I had to take a cut. I got a hold of it and it had great distance for it to have been hit by me. But I pulled it foul and it hit the alley pavement, bounced and rolled all the way to the church in right field.

That got me some respect as the infield backed up a little. Now it was time for the big idea. The next pitch was again a ball and it now made the count two balls and two strikes. The next pitch was low and a ball. Maybe I could draw a walk. The final pitch looked like a strike and I couldn't let it go by. So I played out my big idea and drag bunted the ball. It caught everyone by surprise and I easily made it to first. Now the bases were loaded.

The first baseman commented. "That was clever there four eyes, but this is where it all ends."

I didn't say a word as I took a little lead.

"And where do you think you're going there meat", asked the first baseman as he spit on the ground?

"Home", I said.

"Yeah, you're goin home alright baby cakes, just as soon as we get our bats and blow you kiddies out of the water, chortled the first baseman.

Louie came to bat in the clean up position. Right now, it stank to be him. All the hot air we were blowing around, I now regretted. On his insides the steam valve remained open full throttle. Shouts from the stand could be heard. "Come on", shouted Rachel, "Louie hit it a mile! I know you can!"

The whole team in our dugout was on their feet and my heart was in my throat. The first pitch came in and Louie took his cut. He was going for the fence but over swung. He was way out in front. Disgruntled comments echoed from our bench.

"Ooooh", said the first basemen, "I could feel the wind all the way back here. Is he your big surprise?"

"Shake it off Ray" cried Abe!

"They were lucky you missed that one", screamed Bob!

Tagging up I again took a lead.

The first baseman again commented, "As if you think you're goin somewhere, you're all dressed up and ain't got nowhere to go kiddo."

"We'll see abou that", I finally said.

"Ooooh, it speaks too", laughed the first baseman.

And just at that time, as he was looking at me, and I was staring at him, both of us not payin attention, a crack that sounded like a rifle shot was heard and a ball jetted right past our heads gaining altitude.

"Hah! Look at that! Nothing but a vapor trail", I yelled to the first baseman! "Now I am going somewhere . . . home!"

Thinking about it, I could swear I heard a sizzle when that ball shot past my head. It was just like hearing a fast ball coming into the catcher's mitt but in reverse. Pretty amazing I thought. I'd never seen a ball hit like that except when number 21, Roberto Clemente blasted one at Forbes Field stadium in Pittsburgh. It was a proud moment for Ray and the Ridge Runner team

that day.

I wasn't even running fast because I wanted to see where it landed. It did indeed go the distance. That ball went all the way to the church and bounced clean off the brick wall.

I had read an interview where Babe Ruth was asked how he hit so many home runs and his reply was: "*I swing as hard as I can, and I try to swing right through the ball . . . the harder you grip the bat, the more you can swing it through the ball, and the further the ball will go. I swing big with everything I've got. I hit big or miss big.*"

Babe Ruth seemed to never be afraid of failing. He just got out there and took his licks and swung for the fence and always gave all he had to give.

Ray had caught me daydreaming rounding second and said to me, "Hey Lar, how about completing the round of bases. Get moving before the right fielder throws the ball in and snags us crossing home plate."

I did as he requested and took off. They had thrown the ball in to try and catch us but we were across home plate long before the ball reached the infield.

Our team bench emptied as everyone handed out high fives. Raymond's girlfriend even came out from the bleachers to give him a hug. Grandma was all smiles and gave us the thumbs up sign.

Dad couldn't say much because he was the home plate umpire and yelled out, "Come on let's play ball!"

Our catcher Bob came up to bat and drew a walk. Now we had another runner on. I believe at this point the other team was thinking of changing pitchers.

Dennis our third baseman was now up and said as he headed to the batter's box, "I think that anything I can do short of sprouting wings and flying around the bases won't be appreciated at this point." Dennis did blast a hard line drive. It was hit right to the second baseman who then threw it to first catching Bob off the base for a double play.

Next up was our designated hitter Abe. He went on to take two balls and two strikes but then grounded to the short stop and was thrown out at first. That completed the first inning for us, but what a first it was!

We were jubilant as we left the bench and headed out to take the field. It was a bright sunshiny day. Our spirits were as bright reflecting upon the success of our first inning. But from the opposing team's bench there was much staring, whispering and finger pointing going on. Much of the chagrin from the opposition was being directed at our wild card player Raymond. The other team had what Ray had called a questionably legal staff. But of course we could not say much as Ray was not one of our regulars either.

Skeeter our left hander was pitching great. He had the best arm on the team and used a funny side arm delivery which was confusing to say the least. Nobody around had a wind up and delivery like his. He went on to strike out the first two batters.

Now the mouthy first baseman came to bat. Ray called time all the way from center field so he could talk to his brother Skeeter. He came in to caution him to keep the ball low in the strike zone and mix it up with high outside and high inside pitches. But don't show him anything up in the strike zone to hit, cautioned Ray. Skeeter proceeded as requested but fell behind and the count was now 3 – 0.

This situation put a smile on the batter's face and he let the next pitch go by and took a strike. It was now 3 – 1. On the next pitch the batter took a big swing and just caught a piece of it and the ball fizzled off into the backstop. Three balls and two strikes was the count and I was sweating bullets.

I couldn't imagine how Skeeter felt. This was quickly becoming a stress related situation. Our few fans in the bleachers were calling out but you could hardly hear them over the shouts from the opposing team. I could see that Skeeter was going to try and send one passed the batter. He was going to give it everything he had.

Keep it low I prayed. Just keep it low. Don't let that ball rise. Skeeter leaned back and hurled the ball with every ounce of energy he had. You could hear him grunt as he released his slingshot pitch. The batter was ready and from where I stood the pitch looked way too good.

Swinging with all his might the batter connected and it was off to the races. The ball took flight and was sailing high and away towards right center field. Ray was on the run. It was a well hit ball. It had the distance and height. Our team was thunder struck as we watched the drama unfold.

The other team's bench emptied as they too were hoping for the best. This field was unique in the fact that there wasn't any home run fence. So here, you could even catch the ball for an out no matter where you were. If you could levitate you could catch one off the church steeple.

Ray was doing his best to catch up to the quickly descending ball. I watched and hoped. Yes it was possible that he could make the play and he was almost there. Ray was now racing into the church parking lot. Man he was fast I later thought while replaying his amazing effort in my mind. With gloved hand outstretched he unbelievably dove after the ball in the stone covered parking lot. The dust flew when his body hit the loose dirt and gravel.

Everyone fell silent, reverently awaiting the outcome. For a second we couldn't see if he made the catch or not. The base runner even stopped to have a look before he made it to second.

The teams, the spectators, all were holding their breath. Then out of the dust Ray jumped up holding the ball in glove high above his head. His cap had fallen off, but he was smiling and proudly displayed that he had indeed caught the ball.

"What", the runner yelled! "Impossible", he screamed throwing his cap on the ground in disgust and started jumping up and down on it. The opposing team's bench all aired their sad concerns.

For the other team it was sad but true. That was the third out.

We went back to our bench to start our second inning at bats. As Ray passed the opposing teams bench on his way in, several of the fellows came over to him. Not to show disrespect but to shake his hand on a job well done. My dad had started to go over suspecting foul play but was actually saluted by the other manager.

Suddenly the drama of the game changed. There was no more name calling and chiding. There came from Ray's hard work and sacrifice a new respect that reflected upon all of us.

Ray came into the dugout and had a slight limp. His jeans and cap were dusty and his team shirt was even torn at the shoulder from when he had landed in the gravel. He was picking some small stones from his arm and wore a few scratches on his elbow.

Dad seemed a little concerned and grandma and Rachel came over to see if he was alright.

"Hey everybody, I appreciate the concern! But really . . . I am okay", Ray stated, assuring everyone that he was good enough to continue playing. "I am a little worse for some slight wear. I've taken more lumps diving off the old rickety springboard over at Royer's into shallow water. So lets' play some more baseball and win this thing. I'm just getting warmed up", he shouted!

It was a good day. And this was indeed a very good day. Life is separated by special moments and pieced together like a puzzle. I enjoy pulling out various fragments from life's puzzle, reviewing them, and then placing them back into the picture for later reflection to see just how it all fits together.

Raymond like so many good fellows I have known had certain talents way beyond their own believing. If only we would have channeled them more correctly or maybe had better direction. God gives us all special gifts that we should never waste. We need to constantly pray to Him in order to make sure that what we are doing is what He desires for us.

A story about overcoming great odds from the Bible is found in the Old Testament. It is in the book of Judges 7:2-8. It is the story of Gideon and how God worked through him in order to save the Israelites. God saw his chosen people falling in and out of grace so many times but still He never gave up on them. Working through His people by choosing this man or that woman God would bring the Israelites back into His grace.

The most amazing thing was that God chose Gideon and his clan not because they were the strongest but because they were the weakest. Why the weakest you might ask? Because when they would win the rest of Israelites would know that it was God working through Gideon and not Gideon himself who delivered them out of captivity from their enemies.

Just to prove his point God gave Gideon some incredible instruction before He sent him out to fight the Midianite hoards. After assembling his army of 32,000 men Gideon was told by God that he had entirely too many men. Of course Gideon questioned the reasoning behind this and God said, "If I let you and your' army fight the Midianites and you win then the rest of your people will say it was they who won and that God had nothing to do with it. Therefore tell your army that whoever is afraid may go home." Twenty two thousand were too fearful to fight and this only left Gideon with 10,000 men.

Gideon was stymied when God told him that he still had too many soldiers! By this time I am sure Gideon was in as much disbelief as Noah and Moses ever were, but he continued to follow His instructions.

"Take your men down to the spring", God told Gideon, "And I will test them to see who will go with you and who will not." Gideon along with his army went down to the spring where he was instructed to divide his men in two groups. One group would be those who cup the water in their hands and lap the water like dogs. The other group would be those who kneel down and drink with their mouths from the stream. There were only three hundred who drank from their hands and all the rest got on their knees to drink.

The Lord said to Gideon, with these three hundred I will rescue you and give you victory over the Midianites. Send all the others home. Gideon collected all the provisions and the rams' horns from all the other warriors and sent them home keeping the chosen three hundred with him.

The Midianite camp was waiting in the valley just below from where Gideon was assembling his small army.

Thinking as I do; if I were Gideon I would have some serious doubts as to my own capabilities about commanding only three hundred against the Midianite hoards. But what a test it would be to leap out in faith, simply trust in the Lord.

To find out more about Gideon and whether he achieved the goal that God had prepared for him read on in Judges to find out the whole story.

2 Corinthians 12:9-10 (NIV) But he said to me, "My grace is sufficient for you, for my power is made perfect in weakness." Therefore I will boast all the more gladly about my weakness so that Christ's power may rest on me. That is why, for Christ's sake, I delight in weakness, in insults, in hardships, in persecutions, in difficulties. For when I am weak, I am strong.

Our rag tag crew went on to miraculously win that game. Like so many things in life it was never recorded or thought about again except there, here and now. It was but a tiny fragment taken from a few boys' lives which could have been on any given afternoon in America and elsewhere, wherever dreams are being played out.

CHAPTER 12

Warning; School Daze Ahead

It seemed colder now even though just that afternoon we were playing baseball in the warm sunshine. Now we were packing up the camp along with that summer's memories. The sun was starting to wane in the west and a mild breeze from that direction put a slight chill in the air. This told me that fall was on the way. The coming cool weather will commit the leaves to change color and send them falling to the ground.

Mom will be taking my brother and me shopping for new school clothes during the next few days. It was part of our yearly routine. Still I remember the creaking wooden floors of the old Montgomery Ward's store and the mixed aromas of candy, popcorn and plastic from W. T. Grants. Those stores long since moved out of downtown mid-America everywhere. Both are gone now as urbanization came creeping and sprawling sending the big chains to shopping malls.

At one time, in our local downtowns, stores like Wards and W. T. Grants were surrounded by local mom and pop stores and shops. They reciprocally existed beside one another and that created an individual financial center for each town and the surrounding area. The malls came along advertising plenty of parking, convenience and one stop shopping. In the new malls customers found small franchises disguised as mom and pop stores mixed in and around the large anchor stores. This took away much of the business from small towns and cities turning once thriving downtowns into retail ghost towns. The only thing that remains the same is change and things are certain to change.

I can only now look back in reflection from where I sit, because what does a twelve year old kid know about such things, right? Does he even care? Well no, of course not, because he is too busy being twelve! He is caught up in thinking about the new school year! AND . . . almost forgot there's a whole month of house arrest due me for not telling the truth and for going where I was not supposed to go. Yeah, almost forgot about all of that!

Three days later . . . breakfast time.

"Now that you have so much spare time Larry", grandma said very matter of fact. She was sitting in a chair and knitting and spoke all the while looking out over her glasses at me. We can spend some time on your Bible studies.

The backs of cereal boxes I thought were always pretty cool. They came with games, advertising about decoder rings and other interesting spy gear. Everything that an up and coming super hero needed was right there on the box. I enjoyed reading them from side to side, front and back and top to bottom. I was totally engrossed in the cereal box and in mid spoon of some tasty O's and grandma thought I hadn't heard a word she said. Of course I did, I was just being twelve.

"Earth to the masked hero", grandma inquired, "Do you have your wrist radio on? Can you hear me and are you still alive? Chomp twice if you can hear me!"

Grandma was now coming in loud and clear so I answered. "Yes, masked hero can hear you grandma and I can spend more time with you. Masked hero is ready, willing and able for more communication on Bible studies . . . masked hero over and out."

Grandma stated, "So you can hear me. And all along, I thought that you were ignoring me."

"No grandma", I said. "There are some new things on this box like three-d glasses. You can't read the secret messages without 'em."

"No of course not", grandma agreed and then asked, "You're a super hero and you didn't know that?"

Moving right along I said, "And you have to know what the secret message says in order to complete the mission."

Playing along with my conversation grandma added, "Yes I can see how important that would be, especially you being a super hero and all. You'd have to know what your orders would be if you are to save the world from impending destruction."

"Correcto mundo grandmacita", I said. "And so you do know what being a super hero is all about."

"Not really", grandma confessed, "But I know someone who does. In fact there are really many super heroes in the scriptures. And there are a lot of stories about ordinary people called upon to do amazing things on behalf of the Lord. Many times those called upon by God even question Him for choosing them because they feel unworthy. But the good Lord is patient and I think He is a good salesperson too because He eventually convinces those He chose to go along with the plan."

My little brother suddenly burst into the room with a Superman figurine. He shouted out, "Faster than a bullet, tougher than a train and he can jump over big buildings too! Shhwooosh! Here he goes!" And then he threw the doll over the breakfast bar and the doll landed in the sink.

"Ooooops! I don't know if he can swim though", he said while holding both hands over his ears!

The doll made a splash as it hit the water. A fountain of dishwater hit the window in front of the sink.

"Sorry", Scott replied! He now covered his eyes with his hands and then ducked underneath the breakfast bar.

Mom was following him down the steps. She was far enough behind and hadn't witnessed the plight of the superhero which dumped him into the dark fathoms of dirty dishwater.

"Where did Scott go", mom asked?

Between mouthfuls of O's I gave up the lad as I pointed downward with my spoon. Mom looked under the table and saw him cowering beneath it. "What are you doing down there', she questioned?

I again pointed with my spoon revealing the evidence of splashed water on the window.

"What's that all about", mom asked?

"The last flight of a so called superhero attempting to come clean from his evil ways", grandma chirped.

"Is that what you're hiding from", my mom asked chuckling to herself? "Maybe if you had broken the picture window like your older brother did with a softball. That was a big deal! Come out from under there. This is not a big deal. Still, you shouldn't be throwing toys around."

"Thanks mom for bringing up the softball incident", I said.

Finishing my cereal I placed the dirty dish in the sink put away the cereal box. I turned and cautiously asked grandma what she was referring to about Bible super heroes.

"Clean up from breakfast, sit down and I'll tell you", said grandma, "And little brother can listen too after he retrieves his doll from the sink. A better idea would be, Larry why don't you get Mr. Superhero out from the water and clean him off?"

"I'll get it mom", offered my mother and then reminded us, "Also after a short story time we have to go to the stores to buy clothes for school. School starts in just a couple of days. I hope we haven't waited too long. Most of the good stuff will be picked over. I will finish up the morning dishes and then it's off we go . . . here catch!"

Mom tossed Mr. Superhero back to Scott as she said. "He's all clean and shiny. His cape is still a little wet though, but it'll dry. Don't throw your toys around in the house, okay?"

Scott shook his head in agreement. "Okay mom", he said.

My brother and I walked over and sat down in front of grandma who was still knitting. "Are we sitting comfortably down", she asked? "Good, then I shall begin", grandma replied.

"Now you boys may not believe this", grandma suggested, "But we can all be a super hero. And we can do it on a daily basis too. That little doll that you hold so tightly in your hand Scott can never take flight unless you give it a toss like you just did. But every time we each do something good or kind for someone else we become a hero in God's eyes."

"Back in Bible times", grandma went on to say, "God called upon many ordinary individuals and some were very reluctant and stubborn to do God's wishes. Just to name a few that are on the short list I would have to say who comes to mind are; Abraham, Noah, Moses, Daniel, Shadrach, Meshach and Abednego which you are studying now. There would also be the profit Elijah and Gideon who commanded a small army against all odds. But today we will talk about Samson. We'll talk about him because Scott is so into a character that has amazing strength and is able to run faster and jump higher than anyone else. So yes, I think we will discuss Samson."

"Wasn't Samson the one who had great strength because of his hair and then when it was cut off he lost his power", I asked?

"That's right", said Grandma.

Then I added, "Well that's sorta like the comic book story about Superman where he has secret power but a certain element called kryptonite can destroy it."

"Okay", agreed grandma, "That is a comparison. However, in this case we are not talking about a fictional made up character. We are describing an event recorded in Biblical history in the life of a real human being. His power was not destroyed by an element but rather by the guiles of pagan women and Samson's own selfish desires."

"We as ordinary people can relate better to another who is just like us", advised grandma as she explained, "No matter how many great gifts we have we all fall short of the glory of God because we have the same wants, needs and desires as others around us. Most of all we have trouble with the freedom of choosing between right and wrong. What do you think about that Larry?"

"Your meaning is very clear grandma", I said. Then I asked, "Was Samson born just like me for instance or was it some miracle birth like Christ?"

"That question will be answered in a minute", grandma replied. "First let me say that God chose many to lead his people the Israelites. Either it was from out of captivity or to steer them away from their own sinful nature. During Samson's time the Israelites were in the captivity of the Philistines because they had done evil in the eyes of the Lord. Because of it they were placed in that situation for forty years until Samson was born."

In answer to your question Larry, "The miracle was that Samson was born to a woman who could not have children. Through God's grace she was given Samson in order to begin the process of bringing God's people out of captivity. It wasn't until much later that this task was completed but Samson was there at the beginning. Unfortunately Samson never saw the completion of the task that God proposed for him but he was the element which set the wheels in motion."

"So was he the guy in the Bible with the big muscles", I asked?

"Yes", grandma said as she smiled confirming that Samson was the man with the muscles, "But there is much more to it than brawn and muscle", grandma explained. "He was favored in God's eyes to be the deliverer of His people." God gave Samson's mother certain rules to follow. In Judges 13:5 (NIV): *No razor may be used on his head, because the boy is to be born a Nazirite, set apart to God from birth, and he will begin the deliverance of Israel from the hands of the Philistines.*

"You have to understand boys", grandma went on to explain God's warning and Samson's problem; "Samson would be a hero as long as he was set apart for God. Samson was his own worst enemy though as he sinned terribly, but he accomplished much when he set his endeavors to work for God's purpose."

Being a little confused I had to ask grandma to clarify; "Am I hearing that Samson wasn't such a great hero because he didn't listen to what God wanted him to do? If I was God and gave a special gift like super human strength to someone, I'd be a little upset too if the person I gave it to wasn't using it for the right reasons."

Grandma went forward with the Biblical story and how she viewed it. "In the story it is true that Samson seemed to be going against God's intentions. He was attracted to Philistine women. That was against God's law because they were considered a pagan people. Samson's father protested against his marriage to the Philistine but because of Samson's persistence he gave his consent. What was not realized at this point was that this too was in God's plan. This eventually would bring a confrontation between the Israelites and the Philistines. The stage was set and events were put in play.

There was a wedding feast given by the bridegroom as was customary. The great feast lasted seven days. In that time Samson had proposed a riddle to be answered by those in attendance. If they answered correctly they would win a prize of thirty linen garments and thirty sets of clothes. If they could not find the answer they would return in kind. They coerced Samson's wife to get the answer from him. This she accomplished by continually pleading and crying to him. She went back to her people with the answer and they in turn gave the answer to Samson. But he knew what had happened. She was the only one that could have known the answer. This was a test of her faithfulness to Samson."

Grandma had her Bible open and read; Judges 14:19-20 (NIV): *Then the Spirit of the Lord came upon him in power. He went down to Ashkelon, struck down thirty of their men, stripped them of their belongings and gave their clothes to those who had explained the riddle. Burning with anger, he went up to his father's house. And Samson's wife was given to the friend who had attended him at his wedding.*

"Wow, he took on thirty guys like it was no problem", I exclaimed! "And of course he got rid of his wife because she tricked him. She liked her own people more than Samson, huh grandma?"

"Yes and history was set in motion by those acts", grandma explained. "This was the first in a series of unfortunate events in Samson's life. All the wrong choices that Samson would make placed him right in the middle of the war between the Israelites and the Philistines."

My brother and I were pretty interested in what else Samson had done but my Mother was getting impatient about taking us shopping. She said, "You have ten more minutes and we have to go!"

Grandma quickly continued. "Next boys because the Philistines were so mad at Samson they camped with a huge army of men in Judah. The Philistines told the Israelites that they were there to capture Samson. The Israelites took an army of three thousand men down to where Samson was living in a cave. Samson agreed to go with them as long as it was not they who would kill him. They bound him with new ropes and delivered him to the Philistines."

Again grandma read from the Bible; Judges 15:14-16, 20 (NIV): *As he approached Lehi, the Philistines came toward him shouting. The Spirit of the Lord came upon him in power. The ropes on his arms became like charred flax, and the bindings dropped from his hands. Finding a fresh jawbone of a donkey he grabbed it and struck down a thousand men.*

Then Samson said,

> *"With a donkey's jawbone*
> *I have made donkeys of them.*
> *With a donkey's jawbone*
> *I have killed a thousand men."*

Samson led Israel for twenty years in the days of the Philistines.

Grandma cautioned us as she pointed out, "Even though it was God that gave Samson his

Great strength which gave victory over the Philistines", she then asked, "To whom did he give the credit?"

"Oh yeah", I said and then I made my best uneducated guess, "I think he said that he killed the thousand men and it was he that made them look like donkeys. Is that right?"

"Yes, that is right", said Mom and she added, "Even after God gave him the strength and the battle was won Samson became so full of himself. He quickly asked God, because Samson believed it was through his own accomplishments, that God should immediately quench his need for a drink of water. God agreed and then from a hollow place in the ground caused water to come out and satisfy Samson's thirst. But his needs don't end there right mother."

Grandma said agreeing, "Oh yes, that's right because then along came Delilah . . ."

Little brother put his hand up and said, "That's in my little Bible story book . . . that story about Samson and Delilah. She cut his hair off. That made him bald. He couldn't do anything after that. That's kinda like what's happening to dad."

Scott then curiously looked at his mother and asked, "Mommy are you doin that . . . cuttin off daddy's hair? Is that makin him tired too?"

We all laughed and mom explained that it wasn't her that was cutting off daddy's hair. It was just because he was getting older and it was natural that men start to lose their hair.

"Oh", Scott said. "I don't hope that happens to me anytime soon. I don't want to be tired all the time. Dad's always talkin about how tired he is. So I'll guess now its cause he's losin his hair."

Grandma shook her head and smiled. Mom chuckled and I just wanted the story to continue because I could see mom was getting a little impatient. "Go ahead grandma", I told her and asked. "What happens next?"

She continued, "This next woman in Samson's life was Delilah and she was his final downfall. She beguiled him beyond belief. Samson was so blinded by Delilah's charm that he couldn't see straight about what was really happening to him. Don't take my word for it let me read it to you"; Judges 16:5-6 (NIV): *The rulers of the Philistines went to Delilah and said, "See if you can lure him into telling you the secret of his great strength and how we can overpower him so we may tie him up and subdue him. Each one of us will give you eleven hundred shekels of silver." So Delilah said to Samson, "Tell me the secret of your great strength and how you can be tied up and subdued."*

"You mean to tell me that Samson fell for that malarkey", I asked? "Unbelievable", I exclaimed!

"I would never let a girl get me like that, no way! They're not worth a baseball without a cover on it, or even a jar of dead fireflies that stinks."

"Now wait a minute", said grandma, "It's not over yet. Delilah cried, pleaded and begged three times without getting Samson to tell her the truth. Finally on the fourth try Delilah got him to say that since his birth no razor ever touched his hair because he was set apart for God. Then she put Samson to sleep on her lap and a man came and shaved off the seven braids of his hair. The Philistines entered and took him away. They made him blind, shackled him and put him in prison to push the grinding wheel. But while he was in prison his hair began to grow again along with his strength.

The Philistines brought the blinded Samson out of prison and placed him on public display for their entertainment. They stood him among the pillars of the great temple. Men and women and all the great rulers of the Philistines were there. Also on the roof were about three thousand men and women watching Samson perform for them. Now I'll read the amazing conclusion to the Samson story"; Judges 16:28-30 (NIV): *Then Samson prayed to the Lord, "O Sovereign Lord, remember me. O God, please strengthen me just once more, and let me with one blow get revenge on the Philistines for my two eyes." Then Samson reached toward the two central pillars on which the temple stood. Bracing himself against them, his right hand on the one and his left hand on the other, Samson said, "Let me die with the Philistines!" Then he pushed with all his might, and down came the temple on the rulers and all the people in it. Thus he killed many more when he died than while he lived.*

"So you see kids", grandma said as she began to bring the story to a conclusion, "We need not let our lives go as far out of control as Samson did. The moral of the story is that whenever you need Him God is there to answer prayer for those who truly believe. God still loved Samson and was willing to hear his one final prayer of confession and repentance even though he had fallen really short from His original plan. God heard his prayer and blessed him one final time. And God definitely loves you guys. Believe it, pray on it and he will help you to move mountains, cross oceans, run fast and jump high! Okay, now get out of here before your mother explodes from shopping anxiety!"

We thanked grandma for taking the time to tell us the story. Gee whiz, she had a million of them. I think her head was like the encyclopedia of story time. Grandma could go on and on without a book or rehearsal. I know that from the little plays I was in while back in grade school, when I couldn't remember all my lines, how embarrassing that was. How did she do it?

Mom had this goofy song she sang when we went on a shopping mission. It was sung to the tune, "The Farmer in The Dell." Her words were; a shopping we will go . . . a shopping we will go, high ho the merry 'O a shopping we will go. We'll find our bargains here, we'll spend our money there, high ho the merry 'O a shopping we will go etc. etc. I don't remember the rest of the words, but you get the idea.

Shopping with mom didn't happen often, but when mom decided to shop, it was an all day outing. On those days she must have coined the phrase "shop 'til you drop." I could see later why dad or grandma never went along. Mom had my brother and I try on everything. She said she only wanted to do this once. There were never any returns because she hated having to return anything just about as much as our complaining about going shopping.

After the mission was completed we always stopped at the local burger place called "Biff Burger" and had our gratuitous burger, fries and a shake. It was the first true fast food burger joint in our area.

Now we were prepared for the first half of the school year. The trunk of the car was filled with clothes, tablets, pencils and notebooks.

"We should now be able to make it until after the mayhem of the silly season drives everyone into total holiday madness", mom said hopefully. "After the holidays", she explained. "That is when we will find the real bargains." Mom took bargain hunting as seriously as dad took his preparation for hunting season."

Mom called Christmas the silly season. She told us that she had her own theory about that time of the year. She explained to my brother and me that she didn't want to get into it at that time but went on to say; "Christ wasn't even born on that day and felt that commercialism had taken over the true meaning of the holiday. Christ is the reason for the season but so many have replaced the celebration of Christ's birth with the expectation of gifts. We should be thanking Him for the precious gift of life that He gave us."

Agitatedly she looked at us in the rear view mirror and questioned, "Who do we think we are to desecrate his name in such ways?"

"Gee mom, I don't know", I answered. "I don't think that Scott does." Little brother shrugged his shoulders and shook his head confirming that he didn't know either.

My little brother thought for a moment and then quickly asked mom, "Does this mean we're not having Christmas this year?"

"No that's not what I mean Scott", mom said trying to assure him. Calmly mom smiled and looked into the rear view mirror again at my little brother and suggested, "As you guys grow up you need to find the truth for yourselves."

Mom asserted to us that she felt it was okay to set aside a special day to celebrate the birth of Jesus and what He truly stood for. What the true meaning of the Christmas holiday has turned into she said, plus what the world's intent of it is now, made her very sad.

"Don't get me wrong", mom went on to say, "I am not a Scrooge; I too love the songs, the coming together of family, the food and the love that comes along with the celebration of Christmas. Here too, and just as in all ways, we need to place our Savior in the forefront of all we do and say. Okay kids?"

Scott and I both agreed of course with all mom had said. I was just on the outside of understanding everything mom told us. I felt that my little brother was in fear of not having any Christmas at all.

Making a mental note I wanted to ask grandma about the latest information that mom gave us. I wanted to get her take on the holiday of Christmas, or did I?

What I did know was that the clock for the first big day of school keeps winding down as there are now only three days to go. It's like preparing for summer vacation but in reverse. My heart's just not in it, that's for sure.

A strange time ratio phenomenon occurs during school daze and must be duly noted here and now. This occurrence happens when comparing school days to vacation time. It seems that time slows down during school days and when vacations arrive, time speeds up. I know that doesn't seem possible but some kid should do a study on it and the results be published so that kids everywhere could understand it better. This was discussed among my friends and I and we all agree that there is some kinda black hole that vacations fall into and this causes time to warp.

We noticed that the slowing of time also occurs when the Pastor is giving his sermon. It has also been observed that many of the adults fall into a trance and seem to fall asleep with their eyes wide open. They can't fool me. I know they are asleep, because sometimes they start snoring. Yup, eyes open and snoring. That must be a grown up phenomenon.

CHAPTER 13

Church; Before School Daze

It was warm and hazy. It was a day to make you feel lazy and just a few days ago a message from *"Mother Nature"* told us that fall was on the way. She sent telegrams of sharp cold breezes from a northwesterly direction. The fickleness of the weather in the northeast at this time of the year was evident. Sometimes at the end of August an early frost could occur and in the middle of September it could feel like the middle of July.

My grandpa told me a story about July while we were out looking to see if the wheat was ripe enough to combine. As grandpa hulled a head of wheat in the palm of his hand he related to me; "Back when I was a little boy about your age Larry. One time in July a cold northeast wind blew down from the direction of New York and Connecticut bringing with it lots of rain. The rain froze on the heads of the wheat and just about everything else that it could grab on to. When we woke up in the morning all the farmers in the area got scared and had a meeting concerning the condition of their wheat crops. They were afraid that the ice would destroy the grain and make it unfit to grow into harvest. So you know what they did Larry", grandpa asked?

I shook my head no. How could a kid of twelve even know about such matters?

Pappy went on to say, "The farmers dragged ropes across their fields to knock the ice off of the wheat thinking that they could save their harvest in that way. By the time they got to our farm Larry the sun had come out and melted the ice from the wheat and fruit trees and everything else."

I asked grandpa what happened to his family's crop of wheat since they didn't get to his farm in time.

He laughed and said, "You know everything is in God's hands and he knows best. Sometimes you just have to allow His natural wisdom to guide you. All that good work that those farmers believed they had done was to be of no profit. They thought they were helping themselves but in reality they destroyed most of the pollen that is needed to germinate the plant when it blooms so it can produce the kernels of grain."

"So your wheat was saved", I questioned?

"That's right", grandpa said. "In fact, that year we had a very good crop. The ice actually protected the heads of wheat from that freezing wind and cold. The farmers who dragged that rope across their crops had very little grain to harvest. So you do the best you can and leave the rest up to the good Lord."

"Kinda like Father knows best", I said jokingly?

Grandpa eyed me suspiciously and said, "A-yup, I guess you could say that."

Just thought I'd throw that little tidbit of information in here in case you were ever in that situation and had to make a decision as to rope or not rope your field of wheat. Well, don't do it and leave well enough alone. Now we'll go back to mother knows best.

Mom let us wear some of our new school clothes today to go to church but I had to include some kind of a tie. At least she wasn't going to dress my brother and I alike with our gangster hats again. I checked in my dad's closet to see if there was anything that would match a checkerboard design shirt. There were some hand painted ties with ducks and geese. There were some other kinds with large floral designs. Then I found a string tie with a little silver slide and I didn't know at the time what it was called but I thought it to be kinda cool. Now this tie was different; black cord with a silver clasp. This would match my shirt's checkerboard design. Mom dressed my little brother because he wasn't old enough to know what to wear.

When mom saw what tie I had chosen she asked, "Now where in the world did you find that old thing?"

"In the old trunk with the smelly moth balls in it", I quipped.

"That's an old jazz tie from the late twenties early thirties", she said, "And I have no idea where it came from. But if you want to wear it I guess that's okay. I would have never picked that out for you to wear."

I knew that. Mom of course would not have picked that tie out. She wouldn't be expected to know what a kid of my age would consider as being cool.

The voice of grandma burst through the silence as I checked my look in the mirror that was hanging on the bedroom closet door. "When you're finished loving yourself Mr. Larry", she said, "Breakfast is cooling on the table . . . and if you haven't heard, the church's bell is rallying us to call on the house of the Lord."

The ringing of the bell could be heard in the distance. I always liked that sound. You could hear it from one end of the village to the other. It was a sound that was unique to our village and a sound that I would remember all my life.

After breakfast we started on the short walk to church. My mind was thinking about the passing summer. Memories of last week's camp out came to mind and I looked over at the ball field and listened to the babbling stream next to the road and thought of fishing. The smell of the fresh turned earth where dad plowed over the dead stalks of sweet corn and potato plants reminded me of springtime when he first planted the garden.

Also let's not forget my detention. That had me in a melancholy mood as well. I knew I was going to get busted over my recent arrest for the camp out caper. After the reprieve given to us by dad to let us play the ball game I had not spoken a word to anyone as per house rules; no phone, no baseball, no TV, no, no nothing until further notice.

Thank goodness I took Bob up on the comic book offer. Mom had just bought me new Hardy Boys books the week before. Otherwise, I would be stuck playing trucks and cars with my little brother. Now don't get me wrong. I don't mind doing that as long as the other fellas wouldn't find out that it's my main source of entertainment.

At my age I can't make a steady diet of trucks and cars. After looking at the current Heathkit catalogue I asked mom to order a short wave radio kit. It wasn't that expensive and I would have to put that together capacitor by capacitor, diode by diode and wire by wire. To me that was better than TV or anything else. Mom and dad saw it as a good learning experience. "It is a great learning experience", I told them! I thought it pretty cool to be able to listen in on conversations from all over the world. Yes, of course I had to put it together before that could happen, but the incentive was there.

Mr. Cee drove past us and Abe gave a half hearted wave. Abe's mother Luella was in the front seat. She nodded politely to mom and grandma and his older brother the Snail was in the back seat with Abe. Was it my imagination or did Abe's brother stick his tongue out at him when they passed. I'll have to get clarification on that when we reach the church.

Upon approaching the church I saw people congregating outside and talking. They too must be enjoying the weather since it was really a beautiful day. Grandmother greeted one of her friends by saying, "What a beautiful day the Lord hath made and we should rejoice in it!"

"That is definitely true sister", the lady answered, "and we shall!" They both laughed and shook hands.

Immediately I went over to Abe and stood beside him to ask about the rude tongue incident. "I know we're not supposed to be talking", I said, "but I couldn't help wonder about the rude tongue gesture made by the Snail?"

"Oh . . . yes that. He's been in his glory because I got confined to my room for the camp caper just like you", explained Abe. "It's almost like he now has reason to be more of a creep than usual and mom and dad seem to be letting him get away with it. I'll get him back though. I'm thinking of putting some of mom's hair remover in his hair tonic or hiding a garter snake in his bed. What do you think would be more fun; the snake or the fear of going bald?"

Before I could answer Abe's question his mother Luella clapped her hands and told everyone that it was time for Bible class and that we all needed to come out of God's sunshine and into his house to learn more about him. We filed in one at a time and took our seats.

It wasn't a large church and all the people would simply divide up in the pews according to their learning status. Our age group's class was in the back and to the left. Luella came over with the study book and her Bible and asked how many studied for this week's lesson? About four out of the ten children raised their hands.

"I see", commented Luella who was obviously a little frustrated by the number of hands that were raised. She specifically looked at the guys and asked. "I'll bet if I asked how many home runs were hit by Mickey or Roger this past week someone would be able to tell me that . . . right?"

Abe held up his hand and said, "Okay I'll be the huckleberry . . . one by Mantle in the fourth inning against Detroit on Thursday for sure that I know of. But there could be more?"

"See that, out of the mouth of my own babe came the point I am trying to make", said Luella. "Now that we know that answer let me propose a question. Who or what in this day and age do each of us want to be most like? Ever think about that at all . . . how about you Susie?"

"Yes Mrs. Cee", Susie replied.

Luella asked, "What do you think about when you daydream? Who would you like to be or what do you see yourself becoming when you get older?"

Abe and I snickered and nudged each other and were thinking about the movie "Wizard of Oz". Susie we thought could appropriately portray one of the less desirable characters.

"If I have to separate you two I will", warned Luella who was staring at us from over the top of her reading glasses. Quickly she looked back at Susie, "Go ahead and answer the question Susie and don't worry about what these other people are thinking."

Susie looked over at us and smirked and said, "Thank you Mrs. Cee I would be happy to answer. When I watch TV I see all the beautiful actresses. I especially like the lady on Bewitched and Jeannie on I Dream of Jeanie because they are pretty and they can make whatever they want happen. They have the power to take control over their situations just by a twitch of the nose or a blink of an eye."

Then Susie looked over at a few of us guys, gave us a waspish eyes look and blinked. "But unfortunately Mrs. Cee", said Susie, "When I do it they don't disappear . . . nothing happens . . . but let me tell you, if I could?"

"I know", Luella said sympathetically, "Sometimes I wish I could blink myself out of here but that is not for us to say and do."

Luella then asked, "How about a statement from one you unfortunate guys? Who do you wish you could be?"

Roger raised his hand and said, "Because I am into baseball, I suppose I look at a lot of the big league players and wish I could be one of them. Ya know playing like they do for that kind of money and getting all the recognition for something that you love doing . . . yeah . . . that would be pretty cool."

"Those are good answers", Luella praised and then asked, "How about Elvis? Would anyone here desire to be like the King of Rock n' Roll? How about that? The movies, the concerts and all the adoration of the fans, and of course how about the huge amounts of money . . . who wouldn't want that? Who wouldn't envy or idolize that kind of life", she enquired?

Abe pointed at me and said, "Larry here would be into that since he told me he wants a guitar for Christmas. But he looks more like Buddy Holly than Elvis. Buddy Holly got killed in a plane crash in 1959 . . . saw that on a news reel . . . he could take his place . . . but Larry . . . it's too dangerous to play rock n' roll. So forget about that pal."

"You want a guitar for Christmas . . . is that true", Luella asked? "And what made you want a guitar."

Sheepishly I shook my head yes. Everybody was staring at me and I felt like I had just committed a crime. Searching for an answer I mumbled, "Don't know . . . just thought it might be something I would like to learn how to do."

"Okay", Luella commented, "That wasn't quite the answer I was looking for but hey, it's something he would like to do. That's fair enough, but generally when we are moved to do something it is something we might envy others for doing. Like . . . I want to be a baseball player for the fame and money. I want to be a movie star for others to worship me, or perhaps I want to be a race car driver or whatever. There are many distractions in this world that aren't necessarily things that would please God. This brings us to our story about Daniel and his three friends and king Nebuchadnezzar."

Luella opened her teachers study guide and started reading from her notes. "It was 603 B. C. during the second year of king Nebuchadnezzar's reign. On this particular night the king had a very disturbing dream and he called forth all his wise men; astrologers, magicians, sorcerers and the like. He demanded that these men tell him what he dreamed and give an interpretation. They asked the king to tell them the dream and they would give him the interpretation. Of course the king saw through this trickery because if they were all knowing then they should see the dream and be able to give an interpretation as the king requested. The king also told them that if they could not do this he would have them torn limb from limb and reduce their houses to heaps of rubble."

Looking up from her notes Luella asked, "Class do you think this worried the wise men of Babylon?

"Well yeah, sure", Butch offered up his burley answer. "Nobody alive on this planet knows what another person's thinkin, let alone what somebody's dreamin about. Sometimes I gotta ask myself, what was I thinkin? How can I know what you're thinkin. I'd be pretty afraid havin that kinda pressure put on me for sure. I am sure the king got real angry when the so called wise men couldn't come up with the real goods."

"That's right class", agreed Luella. "In fact he put a death decree on all the wise men of Babylon. Included in this death decree the king told the guards to hunt down Daniel and all his friends as well. When Arioch the commander of the king's guard showed up at Daniels door Daniel was surprised to say the least and asked why this was happening. The commander explained what was going on and Daniel immediately hurried off to see the king. Daniel told the king that he needed more time so he could give the king what he wanted. Daniel then went home and urged his friends Hananiah, Mishael and Azariah to pray to God for mercy by giving them the answer to the king's request."

"What do you think class", asked Luella? "Was the Lord merciful towards Daniel and his friends? She then urgently requested, "Come on this is class participation. Look in your Bibles, come up with an answer. Daniel 2:1-24 holds the answer. When someone finds it hold up your hand."

Susie held up her hand first.

"Yes Susie I see your hand is up", acknowledged Luara as she asked, "What have you found?"

Susie speaks pointing out, "It says here in Daniel 2:19 that God gave Daniel a night vision and the secret was revealed and then from 2:20-23 Daniel gives praise to God for his infinite wisdom and many blessings that he gave not only to the earth and its people but him too."

Luella commended Susie on a good paraphrase and then asked, "So what happened next boys, anyone got that?"

My hand went up.

"Yes Larry", said Luella and asked, "So what have you found?"

Also trying to paraphrase I said, "It looks like Daniel rushes over to the commander of the guard and asks to be taken to the king. Daniel is going to save everyone and himself but all through the giving of this interpretation he praises only God for this revelation. In fact Daniel makes it very clear to the king that this has only happened because . . . and here in Daniel 2:28 it says; *However, there exists a God in the heavens who is a Revealer of secrets, and he has made known to King Nebuchadnezzar what is to occur in the final part of days. Your dream and the visions of your head upon your bed – this it is:*"

Luella put up her hand for me to stop. "Okay", she said. "That is good. So we see here that all through Daniels trials he trusted in whom?"

Abe spoke up. "Daniel showed the king that everything comes only through God."

"That's correct", Luella commended and told us, "As all of you have pointed out it is only through diligent prayer and God's mercy that Daniel and his friends could get through all of this. The Bible tells us in Matthew 7:8 how we should pray. Matthew 7:8 (*NWT*) **For everyone asking receives and everyone seeking finds, and to everyone knocking it will be opened.** Daniel and his friends knew this without doubt, without reservation, and believed in the Lord thy God and they received and were blessed, but it doesn't stop here class."

Luella went on to explain to us the rest of the story. "Because Daniel revealed to the king those secrets of the dream the king showed favor to Daniel. And Daniel asked that his three friends be given administrative positions. Daniel was in the court of the king and was the ruler over all the jurisdictional districts of Babylon.

The revelation of the vision gave King Nebuchadnezzar a big idea and he erected a giant statue of Gold resembling the one from his dream. And just a side note here class; this statue made of gold stood sixty cubits high and six cubits wide. A cubit measured the length from the king's elbow to the tip of his middle finger. This was the rule of measure used in any kingdom during this time."

"The king called all to worship this statue of gold", continued Luara. "He proclaimed that all the heads of power from all over Babylon assemble before the statue and to inaugurate the image at the sound of all sorts of musical instruments they will fall down and worship the image of gold that Nebuchadnezzar the king has set up. In Daniel 3:6 it reads . . . and please read with me from your Bibles." "Class what does it say", our teacher asked?

Daniel 3:16 (*NWT*); **And whoever does not fall down and worship will at the same moment be thrown into the burning fiery furnace.**

Luella took off her glasses and looked at all of us and posed a question. "Well now what? Here you have the three friends of Daniel attending the great celebration as requested. Of course now they have taken on and are known by the Babylonians by heathen names; Shadrach, Meshach and Abednego."

"But have their hearts changed", Luella asked us, "Have they melded so much into this culture that it has changed their beliefs? Let's look at Daniel 3:12-30 for answers. And later from this we must ask ourselves about our own lives? How many times have we been pushed into doing something we don't believe in? Have you stood your ground?"

Roger put up his hand.

"Yes Roger", Luella recognized him and urged. "Go ahead and tell us, what do you see going on?

"I found in Daniel 12", Roger answered, "there are people sort of ratting on the three boys. and telling the king that since these Jews aren't following instructions, why should they? And why not throw these guys into the furnace? What makes them so special?"

"Yes, I see Susie's hand is up", acknowledged Luara and asks, "Go ahead . . . what have you found?"

Susie began to tell the class what she saw in the Bible and again paraphrased. "The king is a little upset. He tells the boys that the next time they hear the music they need to get with the program and bow down. But they say, no way. They don't care what he says. They are sticking with their one God. Basically they say, if it has to be then their God will rescue them. And if not he should know that they still are loyal to their one God. The king didn't like that answer. The king was angry and told everyone that he was heating up the furnace seven times hotter than usual. The king grabbed the three boys, tied them up and was ready to throw them into the furnace.

"That was really good. Thank you Susie and I see you have studied", noted Luella and then suggested, "Now let's all silently read through Daniel 3:21-26" (*NIV*)

21: So these men, wearing their robes, trousers, turbans and other clothes were bound and thrown into the blazing furnace. 22: The king's command was so urgent and the furnace so hot that the flames of fire killed the soldiers who took up Shadrach, Meshach and Abednego, 23: and these three men, firmly tied, fell into the blazing furnace.

24: Then the king leaped to his feet in amazement and asked his advisers, "Weren't there three men that we tied up and threw into the fire?"
They replied, "Certainly, O king."
25: He said "Look! I see four men walking around in the fire, unbound and unharmed, and the fourth looks like a son of the gods."
26: Nebuchadnezzar then approached the opening of the blazing furnace and shouted, "Shadrach, Meshach and Abednego, servants of the Most High God, come out, come here!"

So Shadrach, Meshach and Abednego came out of the fire, 27: and the satraps, prefects, governors and royal advisers crowded around them. They saw that the fire had not harmed their bodies, nor was a hair of their heads singed; their robes were not scorched, and there was no smell of fire on them.

28: Then Nebuchadnezzar said, "Praise be to the God of Shadrach, Meshach and Abednego, who has sent his angel and rescued his servants! They trusted in him and defied the king's command and were will to give up their lives rather than swerve or worship any god except their own God. 29: Therefore I decree that the people of any nation or language who say anything against the God of Shadrach, Meshach and Abednego be cut into pieces and their houses turned into piles of rubble, for no other god can save in this way."

"Has everyone finished class . . . what can we glean from these passages and package for ourselves to take with us", asked Luella? "And by the way, do you think that Nebuchadnezzar now was willing to serve the Hebrew's God alone after seeing how powerful He is?"

"Don't believe so", I said jumping into the conversation. "To believe and have the faith like the three boys . . . that was some miracle . . . and that happened because they believed so strongly in their faith. But what I do know is that even when I get a little burn from doing something dumb around the campfire . . . how bad it hurts for days. I can't imagine that if someone says to me, bow down to an image or else be thrown into a furnace . . . I'd sure have second thoughts. I don't know if I could find in myself that kind of faith."

Abe put up his hand, "I guess in this situation; the boys were protected, god was glorified and they were rewarded."

"Wow", that was a pretty amazing summarization and conclusion", said Luella and then asked curiously. "And where did you find that?"

"In dad's life application and study Bible", confessed Abe. "He said you would be asking a question like this and wrote the answer on this piece of paper I have here."

"At least you brought it out and shared it with all of us. Thank you", said Luella. "I'll speak to your father later about giving you a cheat sheet. Class as usual we are running out of time and this book of Daniel holds an amazing amount of information and correlates so much with prophecy in the New Testament. We haven't even scratched the surface of these texts. Maybe someday time will allow us to get into that part of the study. Stay faithful to your beliefs class and like we said last week . . . don't jump off the cliff just to be part of the in-crowd."

Then someone whispered . . . "The ropes"?

Luella paused and asked, "What did someone say?"

"The ropes", a soft male voice asked? "What about the ropes? Didn't they mean something?"

We all turned to see who was asking the question and it was Russ; the boy who hardly ever spoke up or participated. Most times you never knew he was there. He was a little over weight, had a lot of freckles and thick reddish hair. His mom would drop him off and pick him up again when church was over. Russ seemed like a nice kid who always sat there quietly but never seemed to get involved. This was a first.

"Yes they do or should I say did", Luella pointed out. Then she questioned, "Russ, what do you think the ropes meant?"

Russ cleared his throat and spoke up. "I think from studying the lesson. I took it that since the boys were tied up by the king and thrown into the fire. The ropes were the only things that were burned away and that shows the ropes as being the things of this earth. That's what binds us up and weighs us down. They didn't believe in earthly things or kings. Besides this I think that the boys took one of the Ten Commandments to heart; "You shall have no other gods before me". After all that was what Nebuchadnezzar was asking them to do wasn't he? You know to bow down and worship the big gold statue? Like we were talking about today and what I got from it was that there's a whole buncha things we can get caught up into these days with TV and all. Seems from what my grandparents talk about is that there are way too many distractions nowadays other than just plain livin. Least that's what my grandpa says."

"Okay! That's exciting! What else did you get from the study lesson", Luella inquired of Russ.

"I can't speak for other guys here", continued Russ "But I can relate to some things about school . . . sorta like what Roger was talking about last week. I'm a little over weight and some clowns like to pick on me and call me *"red n' chubby"* and that's okay. Sometimes you like to try and fit in so ya laugh and go along to get along . . . you know that saying. Mom tells me that all the time. Well ya know the girls hang out with the "cool guys" and most of them smoke so it would be like when they offer me a smoke . . . yeah, I might take one to be cool . . . but I don't inhale.

It's like those three boys could have fallen down before the idol and faked like they were worshipping just to get along. They didn't. They stood up for what they believed. They could have thought that even if they did they're really not hurting anybody.

It's like if I would smoke one cigarette mom wouldn't know and I'm really not hurting anybody am I? But then I gotta think about that. The fact is that yeah, I am hurtin someone. That someone is me. Because I know and I am just lie'n to myself and messin up my body . . . which because what I believe now is the temple of God and I can't do that. Just like my eating . .

. it's sorta like cigarettes and I figure that too is addicting . . . I'm workin on that."

After all that being said Russ sat there with a big smile.

"Awesome! Russ! That was well spoken", said Luella praising him for his good commentary. "I guess you did study and you did put together one great package for yourself and thank you so much for opening it up and sharing that testimony. Well done!"

All the rest of us were just silent and I thought to myself that Russ put it all together especially from a kids point of view. Suddenly I thought that good old Russ was kinda cool himself and his grandparents sorta sounded like my grandma. They must have grown up together or something.

Luella stood in front of us smiling and looked at each one of us and then said, "Next week we will learn about a king who grazes with the cattle. That's right, a king who eats grass!" Our teacher then gave a closing prayer but before dismissing us she handed each of us an index card as she said, "Take this card home kids and whenever you feel overwhelmed or pushed into doing something that makes you feel uncomfortable read it, and think about today's lesson and discussion. Life will have many blazing furnaces and we only need call upon our one true living God for deliverance."

I turned the card over and read it to myself. It was Daniel 3:16-18 {NIV) *"Shadrach, Meshach and Abednego replied to the king, 'O Nebuchadnezzar, we do not need to defend ourselves before you in this matter. If we are thrown into the blazing furnace, the God we serve is able to save us from it, and he will rescue us from your hand, O king. But even if He does not, we want you to know, O king that we will not serve your gods or worship the image of gold you have set up.' "*

I placed the card inside my Bible to use as a bookmark. I went over to mom and grandma and sat down for church service. Little brother came over to show us his latest pictures that he got to color for his Bible study. The pictures were various scenes of Daniel talking to king Nebuchadnezzar and Daniel's three friends.

Soon the church service started and we sang and took offerings. I always found the beginning of the service kind of interesting because there was a children's story time where one of the grownups always told a humorous or educational story based on the Bible. But when church gets churchy and the Pastor starts talking about all sorts of things which I have no clue about, that's where I sorta get lost. I'm not being impolite or anything, but just to keep it interesting I start looking around at the old folks. My little brother is usually busy coloring in his book. Mom and grandma are sitting there with their Bibles open and are referencing along with the pastor.

Today our pastor is talking about the book of Genesis and about when God found Adam and Eve in sin. It was God who shed the blood of the first animals in sacrifice in order to cloth and hide the nakedness of Adam and Eve with the animal's skins. He referenced facts all the way through the Bible until Christ died on the cross. The pastor explained that it was the sacrificing of the animals and the shedding of their blood which cleansed the chosen people of their sins. But it was God's ultimate sacrifice that released all mankind from that situation of animal sacrifices.

His descriptions about how the people would bring their best animals and how they would have to hold on to them and transfer their sins into their favorite animal as the high priest would bleed them left me a little sick. I would surely have second thoughts about bringing my favorite pet to some guy I didn't know just to have him take it's life right there in front of me. The pastor went on to say, and as near as I could tell, asked the congregation about what they thought would be the ultimate sacrifice that anyone could give.

As I listened, I heard it said that a person's son or daughter would be the ultimate sacrifice. Hey, wait just a minute. That would be me. I looked at mom and mom was looking at me with a kind smile. If mom was being bad and needed forgiving would she give me up or my little brother? I think that she loves us too much to ever consider that. But the pastor said that is just what God did. He gave his only Son in order to save all of us in the world from sin. Wow, that must have hurt a lot. Because I know how much mom, dad and even grandma care about my brother and me.

Looking over at my little brother, he was just coloring away like nothing had been said about pets or kids or sin. To God the word sin must carry a lot of meaning in order for him to hate it so much that He would make such a huge sacrifice in order to wipe it out. You could say that sin is like polio was and what cancer is now. God is probably getting really upset with us because I see a whole bunch of things that are going on that I wouldn't be very happy about if I were him. The pastor said today that Jesus is the One who can cure all humanity from the disease of sin. Maybe I should think about talking to Jesus so that mom and dad don't stay mad at me about the camping caper.

CHAPTER 14

The Ghost, The Stick, The Car Horn and Seat

The bus to go to school was just a little late. That was normal on the first day. All the west end neighborhood kids waited at the village store under the porch roof. There were only about five of us and of course we all talked about the past summers adventures and what our new teachers would be like. Susie would throw in her boy hater comments and told us how pleased she was that all the boys got busted for doing the things they shouldn't have been doing that summer.

And Susie had to ask. "How long are you Larry and you Abe confined to your bedrooms? I saw you guys flashing signals with your goofy flashlights in some stupid code that's probably so secret even you clowns don't know what it means."

"We were flashing them on and off just for the fun of it Susie . . . it's no big deal", Abe attempted to assure her.

"Just what I was talking about", chided Susie, "Just a couple of little clowns trying hard to become big jokers. Keep trying . . . I'm sure you'll succeed.

Abe was getting upset. "If you weren't a girl Susie I would tear you apart."

Susie just stuck out her tongue.

Roger chimed in, "You know Susie it was just a month ago when you and Abe were listening to records on your front porch. What happened? Maybe it's because he's not giving you enough attention now, huh? But how can he when he's been confined to his room? It's partly your fault you know for being such a tattle tale."

Diving into the conversation I said, "Rog I never looked at it like that but you are a genius. That's it! Susie you are upset at all us guys because we took away your quality time with Abe. And you're pissed off at Abe because he went along with us and we all got into trouble. Wow! This is priceless! So, you're sorta mad at yourself too!"

Susie didn't say a word and turned all shades from pink to red.

Abe looked at us and shook his head and said, "Thanks guys for keepin her quiet but ya didn't have to throw me under the bus to do it."

Speaking of the bus . . . we could hear it rattling and squeaking as it was coming down the road. Soon it pulled up just in time before any more ill feelings were exchanged. It was an old bus and my suspicion was that it was built during the war and should have been retired years ago. But its owner and driver seemed to keep it together with "chewing gum and bailing twine" as my dad would say and he hung in there and kept it running. The bus had old vacuum windshield wipers and in the winter there wasn't much heat. There was a small circular fan that helped push some of the heat to the back of the bus. During the warmer months open windows provided the convenience of air conditioning.

Susie got on first and plopped down beside her best friend and we headed for the back as far as we could go. The older boys had territorial rights over the back seats so we ended somewhere in the middle of the bus.

Because there were so few kids and our homes were scattered across the countryside on farms and in small villages everyone rode the bus from first to twelfth grade. High school and grade school were separated but stood side by side. Grade school was first through sixth and high school seven through twelve. It was a small school district at that time. We didn't have football, just baseball, soccer, basketball, wrestling and softball for sports. It was rural farm country in the good old USA.

The first week of school flew by almost as fast as summer vacation. But I knew that was an illusion. The real school time fun hadn't even begun to bite. There wasn't much homework and we spent most of those days getting to know the teacher and adjust to his or her way of conducting class. Back then in school not much was said about corporal punishment and it was expected if you got out of line. Our teacher that year proudly displayed what he called "*The Board of Discipline*".

"*The Board of Discipline*" was a paddle that was about two and a half feet long with a handle. Holes were drilled through its body to give it less wind resistance on the way to meet the target. The target could be anyone deemed worthy enough to have their backsides meet the " Board of Discipline" in rapid succession.

The only time I really got to see "*The Board of Discipline*" in action, and by the way it was never me on the receiving end, was one time I happened to be walking out of my fifth grade classroom with a bathroom hall pass. Hearing some thwacking sounds from across the hall I saw a guy leaning over that room's teacher's desk.

Aaahh! The swishing of the air, the paddle in motion and then the meeting of the target was almost enough to bring tears to my eyes. I must have been like a deer caught in the headlights as I stood with my mouth agape watching the scene unfold. Just as the teacher was bringing the paddle down the kid who was receiving the whacking saw me and yelled out. "What do ya think you're looking at . . . JERK?"

With that being said I ran off before the teacher saw me and took me before the board. As I left the drama behind the sounds of whacking continued and followed me down the hall to the bathroom. Later that day the kid who received the discipline and caught me staring at him respectfully flipped me the high sign. It was just one of many in a long line of good old golden rule day's memories.

Then it happened. It is as clear to me today as it was back on that one Sunday night when I was preparing for school the next day. I had my clothes laid out and I was about ready to settle into reading a new comic on loan from Bob. Suddenly mom called me downstairs to the telephone. I asked who it was and mom said that it was Susie.

Upon hearing that my heart sank as you know how I feel about conversing with Susie from past events. "Maaooom", I squeaked trying to plead my case I whispered . . . "She is the last person on earth I want to talk to." "What can she possibly want with me", I asked and then reminded her that I wasn't supposed to be talking on the phone.

She gave me the look and stated, "I think it's important."

There mom stood with one hand on her hip, her other elbow rested on the other hip, holding the receiver in the palm of her hand out to me and just shrugged her shoulders and suggested, "Why not just say hellooo?"

So I did . . . "Hellooo Susie . . . and what can I do for you?"

I could hear her breathing but she wasn't speaking. Then she opened up. "Sooo Larry . . . I guess you are up to your old tricks again . . . aren't you Mr. Smar-tee Pants? It's not enough you have to throw cats on my roof and make fun of me in front of all my friends. What you did last night is far beyond anything you have done before. You have insulted me and my mom and my dad. You better march up to my house . . . and right now mister . . . and apologize to my dad!"

I was stymied and first blurted out the obvious question, "What in the world are you talking about? Then I let my natural defense mechanism grip the verbal highway, "You are nuts! You are certifiably insane! I was at home all last night! You can ask my parents! Man, if you were a guy I'd . . . I don't know what I'd do, but it wouldn't be pretty!

My mom now stopped washing dishes and began tuning in to the phone conversation.

"Here Susie . . . do you want to ask my mom about where I was and what I was doing last night . . . doo ya", I asked?

"No, no, no LARRY", screamed Susie . . . "Are YOU not listening? I know YOU are lying because I personally saw YOU. It was YOU in YOUR red hooded sweatshirt and blue baseball cap that I saw running across the field trying to escape to YOUR house. It had to be you. It was your height, your cap, your sweatshirt . . . all going in your direction . . . so yeah, it was YOU, you liar . . . LIAR! I am gonna get you, you sneaky little creep. Like I said you had better come clean and apologize or it's gonna get ugly."

"Susie", I said trying to remain calm after she stopped ranting. Suspecting something was really amiss I waited.

"WHAT", she replied with a snort!

"Please don't start yelling again", I pleaded and then asked. "If we assume it was me that did whatever it was that I supposedly did last night. Shouldn't I know what it was that I did?"

Susie was quiet for a moment and then she started speaking or was it seething through what appeared to be through clenched teeth. She opened up with both barrels blazing, "Do not pretend, do not try to trick me and don't act like a clown Larry. You know it was you who put the stick between the seat and the car horn of my dad's car. He had to run out of the house in his underwear, go across the yard, where he stubbed his toe and turned his ankle on a rock and then he had to quickly hobble into the garage and release the horn. All the neighbors came out to see this going on. Think about how embarrassing this little trick of yours was for my dad . . . in his underwear LARRY . . . all the neighbors were watching LARRY. Do you get the picture? I was looking out from my upstairs window and it was YOU LARRY that I saw running across the field like your butt was on fire."

"No one else saw you, but I did . . . and I know, it was you", Susie uttered ending in a snarly, hoarse whisper.

My mom was now standing in front of me and from the look on her face she was in need of an immediate explanation or she was going to commandeer the phone. "Look Susie" I tried to explain, "My mom is now standing here in front of me and wants to use the phone."

Darla quickly continued, "It's not my folks who are asking for the apology, it is me . . . because it was me who saw you running away. I'm asking you to be a man and fess up to your dirty deed. You think about it and let me know on the bus. I not so patiently await your answer."

"Do your parents know that you are on the phone accusing me of this stuff", I asked?

She hung up the phone with a loud . . . CLICK! There was nothing now but the hum of open line noise.

"Oh yes of course", I said, "No . . . thank you Susie for that information. It was nice speaking with you too", I said speaking into the dead phone. I finished the one sided conversation with, "I hope to see you tomorrow at the bus stop too." I gently hung up the phone and smiled at mom.

Mom was standing before me, arms folded and she was holding a wet dish towel. Wet dish towels were good for whacking too. Her one foot was forward and looked like it was ready to start tapping. "Explanation now mister", was all mom had to say!

"Well, it appears there is a slight case of mistaken identity", I stammered. Suddenly dad poked his head around the corner and appeared on the scene.

"Mistaken identity", he enquired? "How so, and whose mistaken identity might we be talking about?"

"Mine", I said.

"Pray tell", urged mom? "What could it be this time? And this all coming so soon after the saga of "*The Mystery of the Cat on the Roof*" which led to the tale of, "*Local Boys Materialize at Bridg*e" . . . they really weren't there or were they? All good camp caper stuff . . . maybe we should write a book about all this someday?"

Starting out with, "Well last night", I started unpacking the story about the prankish tale of; "*The Ghost, The Stick, The Car Horn and The Seat*". "A kid was seen running away across the field behind a certain garage. Darla thinks it's me because of the red sweatshirt and the blue baseball cap the kid was wearing. It couldn't have been me! Certainly the clothing makes me look very guilty."

"Was it you", my dad asked?

"How could it have been him Ben, he was sleeping", mom said defending me.

"Come on dad, you know it wasn't me", I pleaded.

Dad then, just for a matter of fact, pointed out a few things. "You kids are known to crawl out windows in the middle of the night. And you meet to go riding around. And you peddle over to the creek to fish for a few hours and quickly make it back here before we get up for work. What do you think Larry? Do you see any reason for me to question your possible where-a-bouts?"

Thank goodness grandma wasn't here right now or this conversation would have grown wings and flew out the window.

How'd he know that I wondered? So before speaking I dismissed his prior statement and blurted out some quick kid logic, "Dad the fish aren't biting right now . . . it's too cold for mosquitoes . . . and besides my bike is put away in the barn . . . and Abe's in lock down just like me."

Dad folded his arms and concluded that it seemed like sound logic and a good solid alibi. "Do you buy that mom", he queried?

Mom now started tapping her foot and got one of those straight line smirky smiles like she smelled something fishy and then said, "I don't know Ben . . . it's sounding like the kid's hidin something."

"You'd better come clean about the story kid", she advised and cautioned me, "Before I whack you with this wet dish towel. And it's gonna hurt if I do!"

She paused, then smiled and said, "I don't think it was the kid Ben. His red sweatshirt is definitely in the wash. Oddly though for some reason, the hoodie is in need of serious repair because of a large burn hole in the sleeve and on the back? Looks like you landed in a campfire kiddo. So that lets you off the hook for now." With that said she still hit me with her wet dish towel.

"Hey! What was that for", I asked as I patted my stinging arm?

"That was for even thinking that terrible prank played on poor Mr. Ryan would be considered funny", cautioned mom, "and for ruining your new sweatshirt. Then she demanded, "I wonder how that happened?"

I was silent.

Mom gave me one more swat with the dish towel and said, "That's what I thought." She then turned and went back to her dishes and dad returned to his TV programs.

Later when I thought about it I had to admit that it was humorous even though it was underhanded and sneaky. Too bad it wasn't Susie running out there in her underwear stubbing her toe. Now that would have been priceless. Poor old Mr. Ryan didn't deserve that because he really was a nice guy and never bothered anybody. That whole family pretty much kept to themselves. Susie was actually the only odd banana out of the whole bunch and she wasn't even twelve yet. But she seemed a whole lot older. She was actually taller than any one of us guys. Go figure as they say.

The next day I was sort of put off by the whole west end crew. Even my other buddies were giving me distance like I had some contagious disease or something. For the whole week I pretty much kept to myself and thought, well if this is the way they want it, let em it have their way. They were treating me worse than a common criminal. I had been convicted before I had a proper trial.

All that week on the bus Susie kept prodding me, "You gonna come up to the house and apologize tonight? You'd better before I take care of this myself." When she asked this question just about everybody on the bus would rubber neck and strain to hear my answer. But I wasn't given her the satisfaction of an answer.

For most of the week I sat with Hilltop Rog. We talked about the summer and baseball. We discussed the approaching World Series and about whom we thought would be in it. It had to be the San Francisco Giants and of course the Yankees. Roger all of a sudden was my new best buddy. Even in school we hung out at lunch time. Not being in the same home room we still would hook up when classes changed.

Friday rolled around again and we were on our way home riding on the bus. Roger and I happened to get the front seat right next to the door. That seat was almost as cool as riding in the very back of the bus. Susie was several rows behind us and still had to pop that question. "When Larry . . . when are you gonna apologize?"

The whole bus went stone silent in anticipation of an answer. Oh, the never ending drama of this car horn and seat thing. It just wouldn't die. The entire school must be awaiting the next exciting chapter yet to be written.

Just about at the end of my rope I turned around. Foolishly I stood up and pointed my finger at Susie and nervously said, "Never SUSIE . . . ain't never, NEVER gonna happen . . . because that wasn't me. Can't you get it through your thick Susie skull? I will not apologize for something that I did not do. That's it . . . I am done! Do your worst! Yes, it was me who threw the cat but . . ." then there was a tugging at my shirt and I quickly sat down. Had I lost my mind? And it was not one second too soon upon recovery, because old Mr. Walter was glaring at me in his review mirror.

There was heard a burst of jeers, cat calls, oohhhs and aaahhs filling the air and even some applause. The bus seemed to be suddenly slowing to a stop. There were no stops out here in the Dollar Woods. It was just swamp and pine trees. The clamor in the bus quickly became deathly silent. I began to wonder. Would I be the one walking home from here today?

Mr. Walter was just like the sixth grade teacher and took fooling around as a very, very personal offense. My dad said he was a Navy pilot during World War II and he even had his own small plane and a little runway out on his farm. His tool of trade for disciplinary action was a shaving belt that was about four to five inches wide and didn't need a handle. He would simply loop it around his hand. Mr. Walter would stop the bus, grab whatever kid he deemed at the time that needed a whoopin by the scruff of their neck and went at it. He was even known to drop a kid off at any given location and make them walk the rest of the way home.

Of course we know by today's standards there would be none of these shenanigans going on. A battery of attorneys would be waiting at the home of the abused party even before they arrived back at their residence. There would be search helicopters, there would be news live at five. A follow up and news again at ten. An unending line of specialists all to put their spin on the subject matter would be called in. Then of course there would be the trial for assault and battery of the misbehaving child. Yes, we have come a long way today. Today the kids carry guns and knives and would put up with none of this.

"So Larry", Roger asked. "This whole thing that's going on between you and what's 'er name is because of that car horn thing?"

"Yeah man, it's like she's stuck think'n it was me", I went on to explain. "She thinks it's me just because the person who pulled the prank was wear'n a red hooded sweatshirt and a blue baseball cap like the ones I got. It's almost like a ghost did it. No one's fessed up to it . . . no-body! It ain't me babe I told her. Besides even though it was a really cool prank . . . I like Susie's dad, and I would have to think twice about waking him up in the middle of the night."

Roger's stop was coming up and as he started to get up to leave the bus he asked me a question. "It is a blue ball cap and a red hooded sweatshirt we are talk'n 'bout, right?"

"Yeah", I said confiming. "That's right, a blue cap and a red hoodie. You see my red sweatshirt was in the wash and in need of repair. It couldn't have been me."

"Cool . . . you see my red sweatshirt is not in the wash. And just like you . . . I happen to have a blue ball cap too", Roger stated.

So I whispered, "You mean to say that it was you that . . ."

Roger gave me a wink, a smile and quickly hopped off the bus.

When Roger left Abe moved up and sat down next to me. I wasn't talkin and then Abe spoke up, "Looks like you saw a ghost man. What's up? You haven't been talking to any of us all week. What did we do to get you upset?"

It was all I could do to remain calm as I interrogated Abe, "What's up you ask? You're askin me what's up . . . like you're takin a poll or somethun? For some reason . . . ever since this stupid Susie incident happened. All of you . . . so called good friends and neighbors have treated me like I had the plague. Ooohh, don't want to be seen with Larry. He's the rotten egg. Larry's the black sheep of the community."

"That's not how it is Lar . . . come on", pleaded Abe.

"Then tell me good friend and neighbor", I enquired. "How is it? Explain it to me. I really want to know and guess what?"

Abe asked. "What?"

"And caring about what you have to say . . . I don't give a farmers fig about that", I flatly answered.

"It just doesn't matter now. I know who did the deed and that's all that matters", I told Abe rather pompously.

Abe excitedly inquired. "No way dude . . . who?"

"For me to know and everyone else can find out for themselves", I proudly answered. "I am no rat. So everyone can stuff it as far as I am concerned."

"I'd tell em to go stuff it too", a scruffy voice said coming from the bus drivers seat.

I looked up in amazement to see old Mr. Walter staring at Abe and I in the front seat.

He noticed the questioning look on my face and continued. "I know what goes on in my bus. Don't ever think I don't. Everybody thinks I just sit up here and drive the bus. I hear and can see about everything. Got my special hearing aide turned up so I can. You're getting your tail shaved on this deal kid. Stick to your guns and story. But that's real respectful not to rat out a friend. Everyone's got to have a code of principle. Seems to be no good character left in anybody nowadays and . . . well here's your stop."

Mr. Walter threw open the door and all the kids stood up ready to file out. "Hey kid", he said as I got up and gathered my books. "Have a good weekend", and he gave me a nod.

That was the first time I can remember that Mr. Walter spoke more than two words to anybody and I felt pretty good about it. So good in fact that I just went straight home and didn't say another word to anybody. I did glance back over my shoulder at the porch of the store where Abe, Roger the dodger, Skin and even Susie were engrossed in a heavy conversation. At times they were looking in my direction and pointing. That was okay. For some reason old Mr. Walter's conversation vindicated my feelings and how I handled it. Right or wrong I was feeling pretty good right now. I was feeling kinda grown up as if I was offered an olive branch. It was cool even if it was from the hand of an old guy like Mr. Walter. Everything was going to be just fine, including me.

As soon as I got home I went up to my bedroom. I put my books away and changed cloths. Looking at my mirror I noticed a note hanging there and it had some scripture written on it. It was from grandma. She was always thinking about everybody else. Grandma magically seemed to know what was going on and also knew how to fix what was going wrong.

While sitting on the bed I began to read the scripture to myself. Today it seemed like it was old folk's day. First, it was the bus driver old Mr. Walter who never said a word to anybody. He talked to me and gave me some advice. And now here was a note from grandma.

Psalm (*NIV*) 35: 20-27

They do not speak peaceably
but devise false accusations
against those who live quietly in the land

They gape at me and say, "Aha! Aha!
With our own eyes we have seen it."

O Lord, you have seen this; be not silent.
Do not be far from me, O Lord.
Awake, and rise to my defense!
Contend for me, my God and Lord.

Vindicate me in your righteousness, O Lord my God;
*   do not let them gloat over me.*
Do not let them think, "Aha, just what we wanted!"
*   or say, "We have swallowed him up."*

May all who gloat over my distress
*   be put to shame and confusion;*
may all who exalt themselves over me
*   be clothed with shame and disgrace.*
May those who delight in my vindication
*   shout for joy and gladness;*
may they always say, "The Lord be exalted,
*   who delights in the well-being of his servant."*

Wow! Those are pretty strong words for such a little guy like me to hold on to. But I got the message of what they were talking about. Sounds like those words came from someone who was in distress. Like mom says, "You got to stop worrying. Let the things you can't do anything about in God's hands." Maybe old folks are just a lot closer to God than us kids. Maybe that's how come they know so much. Gotta put that on my research list along with about how they can sleep in church with their eyes wide open.

CHAPTER 15

Bible Study Time

After dinner Friday night grandma said she wanted to talk to me about Bible study. I was starting the study next week on Wednesday evening with our Pastor. Upon entering grandma's room she already had her big Bible ready. It was lying open on the reading stand in front of her. She had many different books on the shelves in her bedroom.

There weren't any comic books though. I figured she would at least have had a whole series of Nancy Drew mystery novels in her collection. There were none of those either. Got to wonder how she keeps herself entertained. Grandma still reads a lot even though her eyes are giving her problems. She said that her vision is unclear and her eyes are easily tired by the small print. Aha! I'll guess that's why she likes her big Bible and why she has a magnifying glass.

Grandma looked up and smiled. "Hey there young fella . . . come in", she said. "Take a seat right here." Her hand invitingly patted the sofa beside her.

Sitting down I saw she also had her magnifying glass ready and on the table, a pencil, note tablet and a cup of hot tea on the end table. She was prepared. It looks like grandma is going to start a Bible study with me right here and now.

Grandma started out. "You know every time you come in here your eyes are inquiring about all my books. And I'll presume you are wondering . . . what they are all about, aren't you?"

"I guess", I said and then asked. "At least I wonder about what kind of books they are? There are so many . . . have you read all of them?"

"Why yes I have", answered Grandma. "I left many favorites behind when I moved into this little room. I probably had four times as many as you see here."

"Wow", I exclaimed and asked. "How'd you find the time?"

"You make time for things that are important", grandma explained. "Knowledge is power. You can only get that from reading. But more important is the understanding of what you are reading and understanding requires study. Many times you can simply read something. But until that magic light comes on by studying what you read you may not ever grasp the meaning."

"Sounds like a whole lot of work", I commented.

"Anything worthwhile is worth doing right", said grandma emphasizing her point by making a fist. "There are no short cuts to knowledge", grandma cautioned. "You have to put in the time. Effort in equal's the quality of the result you are trying to achieve. No good effort in . . . no good results come out."

"Oh", I said. "I guess I understand. I think it is why my teacher in school gets real upset when someone doesn't finish their homework. It seems like I am always doing more and more homework as I go up in grades. Doesn't it get easier? When will I learn all I need to know?"

My grandma just laughed and said. "Boy you will never stop learning. Why do you think I enjoy reading so much?"

"Maybe you like reading your books like I have fun reading my comic books and mystery stories", I stated, "It's just fun! And I am excited to find out about what happens next!"

"Finding out about what happens next is exactly the point", assured grandma. "Every time you discover something new it opens the door to understanding ever wider. Learning turns every sentence into a new day. Are you ready to begin a new journey?"

"About what you just said grandma . . . I am not totally sure", I wondered but then agreed. "Of course, I am with you."

"Great!" Grandma smiled and said, "Then it's unanimous. We two are a committee of one, committed to sailing toward far horizons and new adventures of understanding. Let's begin!"

Smiling all the while, I had thoughts about what mom always says; "*go along just to get along*".

Grandma patted my knee to get my attention and asked, "Did you know there are sixty six books in the Bible?"

"Really", I said. "I thought it was just one big book with a whole bunch of chapters and tales about people from way back when. From what I understand the stories are about special people. Some of them talk to God. Some of them are bad and mess up. God sometimes forgives them and sometimes bad things happen too."

"That's right Larry", grandma said and then went on to explain more. "There are also songs and poems in the Bible. And like you said, stories that tell about things which happened a long time ago. Some of the stories relate to things that will happen in the future. Like I told you kids around the camp fire. The Bible and the information in it are Holy Writings and they are a roadmap to life.

The Holy Book tells us what God has planned for us. It shows by example how we should live. The Bible tells what is wrong in our lives and how to correct those faults and live right. If you do something wrong you can find that somewhere someone in the Bible probably did the same thing. It also shows how God helped that person to correct themselves. The Bible will explain what punishments were handed out by God. It will also show His blessings for doing right as well".

After listening to what grandma was saying I made an observation. "If I understand what you are saying grandma there are a lot of rules to follow. For instance, mom and dad have many rules. I think mom has more rules than dad. But dad seems to deliver the punishment. Mom and you always say; just wait till your dad gets home and hears about this!"

Going on I further explained to grandma that my teacher had rules too. "He hands out warnings on paper like traffic tickets", I tried to explain. "When you get three you're out and you go to visit Mr. Bixby the principal. I learned how to spell principal and principle by remembering that principal was your pal. But when you go to see Mr. Bixby holding three tickets in your hand he is definitely not going to be your pal."

"Okay", said grandma. "I can see that he wouldn't be at that time. But I am sure that at other times he's probably a very nice man."

"Yeah", I agreed. "Other times he does seem like a nice guy . . . he smiles a lot."

Grandma then pointed out. "It is true that God hates sin. He loves a sinner like I said but He hates sin. We can see God is smiling too. Just look all around us. You see the bright sunshine and the flowers and hear the songs of birds. He made us in his own character like image. Yes, and as you know there are rules. They are God's Holy Laws."

"You mean the Ten Commandments", I said guessing.

"Yes", agreed grandma, "The Ten Commandments. And there are others too which I believe to be natural laws or the natural order of things."

"Like what", I asked?

"Well for one there is the law of gravity" grandma explained, dropping a pencil on my head.

"Come on grandma, surely everybody knows that", I said assumingly.

"Now they do", grandma pointed out. "But gravity wasn't discovered until Sir Isaac Newton observed it and asked why does everything that is up there come down here? He didn't ask that until an apple fell from a tree and hit him on the head. And when that falling apple smacked him on his noggin a light turned on in his brain which made him think, "Hey wake up, something happened here that everyone needs to know about". God has to smack us all on the noggin at one time or another just to wake us up."

What grandma was just talking about reminded me of something I did and so I felt that I had to tell her about it. "When thinking about what you just said grandma I can remember times when I thought God tapped me on the head too. I've done some goofy things and have had to ask myself; what was I thinkin . . . or not?"

I told grandma about when I had taught myself how to make gunpowder with the chemistry set that I got for my birthday. But that was back when I was a lot younger I assured grandma. I think I was only ten at the time.

Well I mixed up the ingredients of salt peter, sugar and charcoal and put a match to it, but it wouldn't light to good and only produced a little bit of smoke. The mixture was probably a little damp from being in the basement. So I thought about my model rockets. They have engines. The engines normally ignite by a thin copper wire heated by a battery. I took one apart and ground it up. When I added it to my other mixture and put a match to it. *Ka-Poof*! There was a flash and smoke everywhere.

"After my spankin grandma", I said . . . "That big question came to mind . . . boy, what was I thinkin? At that time it wasn't God tappin me on the head but rather dad tappin me on my backside. Dad was pretty sore at me. Mom was furious and told me that I could have blown myself up, the house and everybody in it by being so dumb. I guess you weren't around all the time back then grandma."

"I guess not", said grandma. "I surely would have remembered that. You could say that was a wakeup call from God about what not to do. The blessing was that no one was hurt and you found out about what you shouldn't be doing. It was a lesson learned."

"That's for sure", I agreed. "The *Ka-Poof* singed my eyebrows and hair and knocked me to the floor. My face was black from the smoke. Dad made me forget all about those things. For a whole week when I sat down my backside remembered the do and don'ts conversation."

"Yes well, I suppose if that was all that got hurt you were very fortunate", grandma stated. Grandma smiled and continued her lesson. "Now getting back to some other natural laws; we know that the sun comes up in the morning and that rain is essential to life and the natural order of things pretty much runs in a cycle. But the most important of all the laws on earth are God's Moral Laws; "The Ten Commandments". Through these Ten Commandments is built our relationship with God. Important also is how we are to treat our fellow human beings."

"Grandma, out of all the Commandments which ones are the most important", I asked?

"You know Larry Jesus was asked that very same question", grandma pointed out, "And that happened as He was approached by the Pharisees when they tried to trick Him. Let me show you right here in Matthew 22:34 - 40 (NIV) Grandma went to her big Bible and turned to the book of Matthew. We read the passages together:

34 Hearing that Jesus had silenced the Sadducees, the Pharisees got together.
35 One of them, an expert in the law, tested him with this question:
36 "Teacher, which is the greatest commandment in the law?"
37 Jesus replied: "Love the Lord your God with all your heart and with all your soul and with all your' mind.
38 This is the first and greatest commandment.
39 And the second is like it: Love your neighbor as yourself.
40 All the law and the Prophets hang on these two commandments."

"Grandma you said that the Sadducees and the Pharisees were trying to trick Jesus. Why would they be trying to do that if Jesus was the Son of God", I asked?

"We should stick to going over the Commandments. Maybe that is a question that would be better answered by Reverend Wright", grandma stated?

She then told me, "I'll just say, that so many times God sent his messengers to His chosen people the Israelites and they rejected all of them.

They were blind to the truth and could not see. Even with all the proof that Jesus offered to them with scripture and miracles they just couldn't grasp it. So it happened; just like they rejected all the rest, the Israelites also rejected Jesus. But this time they killed the only begotten Son of God, the Lord of all, Jesus the Christ."

"That is terrible to think about", I sadly said.

"There's so much more that goes along with this story", grandma assured. "But let's keep it simple for now. Let's just say that Jesus died for us and He is risen and He is right here with us tonight as we discuss His Word. Remember that in Matthew 18:20 (NIV) it reads: "For where two or three come together in my name, there I am with them." That is a comfort isn't it?"

I looked around the room and made a funny face as I said, "A-ha that is what we talked about before, the Holy Spirit. Grandma picked up on what I was doing and smiled.

"That is right and He is here with us in Spirit and that is what we believe. The evidence of faith is us believing in that which remains unseen." Grandma continued, "Children such as you need proper guidance because you absorb like a sponge all that surrounds you. Children are empty vessels who need to be filled with truth, love and understanding."

In 2 Corinthians 4:18 (NIV) it says: 18 *So we fix our eyes not on what is seen, but on what is unseen. For what is seen is temporary, but what is unseen is eternal.*

"Simply stated", grandma said trying to explain to me, "It means that we should not get attached to the worldly things that surround us; like fancy cars, big expensive houses and the buying of every new comic book that comes out Mr. Larry! They will leave us in the end empty and unfulfilled . . . and this life we live . . ." She made a sweeping motion with her hand and uttered, "Whhooosshh, it just fly's on by!"

She pointed at the Bible as she said, "You see Larry we need to be taught very early the things which are truly important. That's why you and I should share together all the truth that we can find in this big old book called the Bible."

Then grandma asked me; "I know we are again moving far from my intended lesson but do you want to hear what Jesus says about little children?"

Shaking my head in agreement I said, "I remember reading or seeing somewhere that he thought children were pretty important."

"Right you are", grandma agreed and added, "When the disciples were asking about who would be the most important in heaven Jesus stopped them and in Matthew 18:2-6 he answered:

2 - He called a little child and had him stand among them.

3 - And he said: "I tell you the truth, unless you change and become like little children, you will never enter the kingdom of heaven.

4 - Therefore, whoever humbles himself like this child is the greatest in the kingdom of heaven.

5 - "And whoever welcomes a little child like this in my name welcomes me.

6 – "But if anyone causes one of these little ones who believe in me to sin, it would be better for him to have a large millstone hung around his neck and to be drowned in the depths of the sea."

"Sometimes it is hard for me to understand what is being said", I told grandma.

She smiled and said, "Let me see if I can help you. Let's pick out a few words. First there is *change* and then there is *humble*. Jesus was speaking to adults who were wondering who would be the most important in heaven right?"

I agreed.

Grandma continued, "Jesus told the disciples that they had to become like children. Children are accepting what adults tell them because they are learning. Children are humble and believing because they look up to adults for information that they can use to grow.

Many adults think they have already learned enough and are set in their ways. They sometimes refuse to accept things other than what they believe to be the truth. Adults are unwilling to bend in their beliefs. Adults have attitudes like: okay, go ahead and prove it to me . . . show me . . . I won't believe it until I see it."

Thinking for a second I then blurted out, "I think I get what you are saying grandma! Back when we were talking about those groups of guys who were trying to trick Jesus . . . we saw that even with all those miracles that Jesus did . . . they still wouldn't accept Him."

"Good thinking", grandma said. "The Pharisees and Sadducees were too prideful to believe that someone else who walked on the earth had a better understanding of the scriptures and was greater in deeds than them. The priests didn't realize that it was the Son of God who was speaking to them. They felt that they were in charge. When it was pointed out that they had been wrong in the way they were influencing all who were in there spiritual care they became offended. There in verse six Jesus clearly cautions those who would try to wrongly influence those who are living in the Word and cause them to sin. Doing that would mean certain spiritual death for anyone."

"Grandma how about *welcome*", I asked. "I pointed to the verse that had the word welcome in it. What do you think that means?"

"That's a good eye Larry", grandma said approvingly. "Yes we sort of skimmed over that", agreed grandma.

She then stated, "I believe that we are all as children when we accept Jesus as Lord and Savior. As we begin our walk with Him it does not matter how old we are. We begin to walk with him step by step learning by faith, being in the Holy Spirit.

We should welcome our brothers and sisters and help them and cause them not to stumble. But if we do make them stray from His grace it will be upon our heads. It will be our fault. This goes especially for you little ones who have no great defense against knowing right from wrong.

That's why when anyone delivers a message to another we must always pray and ask that it not be by our word but we must ask that it be God's Word that we speak delivered by the Holy Spirit."

"Sounds like a warning", I concluded. "I understand now why you always begin our study asking for the Holy Spirit to be speaking through you."

"Exactly Larry and yes it is a warning", said grandma. "There are many warnings throughout the Bible. Just as I said before the Bible is a roadmap. All roads have twists and turns and they also have stop signs too. What are you supposed to do when you see a stop sign?"

"Stop of course", I said.

"What happens when you get caught going through a stop sign", grandma asked me?

"Just like in school you are written up. But in school after three tickets you get to see your pal", I said laughing about my little pun. "But I think this seems a little more serious."

"It is", grandma said cautioning me. "It is much more serious. After knowing what you should be doing spiritually it is a lot more serious. Those who don't know won't be brought to task because they were not aware. Those who know better are written into the book of life and are tried for their sins. So the more you learn and the more you know, the more responsibility you have for yourself and the human race that surrounds you. Our business is humankind Larry."

"There is so much to learn here, my head is spinning and I think I am getting tired", I said complaining.

"So right you are", said grandma trying to comfort me. "It is too much at times for one little boy to handle. I don't expect you to hold and remember everything all at once. We are like gardeners planting seeds in the form of ideas." Grandma pointed to her head and then to her heart as she told me, "Right here is where we want those seeds to sprout and bear fruit."

"You want my head to grow into a bean stalk", I asked smiling?

Grandma laughed and said "You have a good sense of humor too. That will carry you a long way because you can look at the bright side of life. I hope you treasure it and keep it."

We said a prayer together and we said good night. My brain seemed to be on overload and when I got to my room I gazed at my bookshelves. There they all were, my comics, The Hardy Boys books, the UFO magazines, the posters of Roger Maris and Mickey Mantle. There was even a Ted Williams photo and a Babe Ruth too. After getting ready for bed I hit the light switch, plopped into bed and went sound to sleep.

CHAPTER 16

Surprise! Surprise!

Breakfast time on the day we go to church is more chaotic than a school day. Dad has already gone off to work at his usual time of 4:00 am so he never gets involved in this situation. But the rest of the household for some reason becomes like rush hour in New York City. Now only being twelve and a country boy I had not ever experienced up to this point in my life, rush hour in N. Y. C. except on TV. Watching this occurrence on TV seems like there are too many people, going too many places and all have too many problems and there are not enough taxis to go around.

So you might wonder; is that really what our house is like? Maybe it is not that bad. It just seems that way. Grandma is in a rush to have breakfast made and have everyone eat at the same time and on time so she can clean up before we leave for church. No one is ready for breakfast when she has it prepared and that makes her grumpy. Mom is trying to get my brother dressed and he is not co-operating. Grandma points out that the church bell is ringing. Apparently I am taking too much time in the bathroom. And there is my brother who is half dressed and banging on the door because he has to use the toilet. There is only one small bathroom in our house. Mom is becoming agitated. Grandma calls upstairs telling us that we should come and get it or she will throw it out.

"Larry you open this door right now", my mother demanded! "Your brother has to go! If you don't open the door in five seconds or less, you will not be alive to see the sun go down", she threatened as a matter of fact!

"Okay mom", I yelled swiping the comb one last time through my hair! "My hand quickly lifted the latch to the bathroom door and I walked out."

Little brother ran into me and then went into the bathroom. I ran into mom as she stood right in my path. Both her hands were on her hips. "Listen up mister", she said, menacingly pointing her finger in my direction. "It only took the good Lord six days to create the whole universe and it seems that it takes years for you to recreate your image such as it is. What's up with that? Explain yourself?"

"Well mom as you know there's only one bathroom in our house", I explained giving the best kid rational possible. "The Cee family . . . you know have two bathrooms. Otherwise Abe's brother Snail would have been dead a long time ago because he takes forever. Forever . . . that's a lot longer than a year mom. So you have to cut me a little slack. I am getting older. And the older you get the more time it takes to get in shape. That's what grandma told me. She says it takes her much more time to get dressed and do her hair. That's all just because she is getting older. It takes her longer now to get herself back into shape . . . to even get out of her room in the morning. Yup, that's what she says."

"Hmmm, I see", mom pondered for a second then suggested. "So what you're proposing is because you are getting older you need more prep time. My recommendation is that you wake up about one half hour earlier every morning. That way you can accomplish this miraculous feat. There is no need for you to inconvenience the rest of the people in the house because you feel the need to take extra time in the bathroom . . . got it, kiddo!"

Offering out my hand I said, "That'll be a deal we can seal."

Mom looked at me suspiciously and said. "We will have to see about this", and then finally and reluctantly shook my hand.

Running off I quickly went to see what was cooking downstairs. Grandma turned around just in time to see me sliding into my chair in front of the table.

"You are the first", she asked surprised? "How can this be? Usually your mom is yelling up the stairs threatening you with more in house detention. Are you not, or shouldn't you be up to more than a month now?"

"Won't be out of the house until the first real snowfall at this rate", I surmised to Grandma.

Grandma added . . . "You know I remember the time . . ."

Cutting her off in mid-sentence I said, "Grandpa B already told me about the ice storm in July. But it's after July now."

"What I was going to say young Larry", grandma continued showing her frustration that I stifled her speech, "Is that I remember it snowed over two feet one time just before thanksgiving. That's right! Over two feet of snow fell the day before Thanksgiving. People couldn't get anywhere for a week after that with the wind drifting the snow and closing roads everywhere."

"Cool! I wish that would happen tonight so we wouldn't have school for a week", I reveled.

"You would just have to make it up next June when you would be just waiting to get on with summer vacation", grandma asserted.

"Yeah, I hear ya", I said. "A kid can never get a break. It's like we kids have to pay for everything in the end. Doesn't ever get any easier huh, grandma", I asked?

"No, no and no, it definitely does not get any easier", grandma assured me.

Grandma continued setting the breakfast on the table and mom and my little brother came down the steps and sat down.

Mom told my little brother to say a prayer before we ate.

Scott started to pray; "God is great, God is good and we thank him for our food. Please God help Larry in the bathroom so mom doesn't put him in jail. Amen"

Everyone said an Amen and then mom turned to Scott and asked, "What makes you think I'm going to put Larry in jail?"

Out of the mouths of that little babe came; "Well I heard Larry talking to Abe . . . on the phone . . . before school. He told Abe that jail time was addin up. He said he wouldn't be out before Christmas. That made me sad. I don't want Larry to miss-out Christmas."

My good mood was sinking because one of the rules of the camp caper confinement was . . . absolutely no phone. On that particular day mom had gone to work and grandma was outside hanging laundry on the clothes line. I figured I could sneak a call in before we were to walk up to the bus stop. I can't remember what was so urgent that I needed to call Abe right then and there. Looking back I am sure that the conversation could have waited until I met him at the bus stop . . . but nnooo . . . dummy me . . . I had to pick up the phone without thinking. Now here I sit awaiting trial for my action.

There appeared this really funny smile on mom's face. I had never seen this one. And she had many different kinds of smiles. I think it was this certain smile combined with something that was flashing in her eyes that scared me.

Staring not at me but instead into the steaming dish full of scrambled eggs I could tell that something was going on. Even grandma was silent and she was looking curiously at mom waiting for the next word to be spoken at our morning breakfast table.

"Mom, may I have some scrambled eggs?" It was my little brother who broke the silence just as if there were nothing wrong.

Suddenly mom's demeanor changed as if a light switch had been pushed and she said, "Why of course you may sweetie", and mom reached for the eggs like nothing had happened.

Looking up and over at grandma I noticed that her attitude hadn't changed. But I wasn't saying anything and hopefully would navigate through breakfast unscathed. Scrambled eggs were passed to me along with toast and butter. Nothing more was mentioned about the phone call and soon breakfast was over and we were on our way to church. It was the silence that was more nerving than if something had been said.

Outside a gun metal grey sky surrounded us. A slight drizzle was falling and there was a chill in the air as we walked up the road leading to the church. Grandma had the foresight to make the call that umbrellas would be needed for the short walk. Leaves on the trees hung on for their lives as the wind picked up and rustled them about. Too the leaves color seemed to be changing. There was a hint of yellow and a burst of orange here and there as the autumn season began to paint the landscape.

We walked up the hill and approached the small church. I noticed none of the congregation was gathered and chatting outside this morning. The weather wasn't permitting any loitering today. All in attendance were inside waiting to be called to class. The Cee family's Chevrolet was parked in the parking lot, so Abe was inside and Susie's parent's car was there too.

Our church was an old country church and came complete with creaky wood floors. The pews were solid oak and it was hard to stay seated for any great length of time. There were no padded seats. If needed, you could bring your own cushion for extra long sermons.

For air conditioning in the summertime we would just push up the windows to let the breeze blow in if we were fortunate to have a breeze that day. In the winter the church custodian would stoke the fire in the old coal furnace in the basement. As the heat came up the old furnace made banging and clanking noises as the metal expanded and contracted. Hot air was forced through floor vents and that provided the heat for the whole church.

There was no running water at the church so there was never danger of pipes freezing during the winter. I'll bet you are wondering where and how you would go to the bathroom if you had to during church services. Not to worry, you can rewind to a prior chapter where grandma explained the convenience of outside plumbing.

From when I could first remember there had always been light green plaster walls and there was not much that was fancy about our little church. It served a practical purpose and that was as it should be; practical and purposeful. I think that's how Christ always wanted his followers to be in the most simplistic form; practical and purposeful teachers of the faith.

Upon approaching the front door to the church Abe's dad opened it welcoming us inside. "Quick get in here before you catch cold", Mr. Cee urged, "It's warm and comfortable in the sanctuary."

The old country church had a quant ambiance all its' own; the smells, the creaky wooden floor, green painted plaster walls, the rusty old grumbling furnace and the small double hung windows. More importantly there are the memories of the people who were in attendance.

When we entered the small foyer we shook the rain from the umbrellas and the chill from our bones. I pushed open the double entry door and people were sitting about catching up on the past week's news.

Walking past one conversation I could hear a lady telling her friend about a huge pumpkin that one of the local farmers grew. "Surely it will win first prize at the fair as it is well over five hundred pounds" she claimed.

Another story caught my ear. One man was telling another about a problem, "It has to be a fox or a raccoon getting into my chicken house at night! Just about more times than not when I go into feed in the morning there are feathers everywhere and I am missing one if not two of my best hens. I can't understand how a critter is getting in. Guess I'll have to stay up at night with my double barrel and catch whatever it is in the act."

Then a familiar voice halted my eavesdropping. It was Abe motioning me over to where we were to have Bible class. "Over here! I got something important to tell ya", he yelled!

Thinking to myself I wondered. No what could be more important than an overgrown pumpkin or chicken thieves?

Weaving my way through the pews I saw our teacher Luella was also headed for the Bible study area as well. When I got over to Abe he had this great big grin on his face as he said, "I just thought I'd tell you that Susie wants to talk to you. Yeah, I think she wants to apologize!"

"Oh gee wizz Abe, say that is fabulous news", I said sarcastically with a frown and then continued with disdain, "I was listening to some much better news from Fred the farmer and Aunt Fanny what's her name about pumpkins and chickens. Why would I want to even listen to what that twit has to say? Huh, so tell me . . . why would I?"

"Like I said man, she wants to apologize to you", Abe proudly said with a smile. "Susie really means to apologize for all the things that she said about you and . . ."

"And what . . . by apologizing that's supposed to clear her for all the nasty things she has said about me", I asked? "In doing so it is just going to make her feel better . . . so she doesn't feel so guilty?"

I suspiciously eyed Abe and folded my arms over my chest. "Hmmm, I don't think so. Forgiving comes at a much higher price than . . . oh gee, I guess I'll just say I'm sorry so I can feel better . . . oh boo hoo! Why didn't she just come to me herself I wonder?"

Abe quietly said to me, "I guess she thought it might be easier if I told you about her idea first to see how you would react. I know now how you feel and I guess you're still pretty sore."

"Almost Abe . . . and just almost", I told Abe, "I had forgotten about all that stuff. At least it is out of sight and out of mind until I see her twitty face. That's just about every day on the bus and in school. When I see her it's like reminding me that I still got a lump of cold wet sand in my shorts."

Elbowing me Abe said, "Here she comes and here comes my mom too to start Bible study. Let's just sit down and pretend like we never talked about this."

Giving Abe a side long oh yeah look I plopped down on the pew.

Susie passed behind us and made a point to say, "Hi Larry. And then she purposely asked louder than needed, "How are you guys today?" She ran her hand along the back of the pew behind my head?

Feeling the coy cold play in motion I was ready to charge. Abe elbowed me again in the ribs and said, "Just be cool there tiger."

Luella had arrived and was standing in front of us. Looking at Abe and me she asked, "What are you two up to? I see the wheels turning. But never mind, no need to answer."

As Luella addressed the class she let it be known that today there would be a change in procedure, "I thought today I would not go with the normal study plan. Instead . . . because of things that have come to my attention, we will be discussing human events close to home . . . things that bother or affect each of us personally. I will be asking for class participation and I will be more like a director today than a teacher. You will be informing me so to speak, about how far you have come as individuals this summer and how you have applied things you learned in class to your daily lives."

Wondering to myself I thought, what's up with this? I had, upon insistence from grandma, cracked open the lesson book. The rest of the class was a little bewildered too, but some had smiles. It was probably because they hadn't studied and they figured this would be a pleasant break from the routine.

"Today class with the start of school and with summer being over", Luella said and alluded that she believed many of us had anxieties. "I will try to make that plainer as we go along", she explained. "I know that when going into a new situation there are many concerns about the unknown and there are things that frighten us."

Russ the kid that is always quiet put up his hand.

"Yes Russ, would you like to say something", Luella asked?

"Everyone here knows I am the kid that always gets picked on", Russ began saying. "I know what it's like to be afraid and wondering who is gonna say something next? Either it's about my weight or my red hair. This year is even worse cause I'm going into the seventh grade. Now I am just outta the middle school and going into the junior high school. I am with everybody who was always picking on me and then some. Talk about worries and I've got 'em."

"Don't worry Russ", spoke up Butch, "You're in my class man and anybody picks on you just say the word. Both of my brothers are in tenth and eleventh grades and they'll take care of anybody I tell 'em to."

"I think we are back to a prior conversation that we had several weeks ago", observed Luella. "How about to those who do you wrong . . . how about instead of revenge . . . we learn to forgive?"

Butch immediately brought his hand back up and said, "You must be joking Mrs. Cee . . . forgive those creeps who call you names and make fun of you? I remember Russ's speech from last week but I bet if you ask him to think about forgiving them he couldn't do it. I say get the wrecking crew and have at them with some bats and pliers . . . beat them to the punch."

"What do you say Russ", Luella asked?

"Forgive them . . . if it was that easy to stop someone from doing wrong to you I would be all for it", Russ said thoughtfully and then asked, "Wouldn't that show a sign of weakness on my part?"

He then went on to explain . . . "What I mean is if I went up to those clowns and said, *okay guys you've had your fun, ha, ha! Now I forgive you for calling me big fat red, red and chubby and all those other names. They would just laugh and say, good now we're gonna beat the snot out of you to see if you can forgive us for that too.*

There's a lot of pressure in school Mrs. Cee. I don't know if you totally understand. But you must also see, I know where you are coming from. I know what the Bible says about turning the other cheek. I also know too, that because some of us are a little odd . . . people look at us different. I know I am overweight. Yeah, I was born with red hair and I am a freckle face. I accept that and I also accept that other kids sometimes pick on me. I guess even when someone picks on me I silently forgive them because I know how they look at me. I just laugh and go along with it."

Butch sat there with his arms folded and didn't say a word but then he uttered, "Wow man, you are bigger than me! I don't mean that physically, yeah you are bigger, but you are bigger in the sense of how you think. I'd have to start clobbering people. That's just how I am but maybe I can try to look at things a little different. At least I hope I can. Maybe then I wouldn't be visiting the Principals office so much."

Luella suggested, "Let's open our Bibles to see what Jesus says about forgiveness in Luke 18:21-22." She read the passages for us.

21 - Then Peter came to Jesus and asked, "Lord, how many times shall I forgive my brother when he sins against me? Up to seven times?"

22 – Jesus answered, "I tell you, not seven times, but seventy-seven times."

"Now class" said Luella, "I will tell you about the parable that Jesus told to his disciples about the unforgiving debtor. I will condense or paraphrase and tell you how the kingdom of heaven is like a king who wanted to settle accounts with all his servants. One servant owed the king so much money that he begged the king for mercy. The king felt so bad that he forgave the servant all his debt.

When this same servant whom the king had forgiven was approached by a fellow servant to forgive his debt to him he threw his fellow servant in jail for non-payment. When the king was told by his other servants that the servant he forgave did not pass forward the kindness he was shown he was outraged.

He called in the wicked servant and said to him; I canceled all of your debt because you begged me to. Should you not have shown mercy to your fellow servant just as I had on you? He turned the wicked man into the jailers and had him tortured until he should pay back all he owed. Jesus, in Luke 18:35 said speaking to his disciples, "*This is how my heavenly Father will treat each of you unless you forgive your brother from your heart.*"

Luella continued by asking the class a question. "How can we apply this to our daily lives? And how do we understand from this parable what we should do as far as forgiveness to others is concerned?"

Susie who had been uncommonly quiet raised her hand.

Luella recognized Susie. "Yes Susie, what are your thoughts about this parable?"

"When kindness is shown to us we should also be kind to others" Susie said. "But when Jesus talks about his Father he is warning us that if we don't follow His teachings bad things can happen to us later."

"Has anyone here in class ever been forgiven for anything they have done?" Luella asked this as she looked around at all of us and then pushed for a reply. "Come on you are all children and we all make mistakes. Don't be shy. Oh yes, I see my son Abe has finally put his hand up."

"So what can you add to our class discussion, Luella asked?

Starting out slowly and deliberate Abe spoke up, "Everyone knows everybody's business in this village and everybody knows about our camp out problem. I guess my point is that we had to do some asking for forgiveness for some things that we did. You all know Skin and his sister forgave us for throwing 'Fluffy' onto Susie's roof. But there's something that I think should be brought out here and I might have to eat some real crow for bringing it up. But I don't care."

Our Bible class teacher suddenly got one of those quirky mom smiles on her face. I remembered about the conversation Abe and I had before class. This cannot be. Does the term set-up come to mind? I realized what Abe was about to say and I was ready to jab him in the ribs or better yet smack him upside his big idea head.

But before I had the chance to physically drag young Abe outside my vengeful heart was interrupted as Luella asked. "What point are you trying to make Abe?"

Abe went for it as he asked. "What about when someone accuses someone else for no good reason?"

"What do you mean for no good reason", our teacher asked?

Trying to explain the best he could Abe brought up the cop show Dragnet. "Like . . . well for instance even on Dragnet it says that all are innocent until proven guilty in a court of law. People shouldn't just blame someone before knowing if it's true or not . . . even if at first it looks like they did something wrong. This makes a guy look pretty dumb and causes a lot of problems all around."

Questioning her son, Luella asked him what he was talking about. "Is it something you did?"

Feeling pretty uncomfortable I glanced down towards where Susie was seated. She was just staring at the back of the pew in front of her. I was feeling bad for her. Why should I be feeling this way? It wasn't me who caused all these bad feelings by flying off with a big mouth saying things that weren't true. This was the stick, the car horn and the seat incident revisited, oh boy. I folded my arms and prepared for the worst.

Not watching Susie I hadn't noticed that she raised her hand until I heard Luella speak her name. "Susie, do you have something to say?"

Still not sure even to this very day but it seemed like all the conversations in church ceased at that very moment. It was like the whole world came to a sudden stop to hear the next words that would be spoken by this twelve year old girl. I just kept my mouth shut and my eyes focused on the hymnal in the rack in front of me.

"Larry . . . Larry I would like to say something to you" said Susie.

Luella called my attention to what Susie was saying. "Larry I think Susie has something to say and it would be polite of you to look at her when she is speaking."

As I looked up I noticed now that Susie was standing. I said, "Okay I am listening."

"Thank you Larry", said Luella. "Go ahead Susie say what you have to say."

Speaking very softly Susie began with . . . "I know this past summer we have had a few disagreements."

"To say the least", Abe mumbled with a smirk.

"Hey, let Susie say her peace uninterrupted", Luella cautioned.

"Thank you Mrs. Cee" said Susie. And then she continued, "What I am trying to say, and this is hard for me to do . . . I know I have caused some problems between some of my friends and I want to say I am sorry. I am apologizing for thinking that Larry was the one who pulled that prank on us. Although it certainly seemed like it was you Larry. I am sorry. Okay? So there I've said it."

Now that she said what she had come to say, Susie quickly turned around and sat down with a thump.

Dumbfounded I surely was and I just sat there with my arms defensively folded. It was easier to not like Susie. She was always being nosey, squeaky voiced Susie. Now this . . . I was on the spot and I had to say something. All eyes were watching and all the class was waiting for me to say . . . apology accepted and I forgive you. That was the next correct line in this little play. Maybe it's just easier playing the bad guy.

On TV the bad guys appear more interesting even though you want the good guy to win. Like James Cagney when he said, "Look at me ma, I'm on top of the world!" Of course he says that while making his last stand from the top of a huge tank of gas at an oil refinery. Top of the world ma and then boom . . . he along with the tank of gas leave the planet forever. Not too smart . . .

"Isn't that great class", said Luella? "It fits perfectly into what we are discussing. Forgiveness is a wonderful thing. Larry I am sure that it makes you feel good to know that you are no longer considered the bad guy in this case." Luella laughed and then stated, "We all as kids do some goofy things . . . don't we? My son Abe sitting right here is a living testimony to that fact. I must also add that we as grownups act a little bit like children at times too."

Appearing chagrined Abe salutes his mother and says, "Thanks for including me in the lesson study . . . again."

We all laughed and then our teacher focused on me and asked, "What do you think Larry? Do you have something to say to Susie?"

Looking over I saw Susie was again staring at the back of the pew. I was really nervous but I finally managed to stammer out, "Well Susie it was nice of you to admit you were wrong."

Susie then looked at me and gave me a little smirk of a smile but didn't say a word.

Continuing with my one sided conversation I added, "And I hope that we don't have any more disagreements. But you know that we usually don't agree on anything", I rambled on. "I can say the sky is blue and it's a bright sunshiny day. You will say, but it feels like rain."

"And what else", Susie asked?

"Oh, I don't know", I said nervously as the words were stubborn and they just didn't want to come out. " . . . I just don't know . . . what do you think", I said looking at Abe?

"You should accept and forgive to get this over with", Abe advised.

My grandmother got up from her seat and she was headed in our direction and I started feeling guilty. She couldn't have heard all of this. So I calmly but quickly said with a smile, "Susie I accept your apology and forgive you for being . . . well for being the way you are sometimes".

Susie looked at me, returned a smug smile and said, "Thank you Larry, I know that took a lot of thinking on your part . . . and I know how hard that must have been for you. But anyway, thank you for at least saying that you forgive me."

"Yes okay, now don't we all feel better for sharing that", asked Luella?

Russ raised his hand and Luella asked him, "What do you want to add?"

"That was a great show but it lacked truth", observed Russ. "From their attitudes . . . if I was their parents I would have to have a serious talk with both of them."

"Susie I need to point something out to you", said Russ, and he quoted from his Bible, "In Exodus 20:16 it says here, *You shall not give false testimony against your neighbor.*" If nobody knows, that is one of the Ten Commandments. I believe that Larry is definitely your neighbor. If you want forgiveness you should be asking for it in truth and spirit."

Continuing with his observation Russ said, "You two sounded like an old married couple arguing over none sense. Now I don't live with my parents. I live with my grandparents because my parents split up. On the holidays my parents are always arguing over who gets to see me and when and that's how it sounds.

Parents don't realize that even when they're pretending to get a long we kids still know what's going on. We know the difference between playing little polite games and the truth. You guys were polite, but I could see the underlying theme of dislike by just having to talk to each other."

Now it was my turn as Russ turned his attention towards me. Larry . . . my brother, you of course have a huge chip on your shoulder but you need to let it go dude. That chip is gonna make you lopsided. Forgive and forget man.

I want to bring up a point made by Jesus. It happened when the teachers of the law brought a women accused of committing a sin to Him. The Pharisees asked him whether they should stone her . . . Christ than said sure go ahead . . . but first guys . . . let the person among you who is without sin cast the first stone.

That stopped them dead in their tracks and made them think. Soon they all dropped their stones. One by one they slinked away until no one was left to accuse her. Christ did not condemn but forgave the woman and told her to go and sin no more.

My point is Larry, you have done some things that maybe you did or didn't mean to do. Most of them have been forgotten or forgiven. Those problems don't even come to mind anymore. Let this go, so in the future you will be treated just like you should treat Susie now.

"Red", said Luella.

"Yeah", Russ replied.

Luella went on to suggest that maybe Russ should stand up there and teach a Bible class on children's basic common sense. "What do you guys think", she asked the class?

We all felt really good about that idea and what Russ had observed. He made good sense. For the moment I didn't care how creepy Susie acted towards me in the past. Susie was smiling at me and it seemed real. When I looked at Susie she asked me again if I would forgive her and I assured her that I did and all issues were put aside. Even after class, I hate to admit it, but I gave her a hug.

Butch was slapping Russ on the back and told him he should think about becoming a Pastor. I thought that too sounded like a great plan. It seemed that Russ had a gift for taking something complicated and boiling it down so we could relate to it. Now why couldn't I do that? I just get so upset and confused with how I feel in situations that I can't view the whole picture. There will be other Susie situations, more peer pressure and other problems that will come up in my future.

Like Russ did, maybe we can all find the answers in the good book. The Bible seems to hold evidence and conclusion to every situation or combination of situations that could ever come up in a person's life. After all . . . *There's nothing new under the sun.*

As my mom says, *rules to live by.* She should know too, because mom had a lot of rules, especially when it came to my brother and me.

CHAPTER 17

The Really Big Decision

The past Bible class at church seemed to tie up many loose ends in the feelings department about what happened during the summer. Who would have thought that I could ever feel something good about Susie? It seemed like she was always picking on the guys from the neighborhood. In fact, I hadn't a clue that anybody knew it wasn't me who played that nasty car horn trick. I just went on assuming that everyone made up their mind that it was me. Sometimes things just have a way of working themselves out.

My weekly Bible study was coming along rather well and I felt good about the progress I was making. It was a great mid-week break from bedroom detention. Perhaps being sheltered away in the confines of my room is what gave me serious reading time. Looking forward to my final Bible study class coming up on Wednesday I thought I should talk to grandma and bring closure to a big decision I was about to make.

Admiring what Russ had to say in Bible class I was wondering if maybe I should learn more about what Jesus was all about. Russ had a peace that surrounded him. He seemed to forgive all those bullies who made fun of him. Plus he even forgave himself for his own shortcomings as he tried to do something about them. Something was going on with Russ and I admired that.

Grandma should be able to shine a light on these feelings because she has more experience than anyone I know. After dinner that night I asked her if we could have a meeting. She was very surprised and looked forward to talking with me.

As usual Grandma was ready and waiting in her room. Her large Bible was open. Her note pad was ready as well as her cup of tea and of course she was wearing her grandmotherly smile. "Come in", she invited and offered me a seat beside her. "So what is on your mind", she asked? "It certainly must be important for you to ask me for a meeting. Usually I have to grab you by the ear and pull you into my room."

"It has been an interesting summer", I said thinking about it.

Grandma agreed with my observation and pointed out that I packed a lot of living into a very short amount of time. "Choices", she said, "You made quite a few different kinds of choices this summer . . . some good, and some . . . maybe not so good." Then she asked, "What do you think?"

"Yeah, you're right grandma", I said. "But at the time, they seemed like good ideas."

"That's how it is when you're young", cautioned grandma. "You're sort of shooting from the hip as they say. You come up with an idea and you run with it not thinking about the outcome. It's fun at the time. But boy, sometimes the end result can just stink", grandma concluded with a laugh.

Grandma's face turned somber as she said, "I sort of envy you kids, not having to worry about much. With me, at this time, it is a blessing just to have one more day. Even now during my longest days, life appears to be too short. I am thankful for every second."

Sitting and thinking a moment about what grandma just said I had noticed sadness in her tone of voice. Impatience usurped the silent pause and I changed the subject. "You know what grandma?"

"What", grandma asked looking out from over the top of her glasses?

Always I will remember the quick change that she could manage from being what I know now as melancholy to that caring smile of hers. How she was a master of placing her feelings behind the needs of others will always be a trait to be admired.

"Aha", I blurted out. "This past week in church I saw what we were talking about happen right there in front of me . . . the Holy Spirit came. Yup, that is exactly what happened. Susie suddenly had a change of heart towards me. It was almost as if she liked me or something. Here I was thinkin all along that it was because she got a serious talkin to and a whoopin to match. Wow! I guess the Holy Spirit really is a miracle force."

"And what about you", questioned Grandma? "You had a change of heart towards Susie too didn't you?"

"Naaah, felt sorry for her is all", I said . . . "didn't want to see her get all weepy there in church so I said I'd forgive her for just being Susie."

"Hhhmmm", speculated grandma eying me suspiciously, ". . . that so? You know if you want to make a difference you have to come clean about your feelings too. You don't have to always be so macho about girls. It is okay to have feelings even if you pity them for just being Susie."

Pleading my case to grandma I told her that only if there were no other guys around would I admit to having any good feelings about girls. "So don't tell anybody", I pleaded, "especially don't tell Abe . . . and not even mom . . . okay . . . you promise?"

Grandma held up both her hands and stammered out, "Yes, of course, I give up and I promise . . . I can see you are really serious about this, so of course my lips are sealed." Grandma made a motion like she was locking her mouth with a key and then pretended to throw it over her shoulder. "Locked and thrown away", she proclaimed.

It was now Bible Study Wednesday, I made my choice. In the end I did not want to be the unwelcome guest at the banquet table, bound and thrown into a dark street. Recognizing the significance of wearing the proper attire I was ready.

If I chose to walk with God, who could possibly be against me? Choosing this course would bring consequences. After all, look around you, observe where we live. Whatever choices we make, we own them don't we?

The sun was just going down as I headed for the small country church and my final evening of Bible study. When I reached the turn in the road I heard a car pull up behind me. It was Mrs. Cee and Abe. They asked if I needed a ride and I accepted.

As I climbed into the back seat I noticed that it was a new 1962 Chevy Impala and Abe asked, "What do you think of pops new Impala? He's kinda proud about it. He said this year is the company's 50th anniversary. So he picked Chevy's new color called 'Anniversary Gold'."

"Cool", I said. "Smells new . . . sorta like that smell."

"Abe", said Luella, "There's no need to be bragging about your dad's new car. Larry can see perfectly that it is a new car."

"That's okay Mrs. Cee", I said. "Abe's just pointing out some of the facts. I think it's pretty cool. My dad gets a new Plymouth just about every year whether he needs one or not. I don't think the car can wear out in just a year, but he says he gets a better deal that way, with the low mileage trade in and all. I just like the new car smell."

"He has that old Chevy too", I rambled on in conversation, "it has a different smell. He says that's his own personal car. He takes that up into the mountains and onto the old dirt roads. Dad loads Danny and Mike, his two beagles in the trunk when he goes hunting. It kinda has an old funky dusty smell. Dad says this year I can go along hunting. I can't wait for that."

"Well, you be careful when you do that", cautioned Luella. "There are a lot of crazy men running around out there with guns blazing away at anything that moves. You don't want to get mistaken for a rabbit or squirrel."

Abe cracked up laughing and said, "Come on mom, Larry doesn't look anything like a rabbit or squirrel. Maybe he resembles a coyote or a bobcat. Besides mom I'd like to go hunting too. Dad said maybe he would take me this year."

"Hold on a minute there Mr. Abraham", said Luella. "Let me tell you, your dad has not mentioned one word about that and besides you are just a year shy being of legal age. So cool your jets on those thoughts."

Even though I was a year older than Abe I always forgot about our age difference. When you are young and in your kid world you can't wait to get older. You want those perks that come along with the passing of time . . . 12 . . . 16 . . . 18 . . . 21 . . . retirement. What are we talking about . . . retirement? Can't trust anybody over the age of twelve or is that eighteen?

We pulled into the church parking lot and it looked like we were the last ones to arrive. Abe and I got out of the car and Luella observed, "Looks like rain. I will pick you both up here in an hour. Do not even think of walking in the rain. I don't want you big tough guys catching cold."

We agreed and Abe and I slowly walked over to the door of the little white church.

"What are you gonna do", asked Abe?

"What do mean, what are you gonna do", I asked back at him?

"You know, about accepting Christ as your Savior", said Abe? "You know exactly about what I am talking about."

We stopped at the front of the church for a minute to have a little chat about what we were going to do once we went inside.

"I knew what you were asking about", I said. "But that's kinda like personal between me and Him ain't it? Yeah, I see it as being real personal Abe. I know you want to know everything. But I've been doing a whole bunch of thinkin on this. More than I have thought about anything I guess. And as I see it . . . this really is a very heavy decision dude. You can't walk down my path and I can't walk in your shoes. Each of us has to do it for ourselves."

"I mean . . . don't you feel that way too", I asked Abe?

Abe sorta looked down at the ground and kicked a few stones around. "Yeah, I guess I do", he murmured. Then he spoke candidly, "I've been thinkin too. I tried talkin to mom about it. She said something like you just said; it's up to me . . . I had to find out what it all means for myself. I've been studying the lessons. Some things I understand . . . others don't make sense. Some stories seem like fairy tales. Raising people from the dead . . . man that's a little far out. Sounds like something out of the scary movies we see on TV.

I believe that Jesus is the Son of God. I want to follow in his steps and treat people with kindness, but all that other stuff is a little over the top for me. I need to keep it simple. Look at my dad, he's an elder in the church . . . and mom, look at all she does. If I don't understand . . . who's supposed too? I have to admit, the decision . . . it's not all that easy or simple for me."

Quietly I had listened and tried to understand my friends concerns.

"Maybe Abe it is just that", starting with a question I paused and Abe fell silent.

Then feebly I tried giving my kid's point of view? "You're right . . . we need to keep it simple. Why can't we simply accept Christ as a plain and good person who came here to help the people of this world?"

Abe was still silent but I could tell he was thinking.

Continuing I added, "Christ had a lot of great ideas about how we should and shouldn't treat each other. Maybe simply say, we are followers of Jesus Christ and walk with Him for awhile. I look at it as finding a new friend. The rest of the teaching is up to Him. I'm sure he'll teach us what we need to know.

We shouldn't have to worry about what we don't understand right now. Grandma told me that we have to do our part and read the Bible to find the answers we are looking for. He gave us grace and we have to go a little bit on faith is what I think she said."

"What do you think", I finally asked?

Abe glanced at me and I looked at him, without a word spoken we smiled at each other. With a smile and a nod it was a kid's understanding, a code that said we both understood. Together we opened the door and walked into the light.

EPILOGUE

There is a word which was used earlier in the story which I believe needs more space and time donated to it. As it was important at the time of creation it continues to be even more relevant to the lifestyles of our young people today.

Choice . . . it is not a very big word. It is not a small word. I suppose it to be a medium sized pivotal word which provides many inferences. According to the dictionary choice means as follows; an act or instance of choosing; selection: *a wise choice of friends*. The right, the power, or opportunity to choose; an option. The person or thing chosen or eligible to be chosen: Green is my choice of color. An alternative. An abundance or variety from which to choose, ie; a wide choice of styles.

Now here is the definition I like and feel most applicable; *something that is preferred or preferable to others; the best part, something worthy of being chosen; excellent, superior.* **Carefully selected.**

My grandma was always talking about those who stood by their faith through thick and thin and were considered the **chosen** ones. She would quote; ***for many are invited, but few are chosen.***

I wasn't sure what that meant until she directed me to Matthew 22: 1 - 14. You can find it too and summarize for yourself. It is a wonderful story and pertinent to this discourse.

It is "*The parable of the wedding feast*" simply stated; Jesus calls and invites us to become part of His Kingdom. He calls time and time again up until the moment that it will be too late. At that moment only those who have been faithful, only those who believe, will be chosen. Those who have not accepted Christ will be as the man in the parable; ***as if bound hand and foot and thrown into the street, into the darkness, where there will be weeping and a gnashing of teeth.*** I understood the wedding clothes to be the armor of the Holy Spirit around us when we accept Christ as our Lord and Savior.

When Christ was talking to the Pharisees he was explaining to them that he was the Son of God, but they chose not to recognize him. He showed them in the parable that they were too busy and preoccupied with the trivialities of this world in past times to listen to Him. Christ explained that God's own chosen people mistreated those messengers He sent in the past . . . still they **chose** not hear. He then told them that now the door was open to **_all_** who would listen, the *choice* was no longer exclusive to them. **_All_** were now invited to the banquet in the kingdom of heaven. But as we see in future verses and chapters in Matthew the Pharisees had a hidden agenda for Jesus and that did not include listening to Him, but rather they **chose** to murder Christ.

Wow, what a powerful word **choice** is! It sure affects us. It is my choice. It is your choice. It is our choice. Every move we make and everything we do is a choice, and with choice comes an equal and opposite reaction, whether the choices we make are good or bad.

If I choose to extend my hand in friendship with a smile; the reaction I get will be what? If I choose to close my hand into a fist and raise it in anger; the reaction I get will be what? It's your choice, and it really is up to you as to what path you choose to walk. My hope is that we all choose life everlasting.

THE PLAYERS

Larry Bachman, Ben Bachman, Scott Bachman, at Home in
Kissimmee, Pa.

Larry and Scott Bachman

Larry and Scott Bachman (Taken in the Spring of 1963)

Larry at Sixth Grade (11 Years Old)

Larry Bachman & Scott Bachman

Larry's Birthday (Left to Right)
The MBM's, Scott Bachman, Craig Courtney, Lynn Bowersox, Dwight Courtney,
Robert Mitchell, Larry Bahcman

My Mother
Leona Shrawder Bachman

My Outspoken Bible Teacher
Grandmother Bessie Walter Shrawder

AFTERWORD

In conclusion: Everyone's spiritual awakening begins differently. For me as a child, after that final Bible study class so long ago, and after my acceptance, I burst past those church doors like an eagle taking flight. It was a newly discovered exhilarated freedom that carried me down the road and back home. My feet barely touched the ground until I reached that familiar front gate.

My flight through life has been fraught with hidden wind shears and crosswinds ever since. Travel was not always with angels. The itinerary included many stops in less than desirable ports of call. My flight plan, though not always known, brought me back to exactly where the Lord wanted me to be. Landings were not always smooth, as I tended to believe that it was I who was in control. Only when I finally gave up the steering to a more clear minded and experienced pilot did I realize completion and purpose.

How difficult, but how easy it is once you realize that God is the pilot and we are merely co-pilots on this journey. It was said I know; God is my co-pilot. But for me I have realized that it is better to quietly listen. Above the roar of your own desires you will hear and see Him sitting patiently there in the captains chair adjusting the rudders and trim, perhaps slowing the speed, navigating you through the turbulence of life, ready to answer your next question; how, why and where are we going? Amen.

www.ingramcontent.com/pod-product-compliance
Lightning Source LLC
Chambersburg PA
CBHW051140120626
46547CB00012B/883